Setting Limits
in the Classroom

Setting Limits in the Classroom

How to Move Beyond the Dance of Discipline in Today's Classrooms

Robert J. MacKenzie, Ed.D.

REVISED

PRIMA PUBLISHING

Published by Prima Publishing, Roseville, California. Member of the Crown Publishing Group, a division of Random House, Inc., New York.

PRIMA PUBLISHING and colophon are trademarks of Random House, Inc., registered with the United States Patent and Trademark Office.

Illustrations by Karl Edwards

Library of Congress Cataloging-in-Publication Data
MacKenzie, Robert J.
    Setting limits in the classroom : how to move beyond the dance of discipline in today's classrooms / Robert J. MacKenzie.— Rev.
        p.   cm.
    Includes index.
    ISBN 0-7615-1675-1
    1. Classroom management. 2. School discipline. I. Title.
LB3013 .M27   2003
371.102'4—dc21   2002156395

03 04 05 06 07 QQ 10 9 8 7 6 5 4 3 2 1
Printed in the United States of America

Second Edition

Visit us online at www.primapublishing.com

*To the many effective teachers
I've had the pleasure to observe and
work with over the years*

CONTENTS

ACKNOWLEDGMENTS

THIS BOOK BEGAN eighteen years ago as a workshop for teachers. My sincere appreciation goes to all who participated in these workshops over the years. Your experiences, and your willingness to share them, helped refine and improve the methods in this book.

Special thanks also go to those who have supported my workshops in major ways and to those who assisted with the writing of this book.

To Bob Trigg, former superintendent of the Elk Grove Unified School District, for funding and supporting my workshops for teachers for the first ten years.

To Dave Gordon, current superintendent of the Elk Grove Unified School District, for funding and supporting my TRIC (Training Responsible, Independent Children) workshops for teachers during the last eight years.

To the many principals of the Elk Grove Unified School District who have supported my efforts toward staff development.

To the many effective teachers I've had the privilege to observe and work with over the years. You are the real masters of effective classroom management.

To Jamie Miller, Marjorie Lery, and all the other good folks at Prima Publishing for believing in my project.

To Dr. Jonathon Sandoval, professor of education, University of California, Davis, for your technical expertise with portions of the book.

To Jean Seay for your assistance with the many charts and diagrams.

To Lisa Stanzione, special education teacher with the Elk Grove Unified School District, for assisting with my workshops and providing helpful feedback.

To Judy Wyluda, program director; Tad Schmitt, executive director; and all the good folks at Staff Development Resources and the California Elementary Education Association for promoting my workshops on a national level.

To all the parents and children I've seen over the years in my counseling work. Your successes have strengthened my beliefs in the process we've shared together.

INTRODUCTION

I N MANY SCHOOLS, the lessons of classroom management have become part of a "hidden curriculum." They're not discussed at curriculum meetings. They don't show up anywhere in the teacher's daily lesson plan, yet they require as much, if not more, of the teacher's time and energy than any other academic subject. In fact, teachers can't teach their academic subjects effectively until they can establish an effective environment for learning.

Classroom management is simply too important to be neglected or handled ineffectively. The cost to teaching and learning, to our schools, and to our culture is too great. My bias is clear: Guidance and discipline should be taught like any other subject with a sound curriculum, proven state-of-the-art methods, and consistency across grade levels and throughout the school.

As a family guidance counselor and parent/teacher trainer for a large northern California school district, I see nearly two hundred students each year who are not stopping at the signals they confront in the classroom. They don't respect rules or authority, and many lack the basic social skills to be successful students. Some are suspected of having emotional or learning problems, and a few do, but the vast majority is not suffering from any problem at all. They are simply exercising their willpower in the hope they can wear adults down and do what they want. Often, they're successful.

By the time these students reach my office, their teachers have tried a variety of techniques to stop the misbehavior. They've tried lecturing, threatening, reasoning, explaining, bribing, cajoling, writing names on the board, taking away recesses, and making students write apology letters. They've tried making them stand in the corner, sending them to the office, issuing citations, sending home daily behavior reports, and asking parents to spend a day in the classroom—all without success.

Their methods range from extreme permissiveness to harsh punishment and all points in-between, but most of these teachers share at least one thing in common: They're having trouble setting limits in their classrooms. They're doing the best they can with the tools they have, but the tools aren't working, and they don't know what else to do. Teachers need effective methods.

Setting Limits in the Classroom provides you with the guidance curriculum and effective methods you need to stop misbehavior and teach your rules in the clearest and most understandable way. You can say good-bye to all the ineffective methods that wear you down and get you nowhere. No more reasoning, explaining, lecturing, or threats. No more drawn-out consequences or exhaustive attempts at persuasion. And you can say good-bye to all the power struggles, too. Your students will know what you mean when you set clear, firm limits and support your words with effective actions. This book will show you how to do that. The methods should be a welcome alternative to the ineffective extremes of punishment and permissiveness.

In the chapters that follow, you'll learn an approach to child guidance that is clear, systematic, and developmentally appropriate for your students, one that has been tested and used successfully by thousands of teachers and parents. The methods work, and you can use them with children of all ages, from preschoolers to secondary students.

The first five chapters of this book will attempt to do what most books on guidance and discipline leave out—that is, to help you recognize the things you're doing that aren't working for you. Without this awareness, it will be difficult, if not impossible, to avoid repeating your old mistakes, because most of these mistakes are made unconsciously. You'll discover your approach to limit setting, how children really learn your rules, the types of limits you're using, and the type of "classroom dance" you might be doing to get your students to cooperate.

With an understanding of what hasn't worked for you, you'll be ready to learn new skills. Chapters 6 through 13 form the core of the skills-training program. In these chapters, you'll learn how to give clear messages about your rules, stop power struggles before they begin, support your rules with instructive consequences, manage extreme behavior, and how to use the office for back-up support.

In chapters 14 and 15, you'll learn effective motivational strategies for inspiring cooperation, building positive relationships, and increasing on-task time. Chapter 16 will help you get off the discipline treadmill by teaching your students the skills they need to change their unacceptable behavior. In chapter 17, you'll learn how to solve problems with homework.

The final chapter is intended to provide relief for administrators and help them improve the efficiency and effectiveness of their school's guidance program. Whether your program requires a tune-up or a major overhaul, this chapter will help you put the parts back together so they work in an efficient and cost-effective manner.

This book is designed to be a curriculum material for staff development training. Suggestions for getting started are provided in appendix 1. A guide for beginning a teacher study group at your school, as well as teacher study-group questions and discussion topics, are included in appendix 2.

Learning the methods in this book will be the easiest part of your skills training. Most are fairly straightforward. For many of you, the hardest part will be to resist the temptation to revert back to old habits and do the things that haven't worked. Changing old habits is not easy.

You may recognize intellectually that the methods will lead to the type of change you desire, but the methods and the changes they bring may not feel comfortable to you or your students in the beginning. You will likely encounter pressure and resistance to change, not only from your students but also from within yourself. Don't give up. The more you practice, the more comfortable you will feel, and the positive results will increase your confidence.

You should also expect to make mistakes and to have lapses in your consistency when you begin practicing your new skills. That's okay. Mistakes are a normal part of learning. Your goal should be improvement, and you will improve the more you practice. If you encounter unexpected problems with any of the methods, refer back to the pertinent chapters for assistance. Note the specific language used to carry out the techniques in the various examples.

Finally, many of the examples in this book reflect actual cases from my counseling and consulting work with teachers. In all cases, the names have been changed to protect the privacy of those involved.

The methods in this book have helped thousands of teachers regain control of their classrooms and enjoy more satisfying and cooperative relationships with students. If you are willing to invest the time and energy needed to learn the skills, you, too, can share the rewards.

Creating Structure That Works

STRUCTURE IS THE organizational foundation of the classroom. It paves the way for cooperation and learning by clarifying your rules and expectations and by defining the path you want your students to stay on. In a well-structured classroom, many conflicts and behavior problems are prevented because children know what is expected. Rules, procedures, and daily routines are clear. There is less need for testing.

Because structure is so basic, many teachers overlook it and devote too little attention to it at the beginning of the year. They believe they can't afford to take valuable time away from academic instruction, or they assume children should already know what is expected or that they will pick it up along the way. The result is more time spent on testing and disruptions and less time on teaching and learning. Everybody loses. Teachers end up exhausted as they struggle to maintain order in their classrooms, and students lose valuable time for instruction.

This chapter will show you how to prevent the problems that accompany ineffective structure. You'll learn proven techniques for teaching classroom rules and procedures, defining basic student responsibilities, enlisting parent support and cooperation, and solving problems early before they get bigger. By the time you're done, you'll know how to create structure that will work for you throughout the year.

The Cost of Ineffective Structure

THE LESSON OF structure begins the moment your students enter the classroom. There is no way to avoid it. Sooner or later—usually sooner—someone will do something he or she is not supposed to do, and all the students will watch for your reaction. What you do, or fail to do, will define a rule.

> Sooner or later someone will do something he or she is not supposed to do, and all the students will watch for your reaction.

Imagine, for example, that you're an eighth-grade teacher, and it's the first day of school. One of your students arrives in your first-period class wearing a headset and rocking out to one of his favorite songs. You don't like it, but you decide to ignore it. "He'll probably put it away by the time I begin teaching," you say to yourself.

He might, but what is the rule you just taught? Of course, it's okay to arrive in class wearing a headset. What do you think this student and possibly others are likely to do in the future?

The issue is not whether the lesson of structure *should* be taught. It *will* be taught, one way or another. The real issue is who controls the lesson—the teacher or the students? When students control the lesson, the costs to learning and cooperation are much greater. Consider the following.

It's the first week of school in Mr. Johnson's fourth-grade class. The bell just rang, and the kids file back into class. Mr. Johnson stands at the front of the classroom and waits for the kids to settle down.

His lesson has been carefully planned and organized. He scheduled ten minutes for instructions and thirty minutes for seat work. He's ready to get started, but the kids are not. Two minutes have passed since the bell rang, and the noise level is high.

"Let's settle down a little," he says, directing his comments to several boys who are laughing and talking loudly. His words have little impact. The boys continue to laugh. Others are talking, too. Mr. Johnson waits patiently. Another minute passes.

"What's going on?" he thinks to himself. "I announced my rules the first day of class. They should know better." He tries again.

"Okay, class, I'm ready to start," he says in an annoyed tone. He waits a little more. Everyone settles down except two boys.

"Craig, Terry! Are you ready to join us?" Mr. Johnson asks. The boys exchange mischievous smiles, but they stop talking for the moment. Four minutes have passed. Finally, Mr. Johnson begins his lesson.

As he gives directions for the next assignment, Mr. Johnson notices a number of students are not paying attention. "I don't want to explain this again," he says. His warning has little effect. He finishes his directions and passes out the worksheets. "You have twenty-five minutes to complete the assignment," he announces.

"I don't understand," says one student. "Yeah, what are we supposed to do?" chimes in another. Several others look confused. There isn't time for individual instructions. Mr. Johnson is frustrated.

"If you guys had been paying attention, you would know what to do," he says. "Now, listen up." He repeats the directions for the benefit of those who had not listened, eating up another five minutes. Twenty minutes left.

Finally, everyone is working. As they do, Mr. Johnson roves around the room to help those with raised hands and to intervene with disruptions. As he helps one student, he notices Craig and Terry laughing and fooling around again.

"Excuse me, Brenda," says Mr. Johnson. He approaches Craig and Terry. "Guys, would you save it for recess, please?" They smile at each other again but stop for the moment.

Mr. Johnson returns to Brenda, but by this time, other hands are in the air, and other kids are disrupting. He deals with the disruptions first, then the raised hands, and so it goes for the rest of the lesson. Hands are still in the air as the bell rings. Many don't finish.

What happened? Mr. Johnson was prepared to teach his academic lesson but not the lesson of classroom management. His class lacks structure. As a result, he spent more than a third of his time dealing with testing and disruptions.

What did his students learn? They learned the same lessons they had been learning all week: It's okay to enter the classroom noisily. Take your time to settle down. If you don't pay attention the first time, you will get a second set of directions. Worst of all, they learned that testing and disruptions are tolerated. Mr. Johnson is in for a long year. If he continues on this course, he's a good candidate for burnout.

Mistaken Beliefs About Structure

WHY DO SOME teachers like Mr. Johnson devote so little time to structure in the beginning of the year? Often, the problem can be traced back to mistaken beliefs about how rules should be taught and how children learn them. When it comes to teaching rules, there is certainly more disagreement than consensus among educators. Beliefs vary regarding who should do it, how we should do it, or whether it should be done at all. Let's look at some common misconceptions that set up teachers and students for a year of testing and conflict.

1. Teaching rules is the parents' job.
Reality: In the home, teaching rules and setting standards for acceptable behavior is the parent's job, but in the classroom, it's the teacher's job.

Imagine that you're a seventh-grade teacher. You're at home one evening, and a parent of a student in your class calls to complain about her son. "I can't get Jason to clean up his room," says the frustrated parent. "He knows what he's supposed to do. Would you talk to him?"

Would you think this request was a little strange? Aren't parents supposed to be the primary authority figures in the home? Isn't it their job to set standards and enforce their rules? You might offer support and encourage this parent to be firm, but you recognize that the job belongs to the parent.

The same principle applies to the classroom. In the classroom, teachers are the primary authority figures. It's their job to set standards for acceptable behavior and enforce their rules. The kids are counting on them to do it. Parents can offer support, but the essential job belongs to the teacher. Passing responsibility to the parents won't get the job done.

2. Children should know what I expect.
Reality: Students need time to learn the rules and expectations you're willing to enforce.

Some teachers assume that children with any previous school experience should already know what is expected and how to behave. The assumption might hold up if all teachers were exactly alike, but this isn't the case. Their rules, expectations, and methods of enforcement vary. Some overlook misbehavior; others don't. It's not realistic to expect children to understand your specific rules and expectations until they've seen you in action.

3. I can't afford to take precious time away from instruction.
Reality: You can't afford not to.

It's difficult to build a solid house on a shaky foundation. If you attempt to do so, you'll spend a lot of your time with costly repair work. Neglecting structure to preserve time for teaching academics is a false savings. Pay up front and invest the necessary time in teaching your rules effectively, or do a sloppy job and pay as you go. The choice is yours, but paying as you go is more expensive. Effective structure is one of the cheapest and least time-consuming forms of classroom management.

4. If I cover my rules thoroughly in the beginning of the year, I shouldn't need to do it again.
Reality: Rules need to be taught, practiced, reviewed, retaught, and practiced some more.

How many complicated lessons do you teach with full mastery in two weeks or less? Not reading, or math, or spelling, or science, or many others. These subjects require a longer period of instruction, followed by practice, testing, review, more teaching, and more practice. When we're done, mastery is seldom 100 percent. Why should it be different with the complicated lesson of teaching classroom rules and standards for acceptable behavior?

5. Explaining my rules to children should be enough.
Reality: Rules need to be taught with words *and* actions, not words alone.

Announcing rules during the first week of school is an important first step in the teaching-and-learning process, but your words signal only your intentions. The process is incomplete. We need to support our words with effective action if we want children to regard our rules seriously. Words unsupported by action carry little weight.

6. Children won't take me seriously unless I'm strict.
Reality: Being strict without being respectful will not earn the willing cooperation of most students.

Children respond best when rules are communicated with firmness and respect, but firm does not mean harsh. Fear and intimidation provide no lasting basis for cooperation.

7. If children hear my rules often enough, the message will begin to sink in.
Reality: Actions speak louder than words.

Imagine that you're a fifth-grade teacher. You've told your students repeatedly that it's not okay to arrive in class late from recess, but day after day the same group of kids shows up late, and nothing happens but the same old lecture. Why should they take you seriously? What would convince them that you are really serious about their prompt arrival?

Now, let's say you decide to take a different approach. The next time your students show up late, they see you standing at the door with a stopwatch. You click the watch as the last student enters and announce, "You guys owe me eight minutes—two minutes for every one that you arrived late. You'll be staying in class the first eight minutes of your next recess."

These guys really like recess. Do you think the message will get across? What convinced them—your words? Or your effective action?

8. Students resent firm rules and teachers who make them.
Reality: Students respect teachers who establish clear, firm classroom rules, particularly when those rules are communicated in a respectful manner.

When rules are clear, firm, and carried out in a consistent and respectful manner, students know where they stand and what is expected. There is less need for testing, more time for cooperation and learning.

9. When my students sense that I care, they will cooperate.
Reality: Caring is important, but caring alone is not enough to achieve consistent cooperation.

Caring and firm limits work hand in hand, but caring without firm limits will not earn you the respect you deserve, particularly from your strong-willed students.

10. Male teachers make the best disciplinarians.
Reality: In the classroom, power and authority belong to those who exercise them. Gender makes little difference.

Rules in Theory Versus Rules in Practice

CLASSROOM RULES COME in two basic varieties: rules in theory, or the rules you announce to your students; and rules in practice, or the rules you're willing to enforce. Each carries a different meaning and elicits different responses from children. Let's look at how they work.

Rules in Theory

As the term implies, rules in theory operate at the theoretical or hypothetical level. They are words that signal our hopes and expectations for how students should behave. How do they work? Usually they are announced, but they may take the form of requests or directives.

Some teachers set themselves up for conflict by confusing their rules in theory with the rules they actually practice. In reality, the two may be different depending on what happens when our announced rules are tested or challenged. Consider how the following three teachers communicate their rules in theory. Later, we'll examine the rules they actually practice and the actual lessons their students learn.

Mrs. Atkins and the Morning Circle

It's time for morning circle, a daily sharing activity in Mrs. Atkins's preschool class. The kids are all seated on the carpet near the blackboard. As the activity begins, Matthew, age four, presses his foot against the back of the girl in front of him and pulls on her sweater.

"Matthew, we don't put our hands or feet on others when we're in morning circle," says Mrs. Atkins. "We sit like this." She models the behavior she wants by sitting Indian style with her hands in her lap. Matthew decides to cooperate for the moment.

Mr. Larson and the Toys in Class

Mr. Larson, a fifth-grade teacher, notices that some of his students have been bringing small toys or trading cards to class and playing with them during instruction. He decides to put a stop to it.

"If you bring toys or cards to school, you need to keep them in your desk or backpack," he says. "If you have them out during class, I will take them away and return them to your parents at our next teacher-parent conference."

Miss Stallings and Her Tardy Students

Miss Stallings, an eleventh-grade government teacher, is concerned about the number of students who have been arriving late for class. She decides to bring it up with her students.

"Class, I expect you to be in the door before the fifth-period bell rings," begins Miss Stallings. "If you aren't, you will be tardy, and you will have to go to the attendance office to pick up a tardy slip before you can come back to class. If you get three tardies in any one semester, you'll have to spend two hours after school in the silent study center."

Rules in Practice

Rules in practice are defined by your actions or what your students actually experience after all the talking is over. The behavior you're willing to tolerate defines your actual classroom standards.

How do students know your rules in practice? They test, and then watch what you do. Your actions will clarify what you really expect. Now, let's return to our three earlier examples and see what happened when the students decided to test.

Mrs. Atkins and the Morning Circle

Several minutes after Matthew was asked to stop putting his hands and feet on others, he decides to test. He gives Sara another nudge with his foot and tugs the back of her sweater.

"Matthew," says Mrs. Atkins, "you need to sit by yourself for the rest of circle time." She gets out a carpet strip and sets it down about five feet away from the others.

Did Matthew's teacher practice the rule she announced? You bet. She said stop, and that's what Matthew experienced when he decided to test. Her message was clear, and so was her rule. She may need to repeat this lesson several times before Matthew is convinced, but if she does, Matthew will surely get the message.

Mr. Larson and the Toys in Class

Later in the afternoon, after Mr. Larson announced his rule about playing with toys in class, he notices one of his students passing a troll doll to another girl in her table group.

"Mia, what did I say about playing with toys in class?" he asks. "Now put it away, please." He lets it pass with just a warning. The lesson isn't lost on others.

The next day, he catches Dale and Patrick playing with baseball cards. "Guys, do you want to lose them?" Mr. Larson asks. "If not, put them away." Again, he lets it pass with just a warning.

Before the week is over, there are several more incidents and several more warnings. In one case, Mr. Larson actually confiscates some cards but returns them after school with instructions not to bring them back.

What is the rule Mr. Larson actually practices? Of course, it's okay to play with toys in class. All you get are warnings. Why should anyone take Mr. Larson's rule very seriously?

Miss Stallings and Her Tardy Students

The day following Miss Stallings's announcement, three students arrive late for class. She greets them at the door.

"You need to go to the attendance office to get tardy slips," she says.

"Oh, come on, Miss Stallings," pleads one girl. "We had to go back to our lockers to get our leadership reports. We won't do it again."

"Well, the reason is related to class," Miss Stallings says to herself. "Maybe I should give them a break."

"Okay, I'll let it go this time," she says, "but next time, you'll have to get a tardy slip."

The lesson isn't lost on others. There are more late arrivals that week, and each time, the students have good excuses. The pattern continues into the second and third weeks. At the end of the third week, only one student has actually been sent for a tardy slip. He showed up more than five minutes late and couldn't come up with a good excuse.

What's the rule in practice here? Sure, it's okay to show up late for class as long as you can come up with a good excuse. That's what the students learned, and that's what they will probably continue to do. They have little cause to regard Miss Stallings's spoken rule very seriously.

Introducing Rules to Students

TEACHING RULES AND standards for acceptable behavior is similar to teaching academics. Lessons must be taught, practiced, and taught some more before students master them. Compliance is seldom 100 percent, even in cooperative classrooms.

The lesson begins the moment your students enter your classroom. They listen to what you say, and they watch what you do. The more consistency you demonstrate between your announced rules and the rules you practice, the quicker your students will tune in, take you seriously, and give you the cooperation and respect you deserve.

Consistency is the key to your credibility, and consistency takes time. How much time? If you're highly consistent, you should be able to consolidate your authority as the adult in charge within the first three to four weeks. If you're inconsistent, the process will take longer. The best approach is to set aside time during the first four weeks and teach your rules and procedures as systematically as you would any other academic subject. The following tips will help you get started.

On the First Day

- Introduce your general rules or rules in theory. Keep them broad and inclusive, and avoid extensive lists. Many teachers find the three following rules to be sufficient:

  1. Cooperate with your teacher and classmates.
  2. Respect the rights and property of others.
  3. Carry out your student responsibilities.

- Post your general classroom rules in a visible area for elementary and secondary students.

- Describe your classroom procedures for entering and exiting the classroom and for handling transitions such as shifting from whole-class instruction to independent seat work, getting ready for lunch, or preparing to leave at the end of the day.

- Describe the guidance procedures you use when classroom rules are tested or violated. Introduce natural consequences, logical consequences, the two-stage time-out procedure, on-campus suspensions, and parent problem-solving conferences. Pose hypothetical situations, and walk your students through each guidance procedure so they understand how these procedures work. These procedures are described in detail in chapters 8 through 13. Explain that you will make a complete effort to resolve classroom problems with students individually before involving their parents, administrators, or other guidance personnel.

- Be prepared to use your guidance procedures the first time testing occurs. Others won't miss the lesson.

- Announce that you will send home a list of your classroom rules and guidance procedures.

During the First Two Weeks

- Review your general classroom rules daily as well as any specific rules that have been tested or violated. Ask questions to be sure students understand what you expect.

- Set aside time each day to teach classroom routines and procedures. Select a different procedure to work on each day or devote more time to procedures that students have difficulty mastering such as sitting in morning circle, lining up for recess, or going to time-out. Present the lessons in a simple and concrete manner, particularly with preschool and elementary school students. Don't assume that your words will be enough to convey your message. Show them what you mean by modeling the behavior you expect them to use. Walk them through hypothetical situations to make sure they understand what you expect.

- Expect testing, and be prepared to follow through. There is only so much you can teach with verbal instruction, practice, and review. Most of your students will be convinced you mean business when they see how much time and energy you're willing to devote to teaching your rules. They will accept your rules as stated and do their best to follow them. Some of your students, the hard-way learners, will have to experience the consequences of their poor choices to not follow your rules many times before they will be convinced. These lessons won't be planned or scheduled. They might take place at any time during the day. When they do, you will need to follow through and support your rules with effective action.

During the First Month

- Continue teaching your rules and procedures as needed.

- Expect testing and be prepared to follow through. The heaviest testing usually occurs during the first four weeks of school. Be prepared to follow through and support your rules with effective action. Your consistency will buy huge credibility points for later on.

- Set aside time before or after school, during recess, breaks, or lunch for individual or small-group practice sessions for students who need additional practice mastering important skills such as walking the corridor or sitting quietly during instruction. A brief lesson on the student's time can have a huge impact.

- Schedule parent conferences for students who test excessively or fail to comply with classroom rules and standards during the first four weeks. You'll need parent support and cooperation.

Throughout the Year

- Review classroom rules and procedures as needed with individual students or groups of students who need additional practice following your rules and procedures.

- Set aside time for students to practice the skills and lessons they haven't mastered. Arrange for practice sessions to occur during the student's time such as recess, lunch, before or after school, but not during class time.

- Continue to follow through with effective action. Learning to follow rules and respect authority is an ongoing process.

- Schedule parent problem-solving conferences when efforts to resolve problems with students individually do not lead to improvement.

Teaching Good Work Habits and Organizational Skills

ONE OF THE most important lessons children learn in the course of growing up is the lesson of good work habits or how to be responsible for beginning a task, staying with it even when it's difficult, and completing the task in a timely manner. Children who learn good work habits become successful students and successful people. Children who fail to master good work habits face increased risk of failure, particularly at the secondary level, where independent work outside the classroom often counts for 25 percent or more of a student's grade. For many students, good work habits can make the difference between passing and failing.

How do children acquire good work habits? They acquire work habits the same way they acquire other skills—through a teaching-and-learning process. They need instruction, practice, corrective feedback, and opportunities to experience the consequences of their efforts, both positive and negative. The process begins in the home and is reinforced in the classroom. Teaching work habits is a job that parents and teachers share. Teachers can help students develop good work habits by being clear about their expectations, by helping students plan out a study schedule, by acknowledging and rewarding compliance, and by holding students accountable when they do less than their part. The following suggestions should help.

On the First Day

- Share your expectations for basic student responsibilities. Keep your list brief. A sample list might be:

  1. Keep track of your own books and assignments.
  2. Start your work on time and allow enough time to finish.
  3. Ask for help when you need it.
  4. Do your own work.
  5. Turn your work in on time.
  6. Accept responsibility for grades or other consequences.

- Post a list of basic student responsibilities in a visible area in the classroom.

- Share your expectations for homework, and describe homework procedures. Be clear about when assignments are given, when assignments are due, and what happens when work is not completed.

- Introduce your accountability procedures, and explain how they work.

During the First Week

- Review your list of basic responsibilities daily.

- Review your accountability procedures daily.

- Inform your students that you will send home a list of their basic responsibilities, your homework policy, and a description of your accountability procedures so their parents know what is expected.

- Send home a work folder each Friday for parents to review their child's work, make comments, sign, and return with their child on Monday.

Throughout the Year

- Review your list of basic student responsibilities as needed.

- Follow through with accountability procedures.

- Schedule conferences with parents of students who are consistently noncompliant with homework. Discuss your concerns, encouraging them to implement the corrective steps described in chapter 17.

Accountability Procedures

THE LESSON OF responsibility is difficult to learn without accountability. Your students need to know from the beginning that they are expected to do their part and that there will be consequences, positive and negative, associated with their performance. The following procedures will help your students learn responsibility and good work habits by holding them accountable for doing their part.

Friday Work Folders

Friday work folders are a simple and effective method for helping parents stay up-to-date on their child's progress. The procedure is easy to carry out. Each Friday, the teacher sends home a packet of the work the student has completed and turned in for that week. Attached to the packet is a form indicating whether all items were completed and which items remain incomplete (see figure 1.1). Parents review the packet,

Name _____ Week _____

_____ Great week! All work completed.

_____ Work is not complete. Please finish the following
by Monday.

Figure 1.1   Feedback Sheet for Friday Work Folders

sign and date an entry on the inside cover of the folder, make
any comments if they desire, and return the folder with their
child on Monday. Teachers can provide incentives in the form
of points toward course grades or time for a preferred activity
for students who promptly return their folders on Mondays.

Friday work folders have many advantages. They allow parents to closely monitor the quality of their child's class work
and homework. They provide an ongoing communication
channel between school and home, and they serve as an early
detection system so parents and teachers can deal with student
problems early before they develop into more serious problems.

Fun Friday

Fun Friday is a clever procedure used by both elementary and
secondary teachers to acknowledge and reward good work
habits. Teachers set aside a block of time on Friday afternoons
for preferred activities students can do quietly at their seats.
Teachers and students develop an "approved list" of activities,
which are placed in a cabinet or on a shelf in the classroom.
Students become eligible for Fun Friday after they have completed all assigned work for the week. Students who are not

eligible use the time to catch up on incomplete class work or homework. Consider the following example.

It's two o'clock Friday afternoon, and Mr. Hodges, a third-grade teacher, makes an announcement to his class.

"It's time for Fun Friday. Everyone who has completed his or her homework and in-class assignments for the week can select an activity from the approved list. I'll meet with those who haven't at the back table." Some students go to a cabinet to select a game, magazine, or activity. Others use the time to read or draw. Three students take out their incomplete homework and join Mr. Hodges at the back table.

Makeup Sessions for Missed Work

There are ten minutes left until recess, and Jamie, age nine, has fifteen problems remaining on her math worksheet. She's hoping to dawdle the time away and avoid finishing the assignment. Her suspicious teacher intervenes.

"Jamie, you have ten minutes to finish up your math sheet. If it's not finished before recess, you'll have to take a clipboard and finish on the bench during recess."

"Rats!" Jamie says to herself. She races to finish before recess.

This accountability procedure has been a fixture in public school education for generations. The system is very simple. When children dawdle, avoid, procrastinate, or otherwise fail to complete assigned work during class time, they are required to make up that work during their break time or recess. They take their books, writing materials, and a clipboard and continue working on the incomplete assignment. In effect, the loss of break time or recess becomes the logical consequence for not completing their work in a timely manner. The procedure is not recommended for students with attention deficit disorder (ADD) or other special needs who fail to complete work on time because they lack skills or ability.

The Classroom Rental Center

Brad is a bright and capable seventh grader who has a habit of arriving to class unprepared. As he enters his fourth-period Spanish class, his teacher notices that he doesn't have his Spanish textbook or his notebook. She asks the class to take out their books, turn to page 112, and write down the correct vocabulary words for the items on page 113. Brad raises his hand.

"I forgot my book and writing paper," he says.

"Step over to my rental center and select the items you need," says the teacher. "The rent today will be erasing the board after class." Brad's teacher keeps a table with extra books, pens, pencils, writing paper, and blank worksheets next to her desk at the front of the classroom.

Brad collects the items he needs and returns to his desk, when his teacher stops him. She knows better than to trust that he will do the job if there's a chance to sneak off when the bell rings. She asks him to take off one of his shoes and leave it at the rental center for collateral.

"You can have it back when the board has been erased," she says. Brad will probably think carefully the next time he decides to arrive to Spanish class unprepared.

Sure, Brad's teacher could have given him the items he needed, but who would have been responsible for solving the problem? Not Brad. Classroom rental centers are an effective method for teaching responsibility and organizational skills by holding students accountable for arriving to class prepared.

Recess Academy

Recess academy provides students with opportunities to practice, on their time, the skills they haven't mastered during class time. The message is clear: Cooperate during class time, or you can practice improving your cooperation skills during recess. Consider the following.

Todd, a fifth grader, clowns and disrupts instruction for the second time, and it's still early in the day. Each time, his teacher stops the disruption and sends him to the back of the classroom for a ten-minute time-out, but she thinks Todd needs more help mastering the lesson she's trying to teach. As the kids line up for the next recess, she takes Todd aside.

"Todd, you'll be joining me for recess academy for the first five minutes of recess," she announces. "You can read or draw or work on your homework, but I need five quiet minutes without disruption." Five minutes may not seem like long, but to a fifth grader who wants to join his friends on the playground, five minutes seems like an eternity. Todd will think carefully before he decides to disrupt again.

> Brief lessons have a big impact when they're conducted on the student's time.

Recess academy is a great time to help students master skills such as sitting quietly and not disrupting, sitting in a chair or desk correctly, walking instead of running in the corridor, or writing an apology note to another student for making hurtful or unkind comments. Brief lessons have a big impact when they're conducted on the student's time.

As a guidance procedure, recess academy has one disadvantage. Teachers must give up some of their break time, but the small time investment will yield big returns throughout the year in cooperation and respect from your students.

Other Accountability Procedures

Additional effective accountability procedures, appropriate to the secondary level, include after-school detention, Saturday school, on-campus suspensions, and off-campus suspensions. These more "expensive" methods of holding children accountable are discussed in chapter 10.

Enlisting Parent Support and Cooperation

THE FOCUS THUS far has been on helping students get acquainted with the structure of the classroom. We've examined various methods to introduce rules, teach class procedures, and help students develop good work habits and responsibility. The final step in creating a structure that works is to involve the parents in the process. Our structure will not be complete until home and school operate under the same set of rules and expectations.

How do we enlist parental support? There is no one right way, but some guidelines can help you get off to a good start. First, be proactive. Contact parents early, before problems develop. Second, give parents all the information they need to back you up. It is not enough simply to expect their support. Provide them with the information or skills they need to be supportive.

What's the alternative if we don't make early contact or fail to provide parents with the information or skills they need? How will they know what we expect or how to support us? The chances are they won't know, not until we need their help due to a problem that has developed with their child. How are they likely to feel if we seek their support under these circumstances? Defensive? Angry? Embarrassed? Sure. Is this any way to begin a cooperative relationship?

Some teachers wait until their first set of teacher-parent conferences to share the information parents need. This practice has several disadvantages. What parents like to hear at their first conference that their child has been misbehaving or not completing work for the last eight to ten weeks? When we allow problems to develop into patterns, we don't inspire parent confidence in our classroom management skills. Teachers who wait too long to contact parents risk turning a potential supporter into an adversary.

> When we allow problems to develop into patterns, we don't inspire parent confidence in our classroom management skills.

The choices are clear: Either we share our rules and expectations early and start off on a positive note, or we keep parents in the dark and risk alienating them when the focus of our first contact is a problem with their child. The following recommendations should help you get off to a positive start with parents.

During the First Week

- Send parents a letter describing your general classroom rules, guidance procedures, list of student responsibilities, homework policy, and suggestions for how they can support you at home. Ask parents to review the information with their child (see figures 1.2, 1.3, 1.4, and 1.5).

Teacher's name _____

Student's name _____

Dear Parents,

We're off to a good start. I'm enjoying getting to know your child and look forward to meeting you personally during our back-to-school night next week. I'm sure you are as committed as I am to seeing that your child gets off to a good start. For that reason, I am sending a copy of my classroom rules, a list of basic student responsibilities, my homework policy, and a description of some of the procedures I use to keep you informed.

When problems arise in the classroom, I will make a complete effort to resolve the matter individually with the student. If we are unable to resolve the problem, then I often ask parents for support and assistance. Together we can usually resolve problems early and get students pointed in the right direction.

Please support me by reviewing the attached lists of classroom rules, student responsibilities, and homework policy with your child, and indicate a telephone number where you can be reached during school hours. Thanks for your support. I look forward to a great year.

Parent phone number during school hours _____

Figure 1.2   Parent Notification Letter

Classroom Rules

- Cooperate with your teacher and classmates.

- Respect the rights and property of others.

- Carry out your basic student responsibilities.

Figure 1.3 Classroom Rules

Basic Student Responsibilities

- Keep track of your own books and assignments.

- Start your work on time and allow time to finish.

- Ask for help when you need it.

- Do your own work.

- Turn your work in on time.

- Accept responsibility for grades and other consequences.

Figure 1.4 Basic Student Responsibilities

Homework Policy and Friday Folder Procedure

Each week, homework assignments will be sent home with the student on Monday and are due by Friday for full credit. All completed work will be sent home on Friday in your child's Friday work folder. Please review the folder, sign it, make any comments you desire, and return the folder with your child on Monday.

Students who have completed all assigned work for the week by Friday morning are eligible for participation in Fun Friday, a preferred activity period on Friday afternoons. Students who are not eligible will use that time to catch up on remaining work.

Any work that is not completed on Friday will be noted on the student's Friday folder. It is the student's responsibility to complete that work over the weekend and return it in his or her folder on Monday for partial credit.

Figure 1.5 Homework Policy and Friday Folder Procedure

During the First Month

- Schedule a back-to-school night during the first two to three weeks of school. Back-to-school nights are an efficient way to share a lot of information with a large number of people and still provide opportunities for questions and input. Teachers can accomplish in one hour what would take many hours over a period of weeks to accomplish by phone. Topics to be covered during the meeting should include the following:

1. Skills students will learn during the year
2. Classroom rules
3. Guidance procedures
4. Basic student responsibilities
5. Homework policy
6. Friday folder system
7. Specific steps parents can take at home to support you

Be prepared to provide extra copies of the materials you sent home during the first week for parents who may have lost or misplaced them. Set aside time at the end for questions, comments, or input. A well-run meeting will inspire parent confidence and trust that you run an effective, well-organized classroom.

- Make phone contact with parents who did not attend your back-to-school night. Try to limit your call to ten to fifteen minutes and cover the following:

1. Share a positive incident or observation that characterizes their child.
2. Ask whether they have any questions about the materials you sent home during the first week.
3. Encourage them to review the information with their child.
4. Express your appreciation for their support.

- Schedule parent conferences when students persistently test limits, violate classroom rules, or fail to carry out their basic responsibilities. Early intervention is the key to gaining parental support and cooperation.

Space Considerations

MANY CLASSROOM MANAGEMENT problems can be prevented by deciding in advance how to position students in the classroom. You should consider the following questions before deciding on the best seating arrangement: How many students do you have with special needs such as learning disabilities, physical disabilities, ADD, and emotional or behavioral problems?

If you have a number of students with ADD, consider abandoning desk groupings or pods in favor of conventional vertical rows of desks. Most students with ADD or other special needs learn best when placed near the front of the class, near the board and the teacher's desk; away from distractions such as the pencil sharpener, intercom, drinking fountain, and air conditioning vent; and with their backs to as many students as possible. Desk groups or pods, although popular in many schools, surround students with distraction and create opportunities for disruption. Desk groupings are the worst seating arrangement for students with ADD but work fine for compliant students without special needs. The choice is yours, but consider your students, then select the seating arrangement that best fits their needs.

Chapter Summary

EFFECTIVE STRUCTURE IS one of the easiest, least expensive, and least time-consuming forms of classroom management, but many teachers overlook the importance of structure in the beginning of the year. They assume that children should already know what is expected or that they will pick it up along the way—a costly assumption that sets up both teacher and students for a year of testing and conflict.

The lesson of structure will be taught one way or another. There is no way to avoid it. The real issue is who controls the lesson. When students control the lesson, the costs to cooperation and learning are much greater. Time that should be spent in instruction is spent instead handling testing, disruptions, and damage control.

The choices are clear: Either we begin early and invest the time required to teach our rules and enlist parent support, or we exhaust ourselves trying to accomplish these tasks as we go and risk alienating parents in the process. Prevention is always the better way to go. Creating structure early in the year leads to smoother sailing later on.

2

How Teachers Teach Their Rules

Y EARS AGO, WHEN I first began giving workshops, I didn't ask the participants what guidance methods they already used, nor did I spend any time discussing different training models. I just assumed we were operating with a common understanding about what works best, and I jumped in during the first session and shared the methods I knew would be effective. As it turned out, this mistake led me to an important discovery.

After my first few workshops, I began receiving thank-you notes with appreciative comments that really concerned me. "Thanks for helping me become firm with my limits," one teacher said. "I don't nag them all day like I used to. Now I only ask them two or three times, then I give them choices." Another teacher commented, "Limited choices work great. When my students dawdle, I give them a choice—you can finish on time or lose your recesses for a week. They usually finish up."

I became particularly concerned when one fifth-grade teacher told me how much he liked logical consequences. "When my students are disrespectful to me, I make them stay in during recess and write me an apology letter. Then I make them read it to me in front of the class."

"Was this in one of my workshops?" I wondered. How is it possible that someone could so misinterpret the methods I was sharing? But the comments continued, and to my dismay, parents were doing the same thing in my parenting workshops.

Then it occurred to me what was happening. We all thought we shared a common understanding, but we were viewing our guidance methods from very different perspectives. Those who believed in punishment used them punitively, and those who believed in permissiveness used them permissively. Some did both. They all thought they were doing things in new and different ways, but they were simply repeating their old mistakes with new methods. I could see this was not a conscious process.

When I give workshops today, my first task is to hold up a mirror to help the participants become acquainted with their current guidance approach so they can recognize and avoid their old mistakes. I usually begin by demonstrating how a typical discipline problem can be handled in three different ways: permissively, punitively, or democratically. Then we examine the teaching and learning process that accompanies each approach. Most teachers find this helpful. They recognize their approach by examining the methods used by others.

Let's look at how three teachers handle a typical playground problem—rough play. Each uses a different guidance approach.

It's morning recess. A group of boys divides up into teams to play a karate commando game. The teams hide, sneak up on each other, then hold mock battles. It's the last part that leads to problems. Several students have been hurt. The game has been banned from the playground, but some students try to play it anyway.

The mock battle is under way when Mrs. Fisher, the yard duty teacher, notices what's going on. She watches with concern. The boys see her, too, but the game continues with more flying kicks and punches that barely miss.

Finally, one boy is grazed by a kick. He holds his side and grimaces. Mrs. Fisher intervenes. "Guys, that game doesn't look safe," she says. "I'm afraid someone is going to get hurt. Kicks can cause serious injuries. That's why we don't allow that game."

"We're just pretending," says one student. "We'll be careful."

"I know you will, but what you're doing worries me. I really wish you would stop," she says. They do, as long as Mrs. Fisher is in the area, but as soon as she leaves, the battle resumes.

Next recess, Mr. Howard is on yard duty. When he sees the boys playing the karate game, he rushes to the scene. "Stop!" he shouts. "Are you guys playing that karate game again?"

"No, we were just fooling around," says one student.

"Don't lie to me, young man, or you'll find yourself in even more trouble," warns Mr. Howard. He points an accusing finger at the boy and gives him a stern, intimidating look. "Now tell me, who all was involved here?"

Mr. Howard spends the next ten minutes interrogating the group. He listens to their pleas of innocence or guilt and threatens further consequences if he discovers anyone lying. Finally, he's satisfied he has the culprits. He writes up five citations and sends the offenders to the office. "I hope this helps you remember the rules next time you decide to play that game," he adds.

The boys are angry and set on revenge. As they reach the edge of the playground, they get off some parting shots. "You're a great teacher, all right," shouts one student sarcastically. "A great jerk is more like it!" adds another. They all laugh.

"Keep it up, guys!" shouts Mr. Howard. "The principal will hear about this, too. You're just adding to your punishment."

A few days later, it's Mrs. Taylor's turn to supervise recess. When she sees what appears to be the beginning of a mock karate battle, she approaches the group. "Guys, you'll have to choose another game to play," she says in a matter-of-fact tone. "That game is not allowed. If you play it again, you'll have to sit out the rest of the recess on the bench. Thanks for cooperating."

No lectures. No pleading. No threats or accusations. She simply gives them the information they need to make an acceptable choice. Sure, there was some grumbling. The boys weren't happy about it. A few were probably tempted to test, but nobody wanted to spend their recess on the bench. Cooperation was the best choice.

Each teacher in the previous examples was trying to teach a rule about acceptable playground behavior, but only one enjoyed much success. Mrs. Fisher used the permissive approach. Her methods were respectful but not very firm. The boys ignored her and did what they wanted. Mr. Howard used the punitive or autocratic approach. His methods were firm but not very respectful. The boys became angry and retaliated. Mrs. Taylor used the democratic approach. Her methods were firm and respectful. She gave the boys the information they needed to make an acceptable choice, and they cooperated.

Do you think the three teachers in my example would show similar inconsistency if they were teaching a lesson in reading, math, or spelling? Not likely. Why, then, is there so much inconsistency when it comes to teaching rules?

Actually, the teachers in my example are no further apart in their training methods than the rest of us. The methods they use simply reflect the range of practices in our culture at large. We're all over the map. Some believe in permissiveness. Others take a punitive or autocratic view. Some are democratic, and still others flip-flop back and forth between the extremes of permissiveness and punishment.

Most of us teach our rules from one or more of these basic training models. Each model is premised on a different set of beliefs about how children learn, the teacher's role in the training process, and the proper distribution of power and responsibility between adults and children. Each model teaches a different set of lessons about cooperation, responsibility, and your expectations for acceptable behavior. Let's take a closer look now at each of these models.

The Permissive Approach (Respectful but Not Firm)

PERMISSIVENESS EMERGED PROMINENTLY in the 1960s and 1970s as a reaction against the rigidity and autocratic nature of the punitive approach. Many parents and teachers were looking for a new and more democratic approach to raising children based on principles of freedom, equality, and mutual respect.

Putting these principles into practice, however, was not as easy as it sounded. This was uncharted territory for those of us who grew up with the punitive model. How do you do it? Was it a simple matter of relaxing our rules and expectations and giving children more freedom and control? That's what many tried. They experimented with open classrooms, relaxed structure, more freedom and control, and relaxed standards for acceptable classroom behavior. But the experiment often backfired because a vital ingredient was left out—limits.

Freedom without limits is not democracy. It's anarchy, and children trained with anarchy do not learn respect for rules or authority or how to handle their freedom responsibly. They think primarily of themselves and develop an exaggerated sense of their own power and control. The examples of a failed experiment are all around us.

Let's look at how one teacher uses the permissive approach to handle a typical classroom problem—disruption.

Mrs. Weaver, a sixth-grade teacher, passes out worksheets for the next assignment and tells her students they have twenty minutes to finish up before lunch. The students begin working quietly at their seats.

After a few minutes, Mrs. Weaver hears Nate talking to a girl in his table group. He talks softly at first, so Mrs. Weaver ignores it, but his talking continues and the volume increases. She decides to intervene.

"Nate, don't you think it's getting a little loud in here?" she says. "Others are trying to work."

He settles down for a while, but within a few minutes, he talks to someone else, softly at first, then louder.

"Nate, you have fifteen minutes to finish up before lunch," reminds Mrs. Weaver. "You need to do a little less talking and a little more working, okay?"

Five minutes go by before Nate disrupts again. This time, he laughs and jokes with another boy. Mrs. Weaver feels annoyed. She walks over and looks at him impatiently. "How many times do I have to ask you?" she asks.

"I wasn't too loud," argues Nate.

"Well, you sounded too loud to me," replies Mrs. Weaver. "Besides, what you're doing isn't respectful to me or your classmates, and I don't appreciate it. If you don't stop talking, I'm going to move you from your table group. I'm not going to ask you again."

Nate returns to his work, briefly, but within a few minutes, he talks again. Mrs. Weaver intervenes.

"I've had enough of this, Nate!" says a frustrated Mrs. Weaver. "Move your desk away from your group." She points to an area about six feet away.

"But, Mrs. Weaver, that's not fair!" protests Nate. "I was asking Tim for some help. I wasn't bothering anybody."

"You were distracting Tim from his work," counters Mrs. Weaver. "What are you supposed to do when you need help?"

"Raise my hand," says Nate.

"Right!" replies Mrs. Weaver, "and I hope you remember it. This time, it's a warning. If I hear any more talking, I will move you. I really mean it." Nate settles down once again.

What did Nate experience? It wasn't cooperating, at least not for very long. Instead, he experienced a lot of words and very little action. Based on his experience, he has little cause to regard Mrs. Weaver's rule about disrupting very seriously.

Permissive teachers are constantly shifting gears and trying different verbal tactics to convince their students to cooperate. They do a lot of repeating, reminding, warning, offering second chances, pleading, cajoling, bargaining, bribing, arguing, debating, reasoning, lecturing, and trying other forms of verbal persuasion. Consequences, if they are used at all, are typically late and ineffective. By the time everything is said and done, teachers usually end up compromising away their rules and authority or giving in altogether. Often children end up getting their own way. Permissiveness is humiliating to teachers and it's the fast lane to burnout. As a training approach, permissiveness is much worse than punishment for both adults and children. It doesn't accomplish any of our basic training goals. It doesn't stop

> Permissiveness is humiliating to teachers and it's the fast lane to burnout.

misbehavior. It doesn't teach responsibility, and it doesn't teach our intended lessons about rules or authority. Permissiveness does not provide children with the information they need to make acceptable choices about their behavior.

What do children learn from permissiveness? They learn to ignore our words and push us to the point of action to clarify what we really expect. They become very skillful at ignoring, tuning out, resisting, avoiding, arguing, debating, bargaining, challenging, and defying. They don't do it maliciously. They simply do it because it works. Their experiences have taught them that "Rules are for others, not me. I make my own rules, and I do what I want."

Children trained with permissiveness learn they can wear adults down and get their own way. When they can't, there's another reward that's just as appealing—the live entertainment they get from watching their teacher. Permissive teachers unwittingly provide students with a great deal of negative attention, power, and control.

How do you think Nate felt, in our earlier example, each time his teacher tried to deal with his disruption? Was he in control? Clearly. Did he enjoy the show? Definitely. Did his friends enjoy the show? You bet. Permissive guidance is a "reinforcement error" because it actually encourages and rewards unwanted behavior. Let's take a closer look at what happened between Nate and his teacher by examining a diagram of their interaction. We'll place Mrs. Weaver's behavior on the left side of the diagram and Nate's behavior on the right. Visual diagrams often reveal, better than words, the various steps in an interactional sequence (see figure 2.1).

The first thing you probably notice is the length of this diagram. Permissive teachers use a lot of different tactics. Mrs. Weaver is no exception. She begins at point A by attempting to ignore the misbehavior, a strategy that seldom works. Nate

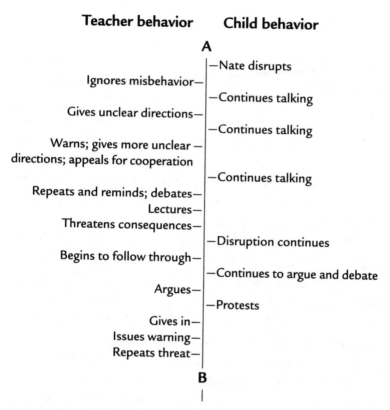

Figure 2.1 Diagram of a Permissive Interaction

continues talking. When his volume increases, she attempts to give him a signal. She asks him whether the noise level is too high and points out that others are working quietly.

Did you hear a clear message that Nate should stop talking? Neither did Nate. He resumes talking a short time later. So Mrs. Weaver tries a different tactic. She points out how little time he has to complete his assignment and asks him to do a little less talking.

What is "a little less talking"? Does that mean some is okay? How much, then? And how will Nate know? Of course, he'll have to test, and that's exactly what he does. He continues talking.

So Mrs. Weaver switches gears again. She tries repeating and reminding. Does this work? No. Nate tries to hook her into an argument. It works.

She takes the bait and argues with him about the volume of his talking, but now the argument is a source of disruption. She lectures him briefly about respect then threatens to move him away from his table group if he disrupts again. Is Nate persuaded by the lecture or threat? Not a chance. He thinks she's bluffing, so he calls her on it. He continues testing.

With her credibility on the line, Mrs. Weaver finally decides to act. She tells Nate to move. It looks as though she might actually follow through, too, but Nate skillfully hooks her into another round of arguments and debates. She listens, tries to be fair, and decides to let the incident pass with just a warning. The encounter ends at point B with Mrs. Weaver repeating her threat to move Nate if he continues talking.

Why didn't Nate cooperate? The reason is simple. He didn't have to. Cooperation was optional, not required. Mrs. Weaver was unwilling to support her words with effective action (consequences). She relied instead on persuasion to get her message across. Can you imagine what things would be like if our traffic laws were enforced in this way? Visualize yourself driving home. The traffic is light, and each time you approach an intersection, you run the stoplight. Eventually, a cop sees you and pulls you over.

"You ran three stoplights," he says. "That's against the law, and our laws are there for your safety and protection. If everyone disregarded stoplights, we would have a lot of serious accidents. I would appreciate it if you would please try to follow the law in the future." Then he gets back in his car and drives off, and that's all that ever happens. Would this stop you from running stoplights in the future? Do you think this approach would serve as a deterrent to others?

Permissive teachers are a lot like the cop in my example. They give lots of warnings, reminders, second chances, and persuasive reasons why kids should stop at their stop signals. They may threaten to write tickets, and sometimes they actually do, but most of the time kids talk their way out of it and things pass with just a warning. Without tickets (consequences) to hold them accountable, kids have little cause to regard their teacher's rules seriously.

Why are permissive teachers reluctant to use consequences to enforce their rules? Most have the best of intentions. They don't mean to be vague or unclear. They're trying to be respectful, but they don't know how to be firm and respectful at the same time. Permissive teachers are afraid that the temporary frustration that accompanies consequences might damage children psychologically.

Let's do a little reality testing with this assumption. Are you accustomed to always getting your own way out in the world? When you don't, do you feel good about it? Aren't we supposed to feel frustrated when we don't get what we want? Isn't that how we learn to adjust to reality? When we prevent children from experiencing the consequences of their behavior, we also prevent much of their learning.

If permissive teachers are reluctant to use consequences to enforce their rules, how do they think they can stop misbehavior? Permissive teachers believe children will stop misbehaving when children realize that stopping is the right thing to do. The teacher's job, therefore, is to convince them to accept this belief.

The belief might hold up if all children were born with compliant temperaments. Compliant children are eager to please. Most will cooperate because that's the right thing to do. But what about strong-willed children or children who fall somewhere in between? Often, the only reason they cooperate is because they have to.

Do you recall our earlier example about the boys and the karate game? Why did they finally stop playing that dangerous game? Was it because stopping was the right thing to do? No, they stopped because they had to. They didn't want to experience the consequence that accompanied the choice to continue. They finally got a clear message about what was expected.

When our words are supported by effective action, children receive a clear signal about our rules and expectations. They understand that our spoken rules are the rules we practice and learn to take our words seriously. When our words are not supported by effective action, however, many children will ignore our words and continue to do what they want. The message they receive comes across like this: "I don't like what you're doing, but I'm not going to make you stop, at least not for a while."

How do kids know when they really are expected to stop? Often, they don't. The only way they will know is by testing our limits to see how far they can go. That's what permissiveness teaches them to do (see table 1).

The Punitive Approach
(Firm but Not Respectful)

THE PUNITIVE OR autocratic approach has been a stable fixture in American schools for a long time. It was the dominant training system prior to the 1960s and remains one of the most widely used training models. Its trademark has been its predictability. Children respond to coercion and punishment the same way today that they did fifty or more years ago. Compliant children cooperate. Strong-willed children rebel.

Table 1.   The Permissive Approach

Teacher's beliefs	Children will cooperate when they understand that cooperation is the right thing to do.
	My job is to serve my children and keep them happy.
	Consequences that upset my children cannot be effective.
Power and control	All for children.
Problem-solving process	Problem solving by persuasion.
	Win-lose (children win).
	Teachers do most of the problem solving.
What children learn	"Rules are for others, not me. I do as I wish."
	Teachers serve children.
	Teachers are responsible for solving children's problems.
	Dependency, disrespect, self-centeredness.
How children respond	Testing limits.
	Challenging and defying rules and authority.
	Ignoring and tuning out words.
	Wearing teachers down with words.

The approach works with children who need guidance the least but backfires with children who need guidance the most—the strong-willed or difficult-to-manage children who cause 90 percent of school disciplinary problems. The punitive approach is a poor match for strong-willed students. It makes them angry and resentful and inspires retaliation and power struggles.

Teachers who rely on the punitive or autocratic approach often find themselves in the roles of detective, judge, jailer, and probation officer. Their job is to investigate children's misdeeds, determine guilt, assign blame, impose penalties, and carry out sentences. Teachers direct and control the problem-solving process, which is often adversarial. Penalties tend to be drawn out and severe. Let's look at how one teacher uses this approach to handle a problem with disruption.

Mr. Stover, a fourth-grade teacher, is writing instructions on the blackboard when he hears giggling at the back of the room. Several students look at Jason, who does his best to appear innocent. Mr. Stover isn't convinced.

> Teachers who rely on the punitive or autocratic approach often find themselves in the roles of detective, judge, jailer, and probation officer.

"Okay, guys, what's going on?" asks Mr. Stover in an annoyed tone. "What's so funny?"

"He made us laugh," says one student, pointing to Jason. Jason shrugs his shoulders. Mr. Stover gives him a stern, disapproving look and then returns to his work on the blackboard.

A few minutes pass, then more giggles, only louder this time. When Mr. Stover turns, he sees Jason making mocking hand gestures to the amusement of his classmates. "That's enough, Jason!" says Mr. Stover angrily.

"I wasn't doing anything," replies Jason, believing he wasn't observed.

"Don't lie to me," says Mr. Stover. "I saw what you were doing, and I don't appreciate it. I expect that kind of behavior from a first grader but not from you. Keep it up and you're going to find yourself in big trouble." He gives Jason another stern, intimidating look.

A few minutes pass, and then Jason makes an even bolder move. When Mr. Stover's back is turned, Jason stands up and shakes his finger in a mock punitive gesture. The giggles turn into laughter. Mr. Stover intervenes again.

"What does it take to get through to you, Jason?" asks Mr. Stover. "Do you enjoy making a fool of yourself?"

"Do you enjoy being such a boring teacher?" counters Jason.

"That's enough!" shouts Mr. Stover, his face flushed with anger. "You've gone too far. Take your chair out in the hallway and write one hundred times, 'I will not be disrespectful to my teacher.'"

Jason spends the next twenty minutes in the hallway. When the bell rings for recess, he tries to join his classmates. Mr. Stover intercepts him.

"Not so fast, Jason," says Mr. Stover. "Where are the sentences?"

"I didn't write them," says Jason defiantly, "and you can't make me."

"You won't go out to recess until you do," says Mr. Stover.

"Oh, yeah? See what I care," says Jason. He would rather sit out the recess than give Mr. Stover the satisfaction of thinking he won.

Sure, Mr. Stover did get his message across, eventually, but what did he really accomplish? Did Jason leave the encounter with increased respect for Mr. Stover's rules or authority? Did Jason receive an instructive lesson in cooperation or responsibility? No. Jason learned what he experienced—a lesson in hurtful problem solving.

As a training model, the punitive approach has many limitations and only partially accomplishes our basic training goals. It usually does stop unwanted behavior in an immediate situation, but it doesn't teach independent problem solving, and it doesn't teach positive lessons about responsibility or self-control. Why? Because teachers make all the decisions, and teachers do all the problem solving. Teachers exercise all of the power and control, and kids are left out of the process. In effect, the punitive approach takes responsibility and learning opportunities away from children.

Let's take a closer look at the methods Mr. Stover used by examining a diagram of the interaction (see figure 2.2).

At point A, Mr. Stover notices the disruption and intervenes with some quick detective work. His tone is angry and adversarial. The focus is on right and wrong, guilt and blame, good guys and bad guys. The kids pick up on the dynamics quickly. They deny their guilt and attempt to place the blame on each other. The game of cops and robbers is under way, but so far the robbers are winning. Mr. Stover's detective work leads nowhere. So he tries intimidation.

Now the students know he is hooked. Their disruption continues, but Mr. Stover gets his evidence. He catches Jason in the act. When Jason denies his guilt, Mr. Stover accuses him of lying and confronts him with the evidence.

At this point, Mr. Stover's anger and frustration take over. He has completely personalized the conflict, and he is determined to make Jason pay for his crimes. The issue of disruption is now secondary to the hurtful and escalating power struggle that dominates the interaction. Mr. Stover begins by shaming and blaming Jason in front of the class; then he adds a challenge. He tells Jason to "keep it up" and threatens further consequences if he does.

Isn't this like waving a red cape in front of an angry bull? What would you predict? Right, the strategy backfires. Jason feels humiliated and retaliates with further disruption and name-calling. Mr. Stover responds on the same level. The drama moves into high gear.

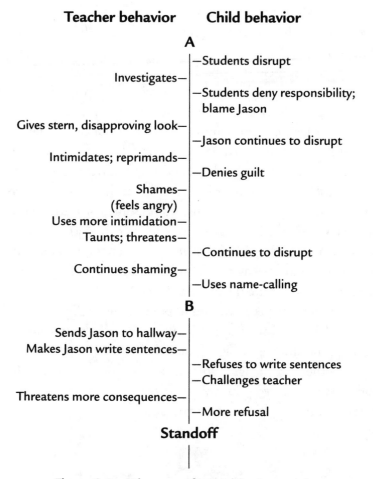

Teacher behavior   **Child behavior**

A

—Students disrupt

Investigates—

—Students deny responsibility;
blame Jason

Gives stern, disapproving look—

—Jason continues to disrupt

Intimidates; reprimands—

—Denies guilt

Shames—
(feels angry)
Uses more intimidation—
Taunts; threatens—

—Continues to disrupt

Continues shaming—

—Uses name-calling

B

Sends Jason to hallway—
Makes Jason write sentences—

—Refuses to write sentences
—Challenges teacher

Threatens more consequences—

—More refusal

Standoff

Figure 2.2   Diagram of a Punitive Interaction

Next, Mr. Stover sends Jason out of the classroom. The consequence, by itself, might have been effective in stopping the disruption, but Mr. Stover doesn't stop there. He adds further humiliation by insisting that Jason write one hundred times, "I will not be disrespectful to my teacher."

Does this stop the misbehavior? Partially. The disruption is over, but not the power struggle because Jason refuses to write. The scene ends in a standoff.

Yes, punishment did stop Jason's disruptive behavior. Does that prove that punishment is effective? This depends on your definition of effectiveness. If your definition is limited to stopping misbehavior, then punishment usually works. But the cooperation it achieves comes at a very high price: injured feelings, damaged relationships, and angry power struggles.

Punishment is humiliating to children. It hurts their feelings, makes them angry, and incites resistance or fearful withdrawal. Often, the hurtful methods are perceived as a personal attack ("You're a bad kid") rather than an attempt to discourage unacceptable behavior ("Your behavior is not acceptable"). The methods obscure the message (see table 2).

Imagine how people would respond if our traffic laws were enforced in punitive ways. Visualize yourself driving home. You approach a traffic signal, and the light turns red. There isn't another car in sight, so you take a chance and run the light. As soon as you do, you see a flashing red light in your rearview mirror. The cop pulls you over.

Table 2. The Autocratic or Punitive Approach	
Teacher's beliefs	If it doesn't hurt, children won't learn.
	Children won't respect my rules unless they fear my methods.
	It's my job to control my children.
	It's my job to solve my children's problems.
Power and control	All for teachers.
Problem-solving process	Problem solving by force.
	Win-lose (teachers win).
	Teachers do all the problem solving and make all the decisions.
	Teachers direct and control the problem.
What children learn	Teachers are responsible for solving children's problems.
	Hurtful methods of communication and problem solving.
How children respond	Anger, stubbornness.
	Revenge, rebellion.
	Withdrawal, fearful submission.

"Are you blind or just stupid?" he asks as he approaches your car. "Couldn't you see the light was red?" He orders you to get out of your car and writes you a citation. But before he hands it to you, he insults you again and hits you twice with his nightstick.

Would your response be to say, "Thanks, I needed that. I understand your point, and I'll be sure to stop next time"? Probably not. More likely, you would feel angry and resentful. You would understand the rule he was trying to enforce, but you wouldn't feel good about the way the message was communicated. You might even consider ways to get back.

When it comes to being humiliated, kids respond much like adults do. Compliant children usually cooperate, not out of respect but out of fear. Strong-willed children become angry and resentful. They rebel, seek revenge, or become sneaky and find ways to fly below our radar.

If punishment has so many limitations, why then do so many teachers continue to use it? Most teachers who use punishment were raised that way themselves. It feels natural to them, and they don't question its effectiveness. They believe the message has to hurt if the student is going to learn from it. When power struggles develop, they assume the problem is the student, not their methods.

The Mixed Approach (Neither Firm nor Respectful)

AS THE NAME implies, the mixed approach is a combination of the punitive and permissive training models. The mixed approach is characterized by inconsistency. Teachers who use it do a lot of flip-flopping back and forth between punishment and permissiveness in search of a better way to get their message across, one that is both firm and respectful. The goal is elusive because they lack the methods to achieve it. So they continue to flip-flop.

There are several variations of the mixed approach. Some teachers start off permissively with lots of repeating, reminding, warnings, and offering second chances, then become frustrated and try punitive tactics—threatening, shaming, blaming, and imposing harsh and drawn-out consequences. Others start off punitively with stern commands, investigation, shaming, blaming, and threats and then give in and take a permissive posture when they encounter resistance.

Still others remain loyal to one approach for longer periods of time. They try permissiveness until they can't stand being ignored or taken advantage of any longer, and then they flip-flop and try punishment until they can't stand how tyrannical they sound. Then they flip-flop back to permissiveness. The cycle of flip-flops just takes longer to repeat itself.

How do kids respond to the mixed approach? Let's see what happens when one teacher uses this approach with a group of disruptive seventh graders.

Miss Carey, a first-year teacher, is teaching a geography lesson when a paper airplane whizzes past her shoulder. She turns and sees a group of boys laughing and taking particular pleasure in her annoyance.

"Come on, guys," she says. "There's a lesson going on here. Would you like to join us?" The laughter stops for the moment, and Miss Carey proceeds with her lesson.

Within minutes, Miss Carey hears more laughter and sees Andrew sitting at his desk with his jacket zipped up over his head. She waits for him to stop, but he just sits there and pretends to follow along. His buddies can barely control themselves.

"Andrew!" exclaims Miss Carey, loud enough to get his attention. He unzips his jacket enough to create a peephole.

"Can I help you?" he asks. His friends continue to laugh.

"You sure can," replies Miss Carey. "You can take your jacket off your head and sit the way you're supposed to. I don't appreciate your clowning around. I really wish you would show a little respect."

"Okay," says Andrew with a smirk. He sits up rigidly in his seat, chest out, eyes forward, as though he were standing at attention. "Is this better?" he asks.

"You know what I mean," she replies. "I don't want to have to tell you again." Andrew relaxes his shoulders slightly and then shoots a quick grin at his buddies. Miss Carey returns to her lesson. Her patience is wearing thin.

A few minutes later, Miss Carey is startled by a loud thud. Andrew is lying on the floor next to his desk. Everyone is looking at him.

"I can't believe it!" he exclaims with feigned surprise. "I fell out of my seat! And I was trying so hard to sit the right way, too." He grins at his friends, who can barely control their laughter.

"I've had it!" explodes Miss Carey. "If you insist on acting like a jerk, then do it outside my classroom." She hands him a referral to the office and points to the door. "Take as long as you want, but don't come back until you can figure out how to cooperate. You'll get F grades on everything you miss while you're gone."

Clearly, Andrew pushed things to the limit, but did his behavior cause Miss Carey to explode, or did she set herself up by allowing things to go too far? Let's answer these questions by examining a diagram of their interaction (see figure 2.3).

What happens the first time Andrew and his buddies disrupt? Do they receive a clear message to stop? No. Miss Carey appeals for their cooperation. She points out that there is a lesson in progress and invites them to join in. Does this mean they have a choice? If it does, their choice is clear. They continue testing.

What happens the second time Andrew disrupts? Does Miss Carey give him a clear signal to stop and tell him what will happen if he doesn't? No. She tells him she doesn't appreciate his behavior and says she wishes he would show a little more respect. What does that mean? How little is too little? Andrew gets right to work trying to find out. He continues to disrupt and to be disrespectful.

What happens the third time Andrew disrupts? Does he finally get the information he's looking for? No. Miss Carey tells

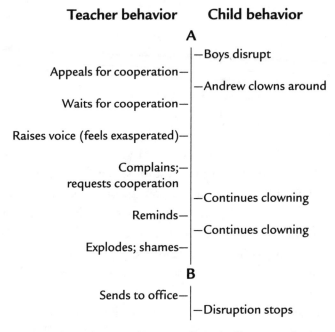

Teacher behavior **Child behavior**

A

—Boys disrupt

Appeals for cooperation—

—Andrew clowns around

Waits for cooperation—

Raises voice (feels exasperated)—

Complains;
requests cooperation

—Continues clowning

Reminds—

—Continues clowning

Explodes; shames—

B

Sends to office—

—Disruption stops

Figure 2.3   Diagram of a Mixed Interaction

him that she doesn't want to have to tell him again. Tell him
what? She probably believes she has been saying stop all along,
but she hasn't been saying it in terms that Andrew understands. She is trying to be respectful, but her message lacks
firmness and clarity.

Let's look at things from Andrew's perspective. He really enjoys negative attention. He disrupted class three times, and each
time, nothing happened to make him stop. Why should he take
Miss Carey seriously? He doesn't. He continues disrupting.

What happens the fourth time? Finally, Miss Carey has
had enough. She is ready to act, but she has allowed things to
go too far. Her anger and frustration take over. She explodes
and ends up using the punitive tactics she tried so hard to
avoid. Like many teachers who use the mixed approach, she

lacks the methods to be firm and respectful at the same time. Miss Carey is on the fast track to burnout.

The Democratic Approach (Firm and Respectful)

EFFECTIVE GUIDANCE REQUIRES a balance between firmness and respect. The punitive approach is firm but not respectful. The permissive approach, on the other extreme, is respectful but not firm. The mixed approach is neither firm nor respectful. All three are based on win-lose methods of problem solving and faulty beliefs about learning. None of them teaches responsibility or accomplishes our basic training goals. What, then, is the alternative?

Fortunately, there is an alternative to the extremes of punishment and permissiveness. I didn't invent it, but I did have the good fortune to observe it, describe it, and eventually teach it to thousands of parents and teachers. As a graduate student in educational psychology at the University of California, Davis, one of my professors asked me to assist him in a research study on teacher effectiveness. The purpose of this 1978 study was to examine teacher behaviors that contribute to time on task with students. Research shows that on-task time correlates powerfully with achievement.

My job in the study was to observe effective teachers in their classrooms and record the specific things they said and did that led to on-task time. This was an eye-opener, because most of these teachers did not have easy classrooms. They had students with ADD, learning disabilities, and behavioral problems, as well as more than a few comedians and attention seekers.

The effective teachers I observed did not give in to misbehavior. They didn't lecture, cajole, bargain, or negotiate. They didn't use threats, intimidation, or long, drawn-out consequences. They didn't compromise their standards.

Instead, they maintained a respectful attitude, held their ground firmly, stated their rules and expectations clearly, and followed through with instructive consequences when their students chose not to cooperate. These teachers were solidly in control of themselves and their classrooms. They made classroom management look easy.

What impressed me most was the fact that their guidance methods worked with the full range of students: compliant students who cooperated for the asking, difficult students who required generous helpings of consequences, students with special needs, and those in between. It didn't matter. The teachers had the tools to get the job done, and they got results. They got the most cooperation, the most respect, and the best achievement from their students. I didn't realize it at the time, but I was getting a crash course in effective limit setting from some real pros.

A few years later, after the study had been published and was collecting dust on some library shelf, I had an opportunity to pilot a teacher workshop series on effective classroom management for a large northern California school district. "Great!" I thought. "I'll use the outcome data from the 1978 U.C. Davis study. We know what works. If I can teach it, others can use it."

The pilot was a success. Teachers found the approach easy to learn and use, and they got results just like the teachers in the study. The workshop became a training program that eventually became a book, but the real credit belongs to the many effective teachers I observed who understood how to create optimal learning environments for children by balancing firmness with respect. I call it the *democratic approach*.

Unlike the other extremes, the democratic approach is a win-win method of problem solving that combines firmness with respect and accomplishes all of our basic training goals. It stops misbehavior. It teaches responsibility. And it conveys, in the clearest way, the lessons we want to teach about our rules for acceptable behavior. Best of all, the democratic approach achieves our goals with less time and energy and without injuring feelings, damaging relationships, or provoking angry power struggles in the process.

> The democratic approach achieves our goals with less time and energy and without injuring feelings, damaging relationships, or provoking angry power struggles in the process.

The democratic approach succeeds where others fail because the process is cooperative, not adversarial. It focuses on what child guidance is all about—teaching and learning. The teacher's job is to guide the learning process by providing clear limits, acceptable choices, and instructive consequences that hold children accountable for their actions. No threats or detective work. No lecturing or cajoling. No flip-flopping back and forth. And no power struggles. The methods don't hurt. Children are simply provided with the information they need to make acceptable choices about their behavior, and then they are allowed to experience the consequences of those choices.

Does the term *democratic* mean that all guidance decisions are put to a vote and decided by consensus? No. The term is used to illustrate how boundaries are arranged and how power and control are distributed in the classroom. In democratic classrooms, the teacher is still the adult in charge, but children are provided with freedom within well-defined limits and allowed to make decisions about their own behavior. The boundaries are neither too broad nor too restrictive. They permit freedom and choices, but children are given only as much freedom as they can handle responsibly. Let's look at how one teacher uses the democratic approach to handle a problem with class disruption.

Josh and Aaron, two second graders, sit across from each other in the same table group. They're supposed to be working on a handwriting assignment, but they fool around instead. First, Josh tosses an eraser at Aaron and hits him in the chest. Aaron flicks it back. Then Josh throws a wad of paper and hits Aaron. When Aaron throws it back, he hits Carly instead. She complains to the teacher.

"Mr. Jordan, Aaron threw something at me."

"Josh threw it at me first," says Aaron.

"No, I didn't," says Josh. "You threw an eraser at me!"

Mr. Jordan intervenes. "Josh and Aaron, you both should be working quietly on your handwriting assignment. Would you like to work quietly at your desks or by yourselves at the back tables?" He keeps two tables in the back corners of the room for cool-downs, time-outs, or when students need to be separated from their table groups. He looks at each for an answer.

"I want to stay here," says Aaron.

"Me, too," says Josh.

"Okay," says Mr. Jordan, "but if there is any more disrupting, you'll have to move to the back tables."

Aaron is convinced. He decides to settle down. Not Josh. He enjoyed the brief soap opera his disruption created, and he's hungry for more. When Mr. Jordan walks away, Josh fires off several more paper wads at Aaron. One hits Aaron in the head. The other sails over Aaron's shoulder and catches Mr. Jordan's attention.

"Pick up your assignment, Josh," says Mr. Jordan matter-of-factly. "You'll have to finish at the back table." Josh heads off to complete the lesson by himself. The disruption is over.

Unlike the teachers in my previous examples, Mr. Jordan succeeds in a firm and respectful manner. He achieves all of his guidance goals and maintains positive relationships in the process. No lectures. No humiliating consequences. No flip-flopping and no angry power struggles. He simply gives the boys the information they need to cooperate and then follows through based on their choice. Let's take a closer look at his methods by examining a diagram of the interaction (see figure 2.4).

Notice how short this diagram is. Effective guidance requires less time and energy and achieves better results. Mr. Jordan is working with a plan. He knows what he's going to do, and he's prepared for whatever resistance he may encounter.

He begins at point A by giving the boys a clear message about what he expects. He tells them they should be working quietly on their writing assignment. Then he gives them some choices. He asks whether they would like to work quietly at their seats or at the back tables. Both boys say they want to

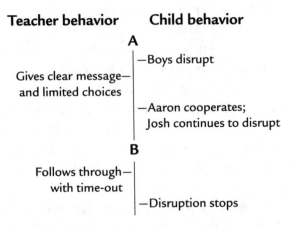

Figure 2.4   Diagram of a Democratic Interaction

work at their seats. So Mr. Jordan tells them they will have to move if there is any further disrupting.

Now the boys have all the information they need to make an acceptable decision. They know what's expected and what will happen if they choose not to cooperate. The way things are set up, they cannot avoid learning the lesson Mr. Jordan intends.

What happens? Aaron decides to cooperate, but not Josh. He decides to test and continues disrupting. So Mr. Jordan simply follows through. In a matter-of-fact manner, he requests Josh to take his work to the back table and finish up. Josh gets a very clear message. Mr. Jordan is teaching his rules effectively.

Can you imagine how much more rewarding your teaching would be without all the reminders, threats, lectures, and power struggles? The goal is achievable (see table 3). The methods are simple and easy to learn. The hardest part is recognizing the things that aren't working for you.

Chapter Summary

MOST TEACHERS TEACH their rules from one of four basic training models: the permissive approach, the punitive approach, the mixed approach, and the democratic approach. Each model is premised on a different set of assumptions about how children learn our rules, and each model elicits different responses from children based on their temperaments and learning styles. The permissive approach is respectful but not firm and often provokes testing and power struggles. The punitive approach is firm but not respectful and often incites rebellion. The mixed approach is neither firm nor respectful and brings out the worst in most children. The democratic approach, in contrast, is both respectful and firm. It achieves all of our guidance goals with the least conflict and greatest cooperation.

Table 3.　The Democratic Approach

Teacher's beliefs	Children are capable of solving problems on their own.
	Children should be given choices and allowed to learn from the consequences of their choices.
	Encouragement is an effective way to motivate cooperation.
Power and control	Children are given only as much power and control as they can handle responsibly.
Problem-solving process	Cooperative.
	Win-win.
	Based on mutual respect.
	Children are active participants in the problem-solving process.
What children learn	Responsibility.
	Cooperation.
	Independence.
	Respect for rules and authority.
	Self-control.
How children respond	More cooperation.
	Less limit testing.
	Resolve problems on their own.
	Regard teacher's words seriously.

In the chapters that follow, you'll discover your training approach, the type of limits you're using, and why children respond to you the way they do. With an awareness of what hasn't worked for you, you'll be ready to say good-bye to old, ineffective methods and create a positive environment for learning that balances firmness with respect.

3

How Children Learn Your Rules

Each day when it's time to line up for recess, Anthony pushes and shoves his way to the front of the line. Then when the bell rings, he sprints down the hallway, sometimes crashing into others, in an attempt to be first to arrive at the tetherball poles.

"I've told him over and over again that it's not okay to push in line or run down the hallway," complains his frustrated teacher, "but he does it day after day. I've explained how dangerous his behavior is. I've even asked his parents to talk to him. Nothing seems to help. I'm beginning to think he has some type of learning problem."

Anthony's teacher believes she is teaching a rule, but Anthony is not learning the rule she is trying to teach. This chapter will show you why. You'll discover how children learn your rules and why the teaching and learning process sometimes breaks down. By the time you've finished this chapter, you'll be a step closer to teaching your rules in the clearest and most understandable way. Let's look at how Christi's teacher does it.

Christi, age four, pretends to cook breakfast in the miniature kitchen in her preschool room. Her friend Beth sits at a small table waiting to be served.

"Would you like some eggs?" asks Christi.

"Yes, please," replies Beth. Christi pretends to scoop the eggs onto a plastic plate, but the pan slips from her hand and falls in Beth's lap. Both girls laugh. Things start to get silly.

"You spilled eggs all over me!" says Beth, still laughing. She grabs her cup and pretends to pour juice over Christi's head. Both laugh. Things get even sillier. Christi picks up a plastic toaster and swings it over her head by the cord. She nearly hits Beth in the head.

> When our words are consistent with our actions, we don't need a lot of words or harsh consequences to get our message across.

"Put the toaster down, Christi," says her teacher matter-of-factly. "You can play with it the right way, or I'll have to put it away."

Christi hears the words, but she's very excited. She continues to swing the toaster. Her teacher reaches over and takes the toaster away. "You can play with it later this afternoon," she says, "if you play with it the right way."

Christi is learning her teacher's rules about using the play items in the classroom. She may need to repeat this lesson before she masters the rule, but her teacher's methods will certainly lead to the desired outcome.

Christi's teacher is teaching her rules effectively. Her words say stop, and her actions convey the same message when she takes the toaster away. When our words are consistent with our actions, we don't need a lot of words or harsh consequences to get our message across. Our message is clear, and so is the rule behind it.

Why Teaching and Learning Break Down

RESEARCH BY THE Swiss psychologist Jean Piaget on children's intellectual development has shown that the thinking and learning of children are qualitatively different from that of adults. Children think and learn concretely. For younger children, immediate sensory experience plays a greater role in shaping their reality than for adolescents or adults.

What does this mean to teachers in the classroom? It means that children's beliefs are largely determined by what they experience with their senses. What they see, hear, touch, and feel determines how they think things are. Their perceptions and beliefs about how the world works are based primarily on their concrete experiences.

Piaget's findings have important implications for how we go about teaching our rules to children. We do this in two basic ways: with our words and with our actions. Both teach a lesson, but only our actions are concrete. Actions, not words, define our rules.

For example, if I tell my son that it's not okay to kick the soccer ball in the house, but he does it anyway, and I overlook it, what is he learning about my rule? Of course, he's learning that it's really okay to kick the ball in the house.

If, on the other hand, I take the ball away each time he kicks it in the house, he and I would probably share the same belief about my rule. He would know that I meant what I said.

When our words match our actions consistently, children learn to take our words seriously and to recognize the rules behind them. When our words do not match our actions, however, children learn to ignore our words and to base their beliefs on what they experience. In effect, we are teaching two rules: a rule in theory and a rule in practice.

This essential miscommunication is the source of most breakdowns in the teaching and learning process, and most adults are not even aware that it's happening. They continue to teach their rules with words while their children learn by actions. This is what was happening to Anthony and his teacher in our opening example, and this is what is taking place in many classrooms throughout the country.

Why Limits Are Important

LIMITS ARE THE messages or signals we use to communicate our rules and expectations for behavior. Limits answer some very basic questions children ask about how their world works. On the surface, limits operate like traffic signals by providing information in the form of green lights (do that) and red lights (stop that) for acceptable and unacceptable behavior. These signals answer the questions "What's okay?" and "What's not okay?"

Beneath the surface, however, limits answer a very different set of questions about the power and authority of the person sending the messages: "Who's in control?" "How far can I go?" "What happens when I go too far?" The answers to these questions define the balance of power and authority in teacher-student relationships and help children determine whether compliance with their teacher's rules is optional or really required.

Limit Testing:
How Children Do Research

HOW DO CHILDREN clarify our rules and expectations? How do they determine whether what we ask is really expected and required? Rarely do they come up and ask, "How much power and authority do you really have? How do I know you really mean what you say? And what are you going to do if I don't do what you ask?" My guess is that you probably haven't had this experience very often, if at all.

Most children don't ask these questions with their words, but they do think about them, and they do ask them with their behavior. They just go ahead and do whatever we asked them not to do, and then they wait to see what happens. This is limit-testing behavior, and this is how children do their research. It answers their basic questions more definitively than words. Much of what we consider to be misbehavior in the classroom is actually limit testing or children's attempts to clarify what we really expect.

Temperament and Learning Styles

All children test limits to determine our rules and expectations. This is normal. But not all children test limits in the same way. Temperament has a lot to do with how they conduct their research.

Compliant children don't do a lot of testing, because they don't require a lot of hard data to be convinced to accept and follow our rules. Their underlying desire is to cooperate. Most are willing to accept our words as all the data they need and cooperate for the asking. Compliant children are easy to teach because they do most of their learning the easy way. The majority of students in most classrooms fall in this category.

Strong-willed children, on the other hand, are aggressive researchers. They test frequently and require a lot of hard data in the form of experience before they're convinced to accept and follow our rules. To strong-willed children, the word *stop* is a theory waiting to be tested, and they know how to find out what it really means. They continue to test and push us to the point of action to see what happens.

> Although strong-willed children constitute less than 15 percent of the school population, they are a powerful minority because they're responsible for nearly 90 percent of classroom discipline problems.

Although strong-willed children constitute less than 15 percent of the school population, they are a powerful minority because they're responsible for nearly 90 percent of classroom discipline problems. Strong-willed children are difficult to teach because they do much of their learning the hard way.

The quickest way to discover what's not working for you is to match your guidance methods with a strong-willed child.

Because compliant and strong-willed students learn rules differently, often they respond differently to the same messages from their teacher. This can be very confusing. Let me illustrate with a personal example. My oldest son, Scott, is usually compliant. He cooperates for the asking. My youngest son, Ian, is strong-willed. He requires hard data before he is convinced I mean business. My boys do their research differently, and I've learned to adjust my signals accordingly.

For example, both boys like to watch TV with the volume cranked up. When Scott does this, I simply say, "Scott, the TV is too loud. Turn it down, please." He always does (at least he has so far), and I've learned to count on his cooperation. He accepts my words as all the data he needs.

If I use the same message with Ian, I know from experience what he's likely to do. He will just sit there and ignore me and wait for a clearer signal. Or, he might give me the words I want to hear and say, "I will," but continue to do what he wants. This isn't really lying. What Ian really means is, "I will when I have to, and I didn't hear that I have to."

Like many strong-willed kids, Ian is thinking, "Or what?" He's looking for concrete, definitive information about what I really expect. So I've learned to provide him with all the data he needs to make an acceptable choice. When the TV is on too loud, I say, "Ian, turn the TV down, please, or I'll have to turn it off."

When Ian hears that word *off,* an interesting thing happens. He gets up, just like his compliant older brother, and turns the TV down. Why? Because he suddenly turned into a compliant person? No. He turns it down because he has all the data he needs to make an acceptable choice. He knows from previous experience that I will turn it off.

Aggressive Researchers

My job as a child therapist brings me into frequent contact with the most aggressive researchers in a large school district. I see the kids who don't stop at the signals their teachers hold up in the classroom, the ones who push everything to the limit. Loren, a second grader, is a good example. He was referred after a series of suspensions for disruptive and uncooperative behavior in the classroom.

"Loren won't listen to anyone," commented his teacher. "He thinks he can do whatever he wants. I've had numerous conferences with his parents, and they say he acts the same way at home. We're all at a loss for what to do."

When Loren arrived at my office with his parents, he plopped himself down in one of my comfortable blue swivel chairs and began sizing me up. Then he went right to work on me. We hadn't exchanged a word, but his research was under way.

What do you think Loren and many other children do when they first sit in my swivel chairs? Right. They spin them, and sometimes they put their feet in them, too. They know it's not okay. Their parents know it, and so do I, but the kids do it anyway. They look at me, then at their parents, and go ahead and see what happens. This is limit-testing behavior. When it happens, I know I am about to learn a great deal about how the family communicates about limits.

I don't need behavior rating scales, standardized tests, or lengthy clinical interviews to see what's going on. I just watch the child, the chair, and the parents for ten to fifteen minutes, and I usually have all the information I need to see what's going on.

Loren's parents responded to his chair spinning the way most permissive parents do. They ignored it. They pretended it wasn't happening and focused instead on telling me about all of the disruptive things Loren did at school. Loren continued spinning. Five minutes passed. Not one signal had been given.

Ten minutes into our session, I could see Loren's father was becoming annoyed. He made his first attempt at a signal. He said Loren's name softly and gave him a look of disapproval.

Loren did what most kids do when this happens. He acknowledged the gesture, stopped briefly, and then resumed his spinning as soon as his father looked away. Loren and his parents were reenacting a script, the same one they go through dozens of times each week whenever Loren misbehaves.

With his behavior, Loren was asking the same questions he asks at home and in the classroom: "What's okay?" "What's not okay?" "Who's in control?" "How far can I go?" "And what happens when I go too far?" He knew his parents weren't going to do anything about his behavior, so he was conducting his research to determine my power and authority and the rules that operated in my office. Between disapproving looks from his father, Loren continued to spin. I waited to see what would happen next.

A few more minutes passed, and then Loren's father did what many other parents do at this point. He reached over and stopped the chair with his hand. His signal elicited the same response as before. Loren acknowledged the gesture, waited for his father to remove his hand, and then continued spinning.

Loren's parents were doing their best to say stop, but Loren knew from experience that stopping was not really expected or required. All of the gestures were just steps in a well-rehearsed drama. The spinning continued. I could see why he wasn't responding to his teacher's signals in the classroom.

Fifteen minutes went by, and Loren still had not received a clear signal from his parents. Their anger was apparent. Finally, his exasperated mother turned to me and said, "See what he does? This is the same thing we have to put up with at home!"

At this point, I intervened and helped Loren answer some of his research questions. In a matter-of-fact voice, I said, "Loren, I'd like you to use my blue chairs, but I have two rules you'll have to follow: Don't spin them, and don't put your feet in them. I'm confident you can follow my rules, but if you don't, you'll have to sit in my orange chair for the rest of the session." I keep an old plastic orange chair in my office for these situations.

What do you think Loren did? Sure, he did the same thing most strong-willed children do. He tested. Not right away, but within a few minutes, he gave the chair another spin and looked for my reaction. He heard my words; now he wanted hard data. He wanted to see what I would do.

So I did what I always do when this happens. I pulled out the orange chair and said calmly, "This will be your chair for the rest of the session. You can try my blue chairs again next session." Then I stood next to him and waited for him to move with a look of expectation. Reluctantly, Loren moved into the orange chair, but he didn't do it in a respectful manner. He rolled his eyes, gave me a look of disgust, and murmured something under his breath I'm sure wasn't a compliment. The bait was skillfully presented and tempting, but I didn't bite. His final attempt to hook me into a power struggle didn't work. What did Loren and I just work out? I just answered his research questions. He heard stop, and he experienced stopping. Now he knows what I expect and what will happen if he decides to test the next time he visits my office. Loren has all the information he needs to make an acceptable choice.

You're probably wondering what happens when children refuse to get out of the blue chair. The interesting thing is that most don't test when they get the information they need to make an acceptable choice. I see more than a hundred chair spinners a year in my counseling work. Only a few continue to test when I bring out the orange chair.

What happens when they do? The process is still the same. The questions haven't changed. They are still asking, "Or what? What are you going to do about it?" So I try to give them the data they're looking for in the same matter-of-fact manner. I turn to their parents and say, "Your child doesn't want to get out of my chair. Do I have your permission to assist him into the orange chair?"

In sixteen years, I've never had a parent say no. Most are so embarrassed over their child's behavior, they can't wait to get out of my office. Others are very curious to see whether I can actually get their child to cooperate.

Once I get their permission, I turn to the child and say, "Your parents say I can assist you into the orange chair, but I'd prefer that you move yourself. What would you like to do?" I take a few deep breaths, remind myself that I'm the adult in this situation, and wait patiently for fifteen or twenty seconds.

> Even aggressive researchers can make acceptable choices when provided with clear signals.

What do you think they do? A very few, maybe two or three each year, wait until I get up out of my chair before they are convinced I will act. Then they move into the other chair. The vast majority move on their own. Why? They move because they have all the information they need to make an acceptable decision. Their questions are answered. Even aggressive researchers can make acceptable choices when provided with clear signals. Their cooperation demonstrates the power of a clear message.

What We Do Is What We Teach

WHEN CHILDREN LIKE Loren misbehave at school, the focus is on their problem behavior, not the hidden forces that operate beneath the surface to shape that problem behavior. This is where my investigative work begins. I try to determine why the teaching and learning process breaks down. Is the problem teaching? Or learning? Or is something else going on? I try to answer these questions by examining the ways rules are taught both at home and in the classroom.

Permissive Rules

Permissive guidance methods often lead to breakdowns in the teaching and learning process because teachers confuse their words for actions and become frustrated when their message doesn't get across. Children learn a different rule than their teacher intends.

For example, Barry, a third grader, tilts back precariously in his chair while his teacher gives a lesson at the board. She notices and gives him a disapproving look. He straightens his chair briefly, but as soon as she looks away, he tilts back once again.

"He's not really hurting anything," his teacher says to herself. She decides to ignore it, and Barry continues to tilt. Ten minutes pass. Then he slips and nearly falls before catching himself.

"That doesn't look very safe to me," says his teacher. "I'm afraid you might hurt yourself. I'd feel more comfortable if you sat the right way."

"I'll be careful," says Barry.

"I know you will," she replies, "but accidents can happen even when you're careful, and I'd hate to see you get hurt. Please sit the right way, okay?" She waits for Barry to comply. He does, and she returns to her lesson, satisfied that her message got across.

It doesn't take long before Barry tests again. This time, he props his feet on the rails of his desk to stabilize his chair while tilting. When his teacher sees what's going on, she feels frustrated.

"I thought I asked you to sit the right way," she says with irritation. "What would the principal say if she walked into our classroom and saw you sitting like that?"

"But it's safe the way I'm doing it," argues Barry. He demonstrates how he can stabilize his chair by putting his feet on the sides of his desk.

"I'm still not comfortable with it," says the teacher. "I'm going to have to insist that you stop."

"Okay," says Barry reluctantly, "but I don't see what it's hurting." He stops tilting.

Do you think Barry and his teacher are finished with this issue? Barry's teacher sincerely believes she's saying stop when she points out the dangers of tilting back in the chair. She becomes frustrated and annoyed when he does not respond as expected. In actuality, she is communicating two messages, but she is aware of only one.

Her words say something that resembles stop, but what does Barry experience? He doesn't experience stopping. Instead, he hears more talking. His teacher's action message is really saying, "Go ahead and do what you want. I don't like it, but I'm not going to do anything about it, at least not for a while."

Barry responds to the mixed message like many children do. He ignores the words and continues pushing with his behavior. He learns from what he experiences. What is Barry's interpretation of his teacher's rule? Sure, it's okay to tilt back in his chair as long as he can tolerate his teacher's attempts to persuade him not to.

Punitive Rules

Those who operate from the punitive model use both words and actions to teach their rules, but their methods often end up teaching a different lesson than they intend. This is what

Mr. Silva experienced when he tried to handle a problem with one of his sixth graders.

Mr. Silva is writing instructions for an upcoming literature assignment when he hears a clicking sound coming from the middle of the room. He turns and sees several students looking at Mel, who slouches in his seat.

"Mel, what you're doing is not respectful," says Mr. Silva.

"It wasn't me," Mel replies.

"Don't lie to me!" says Mr. Silva. "Now sit up and pay attention. If I hear any more noises out of you, you'll spend your next recess on the bench."

"What a jerk," Mel murmurs under his breath.

"What was that, Mel?" inquires Mr. Silva angrily. "Would you like to say it a little louder for others to hear?"

"I didn't say anything," Mel replies.

"Oh, yes, you did," accuses Mr. Silva. "Whatever it was, I'm sure it was disrespectful. You just earned a recess on the bench. Your smart mouth got you in trouble again."

"Oh, ouch! That really hurts," says Mel sarcastically.

"You've just earned another recess on the bench," says Mr. Silva angrily. "Wanna try for three?" Mel clutches his chest in mock agony. "That's three!" says Mr. Silva. "How about all the recesses for the week?"

Mel is tempted to retaliate, but he believes Mr. Silva will follow through on his threat. Mel does not want to lose his recesses. He sits and glares his defiance.

Mr. Silva doesn't realize it, but he is teaching two rules about being disrespectful in the classroom. His words (rule in theory) say, "It's not okay," but what kind of behavior is he modeling? His actions (rule in practice) say just the opposite. He is teaching the same behavior he's trying to eliminate. Which lesson is Mel following?

Lessons at Home Affect Lessons at School

THE HOME IS the training ground for the real world. That's where children first learn the rules for acceptable behavior. They take those lessons with them into the classroom. Steven is a good example. When I first met him, he had been suspended from school four times for hitting, and it was October. The year had barely begun.

His fourth-grade teacher tried everything she knew to help Steven change. She explained the school's rules about hitting. She encouraged him to ask an adult for help whenever he got into a conflict, and she offered her assistance when Steven got into conflicts in the classroom. Nothing helped. She was frustrated and so were Steven's parents.

"Living with Steven is like being around a time bomb waiting to explode," said his mother. "He knows that hitting is not okay, but he does it anyway. He hits his younger brother, he hits other kids in the neighborhood, and he hits kids at school. We've talked to him over and over again, but it doesn't seem to sink in."

"What exactly do you say to him when he hits others?" I asked, curious about their verbal messages.

"Well, I get a little loud," confessed Steven's father. "It makes me angry to see Steven mistreating others, and I let him know I'm not going to tolerate it."

"What do you do to get that message across?" I asked.

"We paddle him when he needs it," Steven's father replied. "We don't believe in all this permissive stuff going on today. Kids need to know you mean business."

"How many times a week does Steven need that kind of reminder?" I asked.

"Two or three times, and sometimes more. He needs to know when he's gone too far," said his father.

"With that many reminders, why do you think Steven is having such a difficult time learning your rules?" I asked.

"We suspect he has some kind of a learning problem," Steven's mother replied. "We're considering having him tested."

As I got to know Steven, I could see he didn't need testing. The problem wasn't learning. It was teaching. Steven was a very capable learner. He was mastering all the lessons his parents were teaching about hurtful problem solving. He was good at yelling, threatening, and intimidating. He knew how to hit, and he was becoming skillful at blaming others when he got caught.

Steven understood his parent's words, but their spoken rules were not the ones they practiced. What did they practice? Hitting. Steven was learning a lesson in violent problem solving. At school, he was simply following the lessons he had been taught.

Permissive training at home also sets kids up for problems at school. James is a good example. He was getting off to a rough start in kindergarten when I first met him. The note his teacher sent was revealing: "James pushes everything to the limit. When I ask him to join an activity, he ignores me and does what he wants. When I insist, he cries or throws a tantrum. He seems to think the classroom rules don't apply to him."

James's mother was equally frustrated. "He's the same way at home," she complained. "He refuses to get dressed in the morning. He won't come in when I call him, and getting him to bed is a nightmare by itself. I have to ask him over and over again. Most of the time, he just ignores me and does what he wants."

Like many children trained with permissiveness, James was accustomed to getting his own way, and he had developed a full repertoire of skills to make that happen. He was an expert at tuning out, ignoring, resisting, avoiding, arguing, debating, bargaining, challenging, and defying. If those tactics didn't work, James played his trump card. He threw a tantrum. His mother usually felt guilty and gave in.

James's intentions were not malicious. He did it because it worked. His experiences had taught him that "Rules are for others, not me. I make my own rules, and I do what I want." James operated on these beliefs both at home and in the classroom.

It wasn't hard to understand why James had such an exaggerated perception of his own power and authority and why he was doing so much testing. At home, the stop signals he confronted did not require stopping, and *no* really meant *yes* most of the time. When he misbehaved, he knew he would hear a lot of repeating, reminding, lecturing, and threatening, but none of those methods required stopping. His training had not prepared him for the real stop signs he was encountering in the classroom.

Teaching Rules Effectively

TEACHERS CAN'T CONTROL the faulty lessons children learn at home, but they can help children move in a more acceptable direction by teaching their rules effectively in the classroom. Let's look at how one teacher does it.

Katy, a third grader, loves to play four square, but she doesn't like to follow the rules. Sometimes when her turn is over, she refuses to leave the court.

"She's cheating again," several kids complain when Mrs. Karim arrives on the scene. "She won't leave when her turn is over." Katy stands in the court with her hands on her hips, refusing to budge.

"You're going to have to play by the rules, Katy, or find a different game to play," says Mrs. Karim matter-of-factly. "What would you like to do?"

"Okay," says Katy as she heads to the end of the line. The game resumes, but within minutes the kids complain again. Mrs. Karim sees Katy standing in the court, refusing to leave.

"I won't do it again," says Katy when she sees Mrs. Karim.

"That's a good choice," replies Mrs. Karim, "but you're going to have to find a different game to play this morning. You can try four square again this afternoon." No shaming. No blaming. No harsh words or lectures. Katy hears the same message she experiences. She may need several more of these experiences before she masters the intended rule, but the methods will surely lead to the desired outcome. Mr. Givens also is effective when he sees one of his ninth-grade students reading a magazine in class.

"Seth, magazines don't belong in class," says Mr. Givens matter-of-factly.

"I'm not disturbing anybody," says Seth, looking for a little bargaining room. Mr. Givens doesn't take the bait.

"You can put it away in your backpack," Mr. Givens replies, "or I will keep it in my desk until the end of the semester."

Now, Seth has all the information he needs to make an acceptable decision. He knows what's expected and what will happen if he decides to test. The way things are set up, Mr. Givens cannot fail to get his message across. There are no payoffs for aggressive research.

Chapter Summary

CHILDREN LEARN CONCRETELY. Their beliefs and perceptions are based primarily on what they experience, not necessarily on what they are told. This fact has important implications for how we go about teaching our rules. We do it in two basic ways: with our words and with our actions. Both teach a lesson, but only our actions are concrete. Actions, not words, define our rules.

When our words match our actions consistently, children learn to trust our words and recognize the rules behind them. When our words do not match our actions, however, children learn to ignore our words and base their beliefs on what they experience. In reality, they are learning two sets of rules: our spoken rules and the rules we practice.

This fundamental miscommunication about rules is why many well-intended guidance lessons break down. Most teachers are unaware it's even happening. They just continue to try to get their message across with their words while their students learn from what they experience.

Children are skillful at determining whether our spoken rules are also the rules we practice. They test. Limit testing is how children conduct their research. Compliant children do not need a lot of data to be convinced to follow our rules. Strong-willed children, on the other hand, are much more aggressive researchers. They need a lot of data to be convinced that our spoken rules are actually the ones we practice.

We can help children complete their research and learn our rules by providing the signals they understand best: clear words and effective actions. These tools are the key to teaching our rules in the clearest and most understandable way.

4

The Classroom Dance of Ineffective Discipline

Teachers who operate with unclear or ineffective limits develop their own special dance of miscommunication, which they perform over and over again when their rules are tested or violated. There's a permissive version of the dance that's wordy and drawn out and a punitive version that's angrier and more dramatic. Some teachers do a little of both. All dances are exercises in ineffective communication that lead to escalating conflicts and power struggles. Over time, the dances become such a familiar and deeply ingrained habit that teachers experience them as their normal way of doing things. They are not even aware they are dancing.

Teachers such as the ones we'll follow in this chapter can easily become stuck in these destructive patterns of communication. Without awareness and new skills, there's no way out. They have no choice but to continue dancing the only dance they know. Awareness is the key to breaking free.

If you suspect that you've been dancing with your students, this chapter will help you break free. You'll learn how your dances begin, how they end, and what keeps them going. Most important, you'll learn how to step off the dance floor so you can move on to more effective forms of communication. Let's look at how one frustrated teacher discovered her dance.

A Permissive Dance

BARBARA, A THIRD-GRADE teacher, was on the verge of burnout when I first met her. Her third year of teaching was starting off as rough as the previous two. The thought of facing another year full of conflicts and power struggles was more than she could bear. Depression was sinking in. Her principal suggested that she give me a call.

"I became a teacher because I like kids," Barbara said when she arrived at my office, "but I don't enjoy them much anymore. I treat them with kindness and respect, but some of them just tune me out and do what they want. I nag them all day long. They're wearing me out!"

She didn't realize it, but Barbara was stuck in an escalating pattern of conflicts and power struggles that she believed the kids were causing. My first task was to help her recognize her dance.

"Pick a typical misbehavior in your classroom and describe, in a very step-by-step manner, exactly what you say and do when your students behave this way."

"The most persistent problem I face is all the talking and clowning around that goes on while I'm teaching. This drives me up a wall."

"What do you when this happens?" I asked. As she described what usually happens, I diagrammed each step in the interactional sequence. Visual diagrams are an effective way to help teachers get acquainted with their dances. When Barbara finished, we both took a moment to reflect on her diagram (see figure 4.1).

"Look familiar?" I asked.

"I must go through that ten times a day," said Barbara. "See what I mean when I say I nag them all day long?" She looked exhausted.

"Yes, that's quite a dance," I replied, giving it the label it deserved. I could understand why she felt so worn-out.

Performing classroom dances is like saving stress coupons. If we collect enough of them in the course of a day or a week, we get a prize—headaches, stomachaches, and a variety of other upsets, even depression and burnout. Barbara's coupon book was full.

"Let's make sure we've captured everything that happens in your diagram," I said. "At what point in the dance do you begin to feel annoyed?"

"I'm annoyed from the beginning," she replied. "I know they're not going to cooperate, but I don't show my anger until later on. I try reasoning and lecturing, then I wear down, and my anger comes out. That's when I get loud."

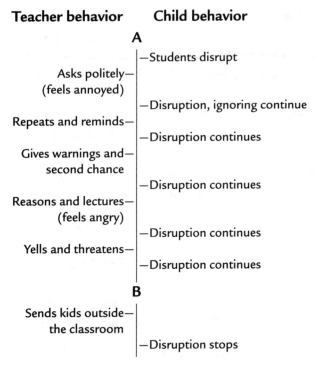

Teacher behavior   Child behavior

A

—Students disrupt

Asks politely—
(feels annoyed)

—Disruption, ignoring continue

Repeats and reminds—

—Disruption continues

Gives warnings and—
second chance

—Disruption continues

Reasons and lectures—
(feels angry)

—Disruption continues

Yells and threatens—

—Disruption continues

B

Sends kids outside—
the classroom

—Disruption stops

Figure 4.1   Barbara's Diagram

At the beginning of Barbara's diagram, I wrote the words "feels annoyed," then, after her lecturing step, I wrote the words "feels angry." The sequence of events was now complete.

I summarized what Barbara's diagram was telling us. "It seems that the more you talk, the more the kids tune you out and the angrier you become. Your dance continues until you can't take any more. Then you stop it with your action step." Barbara nodded in agreement.

Her diagram was revealing. She started off with a polite request to stop. Her requests were usually ignored. Then she tried repeating and reminding followed by warnings and second chances. The misbehavior continued. So she shifted gears again and tried reasoning and lecturing. The resistance continued.

The more she talked, the angrier she became until reasoning and lecturing turned into yelling and threats. When she reached her breaking point, she made disruptive students stand outside the classroom, ending the dance. Repeat offenders were sent to the office.

I returned to Barbara's diagram and drew a circle around all the steps that used words. This took up nearly all of her diagram. I labeled these "verbal steps." Then I drew a box around the step that involved action and labeled this "action steps." The box occupied only a small portion of her diagram (see figure 4.2).

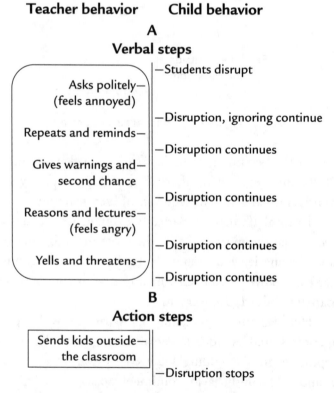

Figure 4.2   Barbara's Verbal and Action Steps

"Which steps take up most of your time and energy and cause you the greatest frustration?" I asked. She pointed to her verbal steps.

"Now, which steps stopped the misbehavior?" I asked. She just looked at me and smiled. She didn't need to answer, because the answer stood right in front of her. Her diagram was proof that she spent most of her time and energy doing things that didn't work. Barbara looked confused and relieved at the same time.

"I thought I was supposed to do all that stuff," she confessed as she pointed to the circled portion of her diagram. "I thought I was giving them every opportunity to cooperate, but I can see I was giving them opportunities *not* to cooperate."

This insight would be her ticket out of the dances. The hardest part was now behind her. She recognized what wasn't working for her. My next task was to help her understand the type of research she was encountering.

"Imagine that you're eight years old," I suggested. "You're skillful at wearing people down and getting your way. When you hear someone say, 'Stop,' your first thought is 'Or what? What will happen if I don't?' Now let's look at your diagram. At what point do you answer these questions?"

"When I send them outside the room," she replied.

"Right," I said. "Your action step answers their research questions. There is no further need for testing." Barbara could see that the kids pushed because she was willing to bend. When she held firm, the pushing stopped. Her ineffective attempts to say stop were beginning to sink in.

"The kids probably get other payoffs from your dances," I suggested. "If you were only eight years old and you could get an adult to do all this stuff by just tuning out and resisting, would you feel powerful? Do you think you might enjoy the entertainment and negative attention?"

"Okay, I'm convinced," said Barbara. "How do I get out of these dances?"

"You've already taken the most important step by recognizing your dance," I said. "Next, you'll need to eliminate all of your ineffective verbal steps. Your dances will end when you put your words and actions closer together." I returned to her original diagram and posed a question.

> Your dances will end when you put your words and actions closer together.

"What would happen if you gave your aggressive researchers all the information they needed at point A, and then moved on directly to your action step at point B if they tested? No repeating. No reminding. No warnings or second chances. No reasoning or lecturing. No raised voices or threats. None of the steps that waste valuable instructional time and wear you out. Your new message might sound like this: 'Guys, you can follow along quietly, or you'll have to spend some quiet time by yourselves. What would you like to do?'"

"I'm ready to give it a try," Barbara replied. Her new diagram soon looked like figure 4.3. So can yours.

A Punitive Dance

PUNITIVE DANCES TEND to be louder, angrier, and more dramatic than their permissive counterparts. The steps are different, but the dances are just another variation of the basic classroom power struggle. They begin with unclear or ineffective messages about rules. They're fueled by anger and resistance, and they lead to escalating conflicts and power struggles.

I recall one punitive dance I witnessed firsthand when a sixth-grade teacher invited me to her classroom to observe one

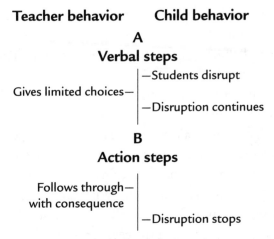

Teacher behavior   **Child behavior**

A

Verbal steps

—Students disrupt

Gives limited choices—

—Disruption continues

B

Action steps

Follows through—
with consequence

—Disruption stops

Figure 4.3   Barbara's New Diagram

of her disruptive students. "Try to arrive about forty-five minutes before we break for lunch," Sharon suggested on the
phone. "Richard usually blows about that time."

She was right. Within minutes of my arrival, Richard disrupted the class. I watched him position several textbooks near
the edge of his desk. Then, while Sharon was explaining a
math problem at the board, he gave the books a nudge with his
elbow. The ensuing crash got everybody's attention.

Sharon turned and glared at him. Her jaw was set. Her
hands were on her hips. "That was real smart, Richard!" she
said with a disgusted look on her face. "Why don't you grow
up and cooperate for a change." She wrote his name on the
blackboard under the frown face.

"Give me a break. It was an accident," said Richard with a
sly smile.

"Sure it was," said Sharon sarcastically. "Just like all your
accidents. I know what you're doing." She glared at him again.

"What?" Richard countered, trying to keep the verbal sparring match going.

"Don't play innocent with me," said Sharon. "I'm sick of your lousy attitude."

"My lousy attitude!" exclaimed Richard, rolling his eyes. "What about yours?"

"That's enough!" said Sharon sharply. "I won't tolerate any more disrespect." She went to the blackboard and wrote a check after his name. "That's your final warning."

"Oh, yeah!" Richard sneered. "What are you going to do? Take my recesses away?" It was only Tuesday, but Richard had already lost all of his recess privileges for the week.

"No. You'll go to the office," replied Sharon. "Keep it up if that's what you want."

"It's better than being here!" Richard shot back.

"I'm glad you like it," countered Sharon, "because that's where you're going." She handed him three sheets of paper. "Don't come back until these pages are full of sentences saying 'I will not be disrespectful to my teacher.'" Richard gave her a defiant look as he headed out the door.

When the bell rang for recess, Sharon and I had an opportunity to talk. "See what I have to put up with?" she began. "He makes me so angry! I never would have talked to my teachers the way he talks to me."

"Was his behavior today typical of what happens?" I asked.

"Yes," she replied, "but he usually stops when I threaten to send him to the office. He hates that almost as much as being sent home. Nothing else seems to matter to him. I've taken away all of his recesses and free activity time, even his field trips."

"Have you spoken with Richard's parents?" I inquired.

"Yes. We're using a daily behavior report card system," she replied. "Each day, I send a behavior report card home to his parents. If he gets sent to the office, his parents make him spend all of his after-school time in his room. No TV, no video games, and no play privileges."

"Has that helped?" I asked.

"We thought it would," said Sharon, "but his behavior is worse, not better." They were digging themselves in deeper with their drawn-out consequences.

I was curious about how Sharon perceived her guidance methods. "What do you usually do when Richard misbehaves?" I asked.

"The first time, I write his name on the board to call his attention to his behavior and give him a chance to correct it. The second time, I write a check after his name as an additional warning. The third time, he loses a recess. The fourth time, he loses all of his recesses for the day. If he misbehaves again that day, and he usually does, then he loses all of his recesses for the week. Next, I send him to the office to write sentences or an apology letter. If Richard is sent to the office twice on the same day, the principal suspends him for the rest of the day. He has been suspended three times this year."

The methods Sharon described were only a partial description of what I observed. "Is she aware of what she's doing?" I wondered. It was time to hold up a mirror and help her see the methods she actually used.

"Sometimes, visual diagrams give us a clearer picture of what's going on," I suggested. "Earlier, when Richard misbehaved, I recorded what he said and did. Then I recorded your responses. May I draw a descriptive diagram of the interaction?" Sharon nodded.

I went to the blackboard and drew a diagram of the interaction I observed, explaining each step as I went. When I finished, I stood back and gave Sharon a chance to check it over (see figure 4.4).

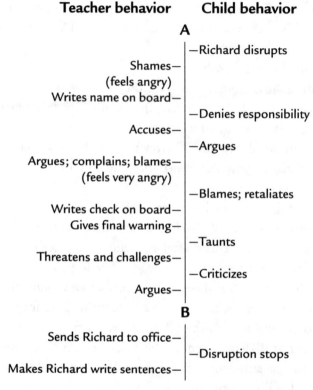

Teacher behavior　　**Child behavior**

A

—Richard disrupts

Shames—
(feels angry)
Writes name on board—

　　　　　　　　—Denies responsibility

Accuses—

　　　　　　　　—Argues

Argues; complains; blames—
(feels very angry)

　　　　　　　　—Blames; retaliates

Writes check on board—
Gives final warning—

　　　　　　　　—Taunts

Threatens and challenges—

　　　　　　　　—Criticizes

Argues—

B

Sends Richard to office—

　　　　　　　　—Disruption stops

Makes Richard write sentences—

Figure 4.4　Sharon's Diagram

"Did I do all of that?" she asked in disbelief, as she pointed to the long series of verbal steps in her diagram. "It seems so angry."

"I call them classroom dances," I said. "The dance you do with Richard is an angry one. You both took quite a few shots at each other." My suspicions were confirmed. She wasn't aware of all the steps she used.

"Let's make sure we've captured everything that happens in your dance," I said. "At what point do you become angry?"

"I'm angry in the beginning," Sharon admitted. "I know what usually follows, but I become angriest when he argues and talks back." I returned to her diagram and wrote the words "feels angry" at the beginning of the interaction and the words "feels very angry" during the arguing and verbal sparring.

Sharon's diagram was now complete, so I summarized what it was telling us. "Richard is skillful at hooking you into verbal sparring matches. The more you talk, the more resistance you encounter, and the angrier you become. Your dance continues to heat up until you finally stop it with your action step.

"Let's take a look at the various steps in your dance," I suggested. I returned to Sharon's diagram and drew a circle around all the steps that relied primarily on words. I labeled these "verbal steps." They took up most of her diagram. Next, I drew a box around all the steps that involved action, labeling them "action steps." They took up a small section at the end of her diagram (see figure 4.5).

"You use two types of steps to stop Richard's misbehavior: verbal steps and action steps." I said. "Which one always stops his misbehavior?"

"My action steps," Sharon replied.

"Right," I said. "Sometimes he stops when you threaten to send him to the office because he knows from experience that your action steps will follow."

Sharon understood where I was heading. She could see that the last few steps in her diagram were the only ones Richard regarded seriously. She was wasting her time doing things that weren't working and becoming angry in the process. My next task was to show her a way to avoid the dance.

"What would happen if you asked Richard to stop at point A and then went on directly to your action steps at point B without any of these other steps in between?" I asked.

"There would be less arguing," she replied.

"Right," I agreed. "And you would be less angry. By eliminating all of these ineffective verbal steps, you could stop his misbehavior with less time, energy, and upset."

Teacher behavior   Child behavior

A
Verbal steps

—Richard disrupts

Shames—
(feels angry)
Writes name on board—

—Denies responsibility

Accuses—

—Argues

Argues; complains; blames—
(feels very angry)

—Blames; retaliates

Writes check on board—
Gives final warning—

—Taunts

Threatens and challenges—

—Criticizes

Argues—

B
Action steps

Sends Richard to office—

—Disruption stops

Makes Richard write sentences—

Figure 4.5   Sharon's Verbal and Action Steps

Next I wanted her to see that long-term consequences actually extended the length of their power struggles. "Let's look at your action steps," I suggested. "Your action steps stop Richard's misbehavior for the moment, but they last a long time, sometimes all week. He becomes angry and resentful and takes it out on you. Then you end up doing many shorter versions of the same dance that end with threats instead of consequences."

"I don't know what else to do," she confessed. "He usually loses all of his recess privileges for the week by Monday afternoon. There isn't much left to take away, but I can't allow him to get away with it, either. He needs to know I mean business." I agreed.

"If there is a way to get that message across without making Richard angry or resentful, would you use it?" I asked.

"Of course," she replied.

"Good. Then let's put a different ending on your diagram," I suggested. "What would happen if you changed your threats to limited choices and used a time-out consequence if he persisted with his disruption? No more loss of recess time or sending him to the office. No more writing sentences or apology letters. No daily behavior reports. And no consequences at home for misbehavior at school. Your new message might sound like this: 'Richard, stop disrupting, please, and follow along quietly, or you'll have to spend some quiet time by yourself. What would you like to do?'"

"It sounds so easy," laughed Sharon.

"The methods are easy compared to what you have been doing," I replied, "and you can use them with your other students as well. The hardest part will be stopping yourself from doing the dance. Richard will probably do his best to get you back out on the dance floor."

"What should I do if he argues or talks back after I give him limited choices?" asked Sharon.

"Don't take the bait," I replied. "Use the cutoff technique." I explained how it works. "If Richard really wants to discuss the matter further, arrange a time during his lunch hour or after school to do so. The time for discussion is not when your rules are being tested or violated."

"And if he persists?" she asked.

"Then, follow through with a time-out, so he experiences what you said," I replied. "No dance. That's a clear signal."

"Sure, I can do that," Sharon replied, eager to get started.

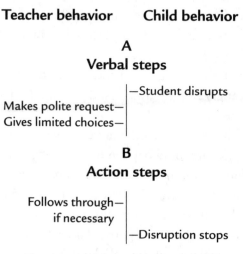

Figure 4.6   Sharon's New Diagram

We spent an hour that afternoon practicing the skills she needed to end her dances. She learned how to say stop in clear and respectful terms and how to use limited choices and the cut-off technique when she encountered testing or resistance. Logical consequences and time-outs replaced the drawn-out consequences she used earlier. She explained the new plan to Richard's parents, and they agreed to put it into effect the next day. Sharon's new diagram soon looked like figure 4.6. So can yours.

A Mixed Dance

MIXED DANCES COME in various forms. Some start off punitive and end up permissive with teachers compromising their limits or giving in altogether. Others start off permissive and end up punitive when teachers react in anger and impose harsh or drawn-out consequences.

Jerry, an eighth-grade teacher, did the latter. He held the school record for sending the most students to the office in a single semester. The feat wasn't winning him many supporters. Parents were beginning to complain, and so was the school's counseling staff. One of the vice principals at his school suggested he give me a call.

"I can only take so much," Jerry complained. "The kids push me too far. That's why I send them to the office. There wouldn't be a problem if they would just cooperate and do what I ask."

He invited me to observe one of his classes and added that his fourth-period class was the worst. I agreed to observe his fourth-period class the next day. We scheduled a follow-up conference for later that afternoon.

I arrived at Jerry's fourth-period class five minutes after the bell rang and took a seat near the back of the room. The kids were curious about who I was. Several turned around to check me out.

Things were calm for the first few minutes, and then the testing started. Two girls began talking and passing notes. Their talking was loud enough to disturb others, but Jerry kept on teaching as though nothing was happening. He ignored their disruption altogether. The girls continued to talk. Occasionally, one giggled, then turned around and looked at me, and then giggled some more. Jerry kept on teaching. Not a word was said.

When the girls saw that I wasn't going to intervene, they became bolder. They talked louder and giggled more. One of them passed a note to a boy and waited for his reaction. He read it and acted shocked, which triggered a new round of giggling. Jerry glanced in their direction several times but kept on teaching. The only change I could observe in his behavior was a slight amplification of his voice as he attempted to be heard above their chatter.

"This is interesting," I thought. "Does he eventually give them a signal?"

On the other side of the room, two boys were flicking bits of mud that had fallen off their shoes at one another. The game was great entertainment for several others nearby, who chuckled each time a shot missed and nodded approval when shots were on target. Jerry seemed aware of what was going on but didn't say a word. He kept on teaching.

Finally, one of the boys did something that couldn't be ignored. He pressed a muddy shoe against the other boy's trousers and left a large print. Jerry looked at both of them impatiently.

"Come on, guys," he pleaded. "We only have thirty-five minutes to go. Can't you save the horsing around for after class?" The two settled down for the moment. Jerry returned to his teaching.

Five more minutes passed, then there was another disturbance. One of the girls who had been passing notes earlier began gesturing excitedly to the boy sitting next to her. Everyone was watching. Jerry stopped once again and looked at her impatiently.

"Jana, would you get yourself under control, please," he requested politely. "I don't want to have to ask you again." He waited for Jana to settle down. She did, and he resumed his lesson. Meanwhile, the mud-flicking game started up again on the other side of the room.

Jerry looked frustrated. "How much longer can he hold out before he gives a stronger signal?" I wondered. Jana answered my question. Without warning, she jumped up out of her seat and tried to intercept a note passed to Mark. The whole class watched as the two girls wrestled for the note. Jerry exploded.

"I've had it!" he shouted. "Jana and Shannon, you're out of here." He handed them both passes to the office. "Mark, you'll be joining them shortly if you don't settle down."

A tense silence fell over the class. Glances were exchanged, but no one disrupted. Even the mud-flicking game stopped. They knew he had reached his limit.

When I arrived for our afternoon conference, Jerry was still angry. "See what I have to put up with?" he said.

"Yes," I agreed. "They pushed you pretty far. Do you usually handle disruptions the way you handled them today?" I inquired.

"Yes," he replied, "but they don't usually push me to the point where I have to send them to the office. That only happens a few times each week." Jerry was willing to overlook a lot. I wondered whether he was aware of the mixed messages he sent his students. I decided to check it out.

"May I draw a diagram of the interactions I observed during your fourth-period class?" I asked. He nodded. When I finished, we both paused to look at it.

"Look familiar?" I asked.

"It sure does," he replied. "That's what I go through all day long."

"I call them classroom dances," I said. "Your dance starts off politely and ends with an angry explosion. Were you aware of all the disruptions that took place before Jana and Shannon wrestled for the note?" Jerry nodded that he was.

"When did they begin to bother you?" I asked.

"I was annoyed when Greg wiped his muddy shoe all over Randy," Jerry replied. "And I was annoyed with Jana when she made all those dramatic hand gestures and showed off for Mark. But Jana and Shannon went much too far when they started wrestling for that note. That's when I lost it."

I returned to Jerry's diagram and wrote the words "feels annoyed" after the incidents he described and the words "feels very angry" after the wrestling incident. Jerry's diagram was now complete (see figure 4.7).

I summarized what his diagram was telling us. "The kids test you with various forms of disruption, but your first response is to ignore their misbehavior. You overlook as much as

Teacher behavior   **Child behavior**

A

—Students disrupt

Ignores disruption—

—Disruption continues

Continues to ignore—

—More disruption

Continues to ignore—

—Boys flick mud

Ignores disruption—
(feels annoyed)

—Wipes muddy shoes

Pleads and cajoles—

—Pass more notes;
gesture with hands

Requests cooperation—

—Continue flicking mud

Continues to ignore—

—Girls wrestle for notes

Explodes—
(feels very angry)

B

Sends girls to office—

—Disruption stops

Threatens Mark—

Figure 4.7   Jerry's Diagram

you can until you become annoyed. Then you try pleading, cajoling, and polite requests. The disruption continues. When it reaches the point where you can't take it any longer, you stop it with your action step." He nodded in agreement.

"At what point in the diagram is their disruptive behavior unacceptable to you?" I asked. He looked at me like I was crazy.

"It's never okay to disrupt," he replied.

"I agree with you, in theory," I said, "but let's look at the rule in practice. If their disruptive behavior was not okay at the beginning of the period, then why did you allow it to continue for twenty-five minutes before you finally decided to stop it?"

Jerry didn't have an answer, but he understood what I meant. He could see that he was sending a mixed message.

"Let's take a closer look at the steps in your dance," I suggested. "You use two types of steps: verbal steps and action steps. We'll include ignoring as part of your verbal steps." I drew a circle around all of his verbal steps, including the ignoring, and a box around his action steps at the very end of his diagram (see figure 4.8). "Which steps stopped the misbehavior?" I asked. He pointed to his action steps.

"Exactly," I replied. "That's the first time the kids get a clear signal that you expect their disruption to stop. None of the circled steps have any lasting impact on their behavior. How do the kids know how far they can go before they've gone too far?"

"They don't know," Jerry admitted. He could see that's why they keep pushing. "How do I get out of this dance?" he asked.

"The solution is simple," I said. "Since the kids want to know how far they can go, what would happen if you gave them the information they want the first time they disrupt? Your new message might sound like this: 'You can stop disrupting, or you'll have to spend some quiet time by yourself. What would you like to do?'"

"There would be much less disruption," replied Jerry, "but I still would be sending kids to the office."

"Then let's use a more effective action step," I suggested. I showed him how to use the two-stage time-out procedure. He introduced it to each of his classes the next day. As expected, his aggressive researchers tested it out to see whether it worked. It did. They soon learned that disruptions would no longer be tolerated. Jerry's new diagram looked like figure 4.9.

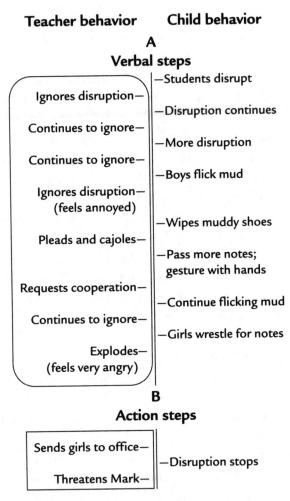

Figure 4.8 Jerry's Verbal and Action Steps

Chapter Summary

CLASSROOM DANCES ARE destructive patterns of communication and problem solving that play out over and over again when classroom rules are tested and violated. For some students, the dances are a great source of live entertainment or "a

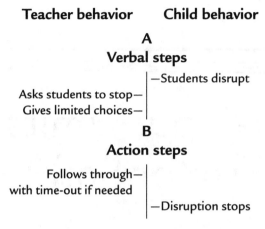

Figure 4.9   Jerry's New Diagram

reinforcement error" because they actually encourage unacceptable behavior. Students are the producers and directors, and teachers are the actors and actresses. For teachers, classroom dances are anything but fun. They're a major source of stress and wear and tear that leads to burnout.

Classroom dances come in many forms. There's a permissive version and a punitive version, and some teachers do both. All dances begin with unclear or ineffective messages about our rules. They're fueled by anger and misunderstanding, and they all lead to escalating conflicts and power struggles. Over time, classroom dances become such a familiar and deeply ingrained habit that teachers experience them as their normal way of doing things. These teachers are not even aware that they are dancing. Awareness is the key to breaking free.

The best way to stop a classroom dance is not to start one. Teachers can avoid dances altogether by starting off with a clear verbal signal and by supporting their words with effective action. The process is easy once you discover the things you're doing that aren't working for you. The next chapter will help you do that.

5

Are Your Limits Firm or Soft?

I F YOU WANTED to stop cars at a busy intersection, would you rely on yellow lights alone to get the job done? Not likely. Most motorists don't stop at yellow lights, and neither do children when they confront these signals in the classroom. Children don't stop for the same reason adults don't. Stopping is optional, not required.

If we really want someone to stop, we need to present the right signal: a red light. Motorists respect red lights. They associate them with consequences: collisions, tickets, and higher insurance rates. Children respond in much the same way. They're more likely to comply with our requests when we support our words with effective action.

Many teachers hold up the wrong signals to stop misbehavior in the classroom. They don't realize that their stop signs don't really require stopping or that their attempts to say no

sound like yes, or sometimes, or maybe to their students. The problem, in most cases, is unclear communication about limits.

Limits come in two basic varieties, soft and firm. Each conveys a different message about our rules and expectations. In this chapter, you'll discover which type of limits you use and why your students respond to you the way they do. You'll learn how to minimize the need for testing by starting off with a clear message children really understand. Let's begin by examining the messages that don't work for us. It's time to get acquainted with soft limits.

Soft Limits: When No Means Yes, Sometimes, or Maybe

RAYMOND, AGE NINE, knows he's not supposed to eat snacks during class, but when his teacher isn't looking, he pulls out a bag of corn chips and starts crunching away. He's halfway through the bag before his teacher notices what's going on.

"Raymond! You know you're not supposed to eat during class," she says with disapproval. "Put that bag away, please, and wait until lunch."

"Sorry," says Raymond, as he sticks the corn chip bag back in his desk.

A few minutes pass before Raymond tries again. When his teacher's back is turned, he sneaks a few more chips out of the bag and chews them softly, one at a time. No one notices, so he grabs a small handful. He gets caught a second time.

"Raymond!" says his teacher with exasperation. "Are you eating chips again? I thought I told you not to." He looks apologetic. "If I let you eat during class, then I have to let everybody do it," she explains. "It's not fair to others. I really wish you would put them away and wait for lunch."

"Okay," says Raymond contritely. He puts the chips back in his desk.

Raymond's teacher is using soft limits. She believes her message is getting across, but what did Raymond experience after all the reasons and explanations? It wasn't stopping. Instead, he finished most of the bag!

What did Raymond learn from this experience? He learned that eating snacks during class is really okay if he can endure his teacher's attempts to convince him not to. His teacher communicated a different message than she intended.

Soft limits are rules in theory, not in practice. They invite testing because they carry a mixed message. The verbal message seems to say stop, but the action message says that stopping is neither expected nor required. Raymond understood this clearly and responded the way most drivers do when the light turns yellow. He acknowledged his teacher's signal but continued on his way. Raymond and his teacher will likely have many more of these encounters as long as she uses soft limits.

From a training perspective, soft limits do not accomplish any of our basic goals. They don't stop misbehavior, they don't encourage acceptable behavior, and they don't promote positive learning about our rules or expectations. They simply don't work. Worse yet, they frequently achieve the opposite of their intended effect by inviting testing and power struggles. Soft limits are the cause of most classroom dances.

> Soft limits are the cause of most classroom dances.

Soft limits come in a variety of forms. They can be ineffective verbal messages or ineffective action messages. Sometimes, they are both at the same time. All share the common message that compliance is neither expected nor required. Let's look at some typical examples.

Wishes, Hopes, and Shoulds

Rhonda, age four, knows she's not supposed to use painting materials in the carpeted areas of her classroom, but both easels are in use, and she really wants to paint. She grabs a brush and a tray of paints and heads to the nearest table. Her picture is nearly complete when the teacher discovers what's going on.

"Rhonda, you know you're not supposed to use paints near the carpets. You might spill."

"I'll be careful," says Rhonda.

"I know you will," says her teacher, "but accidents can happen even when you're careful. That's why we put the easels in the tiled area. I really wish you would put the paints away and finish your picture later, when an easel is free."

"Okay," replies Rhonda, but she continues to paint.

Her teacher waits, but nothing happens. So she tries again. "Rhonda, do you know how difficult it is to get paint stains out of the carpet? I hope you put the paints away before there is an accident."

"I'm almost done," says Rhonda, as she dabs the brush into the blue paint jar.

"Rhonda! I'm starting to get mad," exclaims her teacher. "Is that what you want? Please do what I ask before I get even madder." Rhonda paints quickly.

Did you hear a clear message that Rhonda was required to stop painting? Rhonda didn't, and she responded the way many children do when they receive this type of mixed signal. Wishes, hopes, and shoulds are another way of saying, "Stopping is nice, but you really don't have to until you're ready." Compliance is optional, not required. Often, when children confront this type of signal, they test for clarification. That's what Rhonda did when she ignored her teacher and continued painting.

Repeating and Reminding

Algebra is Chad's least favorite subject. While his teacher explains equations at the board, Chad pulls out a comic book and starts reading. His teacher notices.

"Chad, I think it would be a good idea if you put that away," suggests the teacher. Chad places the comic under one of his books and looks up attentively. As soon as his teacher returns to the lesson, Chad pulls the comic out and continues reading. Several minutes go by before he's discovered.

"Chad, how many times do I have to tell you?" asks his annoyed teacher. "Put the comic book away!"

Chad puts the comic away and waits a full fifteen minutes before he pulls it out again. This time, he conceals it under his binder and looks up periodically to give the impression he's paying attention. His teacher isn't fooled. He walks over to Chad's desk and lifts up the binder.

"That's enough!" says the teacher. "Put the comic in your backpack, or you can give it to me and pick it up after school." Chad puts the comic in his backpack.

When Chad ignored the first request, nothing happened, so he decided to test and try again. The second request followed the same pattern. If the teacher did not mean what he said the first two times, why should Chad take his words seriously the third time?

> Teachers who repeat and remind are teaching kids to ignore and tune out.

Teachers who repeat and remind are teaching kids to ignore and tune out. Like many students who wonder how far they can go, Chad doesn't comply with his teacher's request until he has to.

Speeches, Lectures, and Sermons

Robin, a fifth grader, strolls into class five minutes late from recess. "Where have you been, Robin?" asks her annoyed teacher. "The bell rang nearly five minutes ago."

"I had to use the restroom," Robin replies.

"You need to take care of bathroom trips before the bell rings," admonishes her teacher. "I don't appreciate your lack of consideration. I've already given directions for the next assignment, and now I have to repeat them just for you. You're holding everybody up. What kind of a class would this be if everyone showed up when they felt like it? It isn't fair. Now, take your seat, please, so we can started."

Did you hear a clear message that showing up late would not be tolerated? Robin didn't. Will the lecture help her arrive on time in the future? Probably not.

What did Robin learn from all of this? She learned that showing up late is really okay if she can tolerate her teacher's lectures. This is not a bad deal for someone who wants to avoid classwork and extend recess time. Robin knows from experience that she can count on her teacher to provide a set of personal instructions when she arrives late.

Warnings and Second Chances

It's a sunny day, and Mrs. Adams decides to take her second graders outside and read them a story. When everyone is seated, she begins. Within minutes, several students begin horsing around.

"Carlos and Daniel, would you like to sit together?" asks Mrs. Adams. They both nod. "Then you will have to follow along quietly. That's a warning."

She resumes her story. A few moments later, the boys poke and tickle each other again. Mrs. Adams puts her book down. "Guys, didn't I ask you to follow along quietly?" she asks. They both nod. "Well, I meant it, too. This is your final warning." She returns to her story.

This time, things are quiet for a full five minutes, and then Daniel lets out a yelp. "He pinched me!" complains Daniel.

"It was an accident," says Carlos.

Mrs. Adams isn't sure what happened. "Okay, this is your last chance," she says. "If I hear any more disruptions, I'm going to separate you. Do you understand?" The boys nod. She resumes her story.

Do you think she has seen the last of their disruptions? Not likely. The boys violated her rule three times, and each time they received a warning and another chance. They'll probably continue to test until they receive a signal that requires stopping.

Cooperate, Okay?

Three-year-old Shelly knows she's supposed to put her materials away when she's finished with them, but she leaves her completed puzzle on the floor and begins playing in the sand trays. Her teacher notices.

"Shelly, you left your puzzle on the floor," says the teacher. "You're supposed to put it away before you begin something new. Okay?"

Shelly acknowledges her teacher's words but continues to play with the sand trays. Her teacher tries again. "Shelly, if everybody left their projects laying around, our classroom would be a mess. Please pick up the puzzle and put it away, okay?" This time, Shelly doesn't even look up.

What does it mean when we ask a child to do something and then add "okay?" at the end of our request? Okay with whom? The child? Or the teacher? What happens if it's not okay with the child? Does that mean cooperation is optional? And who decides? Shelly seems to have made up her mind. When we add "okay?" to the end of our requests, we obscure the clarity of our message.

Statements of Fact

The sixth-period bell rings, and Mr. Gilbert moves to the front of the class to begin his lesson. He's ready, but many of his students are not. They talk and joke around. Several haven't even made it to their seats. Mr. Gilbert waits patiently.

"I'm ready to start," he announces, but his words have little impact. The kids continue to talk. Mr. Gilbert waits a little longer. "I can't get started until it's quiet," he says. The talking continues. Mr. Gilbert is angry.

Did you hear that the students were required to stop talking and get in their seats? Neither did they. Many continued to test for that message. Mr. Gilbert is not likely to get the cooperation he expects until he gives a clearer signal. Statements of fact do not convey the intended message.

Ignoring the Misbehavior

Lyle, a sixth grader, enjoys being the class clown. Each day, he pulls a series of gags and stunts to amuse his classmates. His teacher is not amused. She finds his behavior irritating and tries to ignore it in the hope that it will go away. She encourages his classmates to ignore him, too, but Lyle shows no sign of slowing down.

Is the absence of a green light the same as a red light? If it was, Lyle would have stopped his clowning long ago. When we ignore misbehavior, we are really saying, "It's okay to do that. Go ahead. You don't have to stop." That's the message Lyle follows.

> When we ignore misbehavior, we are really saying, "It's okay to do that. Go ahead. You don't have to stop."

If Lyle's teacher wants to stop his clowning, she needs to give him the right signal. She needs to say stop with her words and, if needed, follow through with her actions by temporarily removing Lyle from his audience. Lyle will learn his teacher's rule when he experiences the consequences of his unacceptable behavior.

Reasoning and Explaining

Several fourth-grade boys have invented a variation of the game of tag. When someone is tagged, the tagger yells out for the others to pile on the new person who becomes "it." The game is great fun, but not very safe. When the yard duty teacher sees what's happening, he intervenes.

"Guys, that game doesn't look safe. Someone could get hurt. You can play tag without piling on."

"Come on, Mr. Kearney," pleads one boy. "No one is going to get hurt. We'll be careful."

"I know you will," replies Mr. Kearney, "but the blacktop is hard, and Christopher could have been hurt when you guys piled on him. I'm concerned."

"But Christopher didn't mind," says one boy. "Yeah, he liked it," says another. Christopher nods in agreement.

"Well, it's still not a good idea," says Mr. Kearney, "It's best that you stop."

The boys grumble a little but head off. A few minutes pass, then Mr. Kearney hears, "Pile on Jared!" This time, he sees the same group of boys piling on Jared. Mr. Kearney calls them over.

"Guys, didn't I ask you not to do that?"

"You said it wasn't okay on the blacktop," says one boy. "We're on the grass. It's safe here."

"Piling on is not safe anywhere," insists Mr. Kearney. "Someone might get hurt. You guys would feel terrible if that happened and so would I. That's why we don't allow rough games on the playground. They lead to problems. Do you understand?"

The boys nod and head off once again. This time, they select an area well away from Mr. Kearney before they resume the game. Mr. Kearney decides to check it out. Sure enough, the boys are at it again. He calls them over.

"Guys, you don't seem to understand what I've been trying to tell you," says a frustrated Mr. Kearney. "That game is dangerous. I'm not going to wait for someone to get hurt before it stops. If I see any of you piling on again, you'll spend the rest of your recess on the bench." No one wants to spend their recess on the bench. The game stops.

Mr. Kearney believes he said stop each time he gave reasons and explanations about the dangers of piling on, but what did the boys experience? They didn't stop. Cooperation was optional, not required. The boys knew it and continued to pile on until they experienced a signal that required them to stop.

Is there a time for giving reasons and explanations? Yes, but that time is not when our rules are being tested or violated. When children test or go too far, they need to know the consequences of their behavior. Reasons and explanations do not provide them with the data they need to complete their research.

Bargaining and Negotiating

Lynn, a high school sophomore, knows she's supposed to turn in her biography assignment on Wednesday, but it's Monday, and she hasn't even started. She asks for a deadline extension.

"Mr. Edwards, may I have a few extra days to complete my biography assignment?" Lynn asks.

"You've had three weeks," says Mr. Edwards. "That should have been plenty of time for a project under ten pages."

"I know, but it's taking longer than I expected. May I turn it in on Monday?" she asks.

"No, but you can turn it in on Friday for full credit," he replies.

"Oh, please! Mr. Edwards," Lynn pleads. "I'll do a better job if I can have a few more days. May I have the weekend, please?"

"Okay," concedes Mr. Edwards, frustrated by his weakening position, "but just this once. Next time, you'll have to finish on time like everybody else."

Did you hear that getting assignments in on time was expected and required? Lynn didn't. Her teacher was willing to bargain and negotiate about the due date for the assignment. In effect, Mr. Edwards is saying, "My rules are negotiable. Let's make a deal." Lynn tested to see how far she could go.

To children, negotiable feels a lot like optional. By the time the negotiation session is over, Lynn understands the real rule is "Complete your assignments on time unless you can talk your way out of it." Teachers who bargain and negotiate over their rules invite children to test and redefine those rules.

Arguing and Debating

André, a second grader, knows he's supposed to clean around his desk before he leaves in the afternoon, but he tries to sneak out the door unnoticed. His teacher calls him back. "André, you can't leave until you pick up around your desk and put your books and papers away," she says.

"I don't see why I have to clean up when Shelton doesn't," says André.

"Shelton's desk is clean, and he put his books away," replies the teacher. "That's what you need to do, too."

"Well, it didn't look that way yesterday," argues André, "and you let him go. It's not fair."

"We're not talking about Shelton," replies his teacher. "We're talking about you, and you know what you have to do."

"You're not fair," André complains, looking for a little bargaining room. "Why do I have to do things others don't have to do?"

"I'll keep a closer eye on Shelton's desk from now on," says the teacher, "and I'll make sure he follows the rules just like you."

"Well, they're stupid rules!" says André.

"Stupid or not, they won't change all year," says the teacher. She walks to her desk and begins to correct papers. When André realizes that he can't talk his way out of it, he heads over to clean up his desk.

What was not happening while the arguing and debating was going on? Of course, André was not cleaning up his desk. That won't happen until the argument is over. Some arguments can last a long time.

What is the message André's teacher sends by arguing and debating over her rules? Isn't she saying that her rules are subject to further discussion and debate? That's what André thinks. She invited resistance and a power struggle by allowing André to test her limits and prolong his resistance.

Pleading and Cajoling

It's snack time, and four-year-old Trent decides to amuse his friends by spitting gobs of chocolate pudding on the table. "Ooh, gross!" says the girl sitting next to him, but Trent keeps it up. *Plop.* Another gob hits the table. His teacher intervenes.

"Come on, Trent," she says. "It's not nice to eat like that. The kids think you're gross. Show me you can eat like a big boy." The words barely leave her lips when the next gob hits the table. *Plop.* Trent smiles mischievously.

"Okay, Trent, you've had your fun. Now, let's eat the right way, okay?" she pleads. But Trent is having a ball. He spits out two more gobs. "You usually have such good table manners," she says. "We all would feel better if you stopped that."

Did Trent hear a message that stopping was expected and required? No. He heard a lot of pleading and cajoling and a message that said it would be nice if he stopped. Trent thinks it would be nice if he doesn't. If Trent's teacher really wants him to stop, she needs to say stop clearly with her words and remove the pudding if he doesn't. Without a clear signal, he's not likely to give up his game.

Bribes and Special Rewards

Every day, Mr. Sawyer complains in the staff lounge about one of his disruptive fifth graders. "Why don't you offer him some special rewards for better classroom behavior?" suggests a well-meaning colleague. "Maybe you can buy his cooperation."

Mr. Sawyer is desperate. He decides to give it a try. The next day after school, he calls Carl to his desk and asks about the things Carl enjoys most. Carl shares the typical list—pizza, ice cream, video games, baseball cards, skateboarding, and street hockey.

"How would you like to earn a pack of baseball cards every day at school?" Mr. Sawyer asks. Carl perks up. "All you need to do is complete a whole day without disrupting class," says Mr. Sawyer. "Do we have a deal?" Carl nods.

The agreement resulted in a dramatic turnaround in Carl's behavior. He earned four packs of cards the first week and five packs during weeks 2 and 3. Carl liked the new arrangement, but Mr. Sawyer was having second thoughts. By the end of the third week, he had paid out nearly twenty dollars. Carl's cooperation was expensive.

"None of my other students have to be paid to cooperate," Mr. Sawyer thinks. "Carl has already shown that he can do it. I shouldn't have to pay him any longer." The more he thinks about it, the madder he becomes. He decides to revise the terms of their agreement.

> When we offer children bribes and special rewards in return for cooperation, aren't we really saying with our actions that we don't expect them to cooperate unless we pay them off?

When Carl comes up to collect his cards the next day, Mr. Sawyer says, "Carl, I don't think we need to do this anymore. You've shown that you know how to cooperate."

"No way!" says Carl. "I'm not doing it unless you give me the cards." Carl's cooperation stopped as soon as the reward was withheld.

When we offer children bribes and special rewards in return for cooperation, aren't we really saying with our actions that we don't expect them to cooperate unless we pay them off? That's what Carl thought. Bribes and special rewards are another form of soft limits.

Unclear Directions

Mrs. Robie, a seventh-grade teacher, selects two students to return an overhead projector to the school's equipment room. She suspects they may try to stretch the trip out longer than it should be. "Don't take too long," she says, as they leave the room. "I want you back on time."

What does "too long" mean to a couple of seventh graders who enjoy being out of class? Five minutes? Ten minutes? Fifteen minutes? And who decides? Isn't Mrs. Robie making an assumption that she and her students share the same belief about how long the trip should take?

Unclear or open-ended directions invite testing and set up both students and teacher for conflict. If Mrs. Robie expects the students back in five minutes, she should say, "I expect you back in five minutes."

Ineffective Role Modeling

Mr. Allen, a high school teacher, sees two boys in the hallway yelling, threatening, and calling each other names. They're squared off and ready to fight. He intervenes.

"Knock it off!" he shouts, as he pushes the boys apart. "You're both acting like a couple of jerks. If you want to make fools out of yourselves, do it on your own time. Now, get to class before I send you to the office!" Reluctantly, the boys head their separate ways.

What did the boys learn from this encounter? They attempted to resolve their conflict with yelling, threatening, and name-calling. What did Mr. Allen do? He resolved the conflict with yelling, threatening, and name-calling. In effect, he was teaching them to do the very thing he was reprimanding them for.

Inconsistency Between the Classroom and the Office

There are two minutes until recess, and Madison, a second grader, has art supplies spread out all over her desk.

"You can't go out for recess until you put your art supplies away," says the teacher, as she passes by Madison's desk. Madison tries to bargain her way out of it.

"If I do it now, I'll be the last one in line for hopscotch. Why can't I do it after recess?" Madison pleads. Her teacher holds firm. When the bell rings, Madison tries to sneak out. Her teacher intercepts her at the door.

"Not so fast, Madison," says the teacher. "First, you need to put your things away."

"I won't do it!" says Madison defiantly.

"That's up to you, but you can't leave for recess until you do," says the teacher.

"I still won't do it," says Madison.

Her teacher is not about to spend her break period arguing with Madison. She gives Madison some choices.

"You can clean it up now or work the problem out with Mr. Thompkins, our principal, if you prefer," says the teacher. She escorts Madison to the office and explains the situation to Mr. Thompkins.

When she's finished, Mr. Thompkins calls Madison into his office and listens to her side of the story. "I don't see what difference it makes if she picks up before or after recess," Mr. Thompkins thinks. He decides to let her off the hook. "Okay, this time, I'll let you go out to play, but it's important to cooperate with your teacher. Now, run along."

What did Madison learn? In effect, two sets of rules are operating: the teacher's rules, which say pick up your mess before you can go out to play; and the principal's rules, which say you don't have to if you have a good reason not to. Which set of rules will prevail?

What do you think Madison will say next time her teacher wants her to pick something up before recess? Sure, she'll probably play the principal against the teacher by saying, "Mr. Thompkins says I don't have to do it."

If Mr. Thompkins decides to hold firm next time, Madison will probably say, "Last time you said that I didn't have to do it." Inconsistency between the classroom and the office sets up Madison for testing and all three for conflict.

Examples of Ineffective Verbal Messages (Soft Limits)

"Would you cooperate just once in a while?"

"Come on, get your act together!"

"Would you do me a favor and pay attention?"

"Can't you see I'm trying to teach a lesson?"

"Would you yell a little softer?"

"You better shape up."

"I don't care for your attitude."

"I don't believe it. You actually did what I asked."

"Would you like it if I interrupted you?"

"Stop acting like a jerk!"

"Is it asking too much to have a little cooperation?"

"I've had enough from you!"

Examples of Ineffective Action Messages (Soft Limits)

Allowing students to walk away from a mess

Cleaning up students' messes for them

Overlooking misbehavior when you're in a good mood

Overlooking misbehavior to avoid embarrassment

Giving in to persistent nagging

Giving in to a tantrum

Firm Limits: When No Really Means No

ARTIE, A KINDERGARTNER, thinks it's funny to wipe finger paint on Selena, the girl who sits next to him. Selena doesn't share his humor. When he touches her, she complains.

"Artie, keep your hands away from Selena," says the teacher. "If you do that again, you'll have to put your picture away and sit by yourself for a while. Is that clear?"

Artie nods, but as soon as the teacher walks away, he reaches over and wipes a gooey streak of finger paint all over Selena's arm.

"He did it again!" complains Selena.

"It's time to clean up, Artie," says his teacher matter-of-factly. She helps him up from his seat and leads him over to the sink. "You can draw quietly at the back table until the others finish." No shaming or blaming. No disapproving lectures or negative attention.

Artie's teacher is using firm limits to teach her rule. Her words say stop, and so do her actions when she separates Artie from the others. Artie has all the information he needs to make a more acceptable choice next time he's tempted to wipe finger paint on a classmate.

Firm limits send clear signals about our rules and expectations. Children understand that we mean what we say and learn to take our words seriously. The result: less testing, better communication, and no classroom dances. Firm limits are effective teaching tools.

Chapter Summary

LIMITS COME IN two basic varieties, firm and soft (see table 4). Soft limits are rules in theory, not in practice. These ineffective teaching tools contribute to miscommunication and testing as children attempt to clarify what we mean. Soft limits take many forms. They can be ineffective verbal messages or ineffective action messages. Sometimes they are both. All soft limits are mixed messages that invite power struggles and dances.

Table 4. Comparison of Firm and Soft Limits

	Firm limits	Soft limits
Characteristics	Stated in clear, direct, concrete behavioral terms.	Stated in unclear terms or as mixed messages.
	Words supported by actions.	Actions do not support intended rule.
	Compliance expected and required.	Compliance optional, not required.
	Provide information needed to make acceptable choices and cooperate.	Do not provide information needed to make acceptable choices.
	Provide accountability.	Lack accountability.
Predictable outcomes	Cooperation.	Resistance.
	Decreased limit testing	Increased limit testing.
	Clear understanding of rules and expectations.	Escalating misbehavior, power struggles.
	Regard teacher's words seriously.	Ignore and tune out teacher's words.
What children learn	No means no.	No means yes, sometimes, or maybe.
	"I'm expected and required to follow the rules."	"I'm not expected to follow rules."
	"Rules apply to me like everyone else."	"Rules are for others, not me."
	"I am responsible for my own behavior."	"Adults are responsible for my behavior."
	Adults mean what they say.	Adults don't mean what they say.

How to Be Clear with Your Words

A CLEAR MESSAGE BEGINS with our words, and most often, that's where communication breaks down because we say or do more than is needed. Anger, drama, and strong emotion can easily sabotage the clarity of our message and reduce the likelihood of cooperation. It's not only what we say that matters; it's how we say it. Our words are an important guidance tool.

This chapter will show you how to use your words in the clearest and most understandable way. By following a few simple guidelines, you'll learn how to give your aggressive researchers all the information they need to make an acceptable choice and cooperate from the beginning.

Guidelines for Giving Clear Messages

THE KEY TO giving a clear message with your words is to say only what needs to be said in a clear, firm, and respectful manner. The following tips will help you get started.

1. Keep the focus of your message on behavior.

Keep the focus of your message on what you want the child to do or stop doing, not on attitude or feelings or the worth of the child. Remember, our goal is to reject unacceptable behavior, not the child performing the behavior. Messages that shame, blame, criticize, or humiliate go too far. They reject the child along with the behavior and obscure the clarity of the guidance message. The focus is misdirected. A clear behavioral message is less likely to be perceived as a personal attack.

For example, if you want Sharon, a tenth grader, to stop talking during your lesson, your message should be "Sharon you can talk with your friends during lunch or after class but not now." Your message should not be, "Sharon, do you have to be so annoying?" or "Why are you being so rude?" or "Would you like it if I interrupted you while you were trying to teach?"

2. Be direct and specific.

A clear message should inform children, directly and specifically, about what you want them to do. If necessary, be prepared to tell them how and when you want them to do it. The fewer the words, the better.

For example, if you want Kyle, age nine, to clean up his desk before he leaves for home, your message should be, "Kyle, pick up thoroughly around your desk before you leave. That means picking up all the crayons, pencils, or any other items that are on the floor, and putting away all your books and papers. If that's not finished, you won't be ready to go."

Avoid indirect unclear messages such as "I hope you do a better job picking up around your desk today." What is "a better job"? And who decides? You or Kyle? What happens if your definition is different from his? Without a direct and specific message, Kyle's performance will probably fall short of your expectations.

3. Use your normal voice.

The tone of your voice is important. Your normal voice expresses control, whereas your raised voice sends the opposite message—loss of control. Your tone should convey that you are firm, in control, and resolute in your expectations that the children do what you've asked. The best way to communicate this expectation is simply to state your message matter-of-factly in your normal voice.

Firm limits are not stated harshly. There is no need to yell, scream, or raise your voice to convince children that you really mean what you say. Your actions will convey your resolve more powerfully than words.

Maintaining a matter-of-fact attitude in guidance situations is easy for some teachers, but not for others—particularly those who grew up in homes where yelling, screaming, and angry dances were commonplace. The urge to yell becomes a deeply ingrained habit and a nearly automatic response in conflict situations. These old habits won't disappear overnight just because you're inspired to do things differently. You have to work at it. Managing anger is a skill you can learn; but like most skills, the learning process requires time, patience, and lots of practice. The more you practice, the faster your new skills will improve.

4. Specify the consequences for noncompliance.

Remember, strong-willed children want to know the bottom line or how far they can go when they decide to test or resist your rules. When you ask them to stop misbehaving, they ask themselves, "Or what? What are you going to do if I don't?" Teachers can prevent a lot of testing and power struggles by providing students with all the information they need to make acceptable choices from the beginning.

If you expect a student to test, tell him, in your normal voice, what will happen if he doesn't cooperate. This isn't a threat. You're just being clear by giving your aggressive re-searcher all of the information he needs to make an acceptable choice to cooperate.

For example, if you ask Larry, a second grader, to put away his Silly Putty during class, but you expect him to test, your message should be, "Larry, put away the Silly Putty, please. If you have it out during class again, I'll have to keep it in my desk until the next parent-teacher conference."

> Teachers can pre-vent a lot of testing and power strug-gles by providing students with all the information they need to make acceptable choices from the beginning.

Now, Larry has all the infor-mation he needs to make an ac-ceptable choice. He may still decide to test, but if he does, all you have to do is follow through with your action step and take the Silly Putty away. Larry will learn you mean what you say.

5. Support your words with effective action.

Your words are only the first part of your total message. In many cases, your words will be all you'll need, but even the clearest ver-bal message will be ineffective if you fail to support your words with effective action. Be prepared to follow through.

Examples of Effective Verbal Messages (Firm Limits)

"Stop pushing now."

"It's not okay to interrupt."

"I expect you back in five minutes."

"If you wipe the glue stick on others, I'll have to take it away."

"You can play by the rules or find another game to play."

"If you shove, you'll have to go to the back of the line."

"You won't be ready to leave until your desk is clean."

Examples of Effective Action Messages (Firm Limits)

Using a time-out consequence for persistent disruption

Removing a toy from a child who does not put it away
when asked

Revoking a play privilege temporarily for failing to
play by the rules

Separating a child from others for misbehaving in
the cafeteria

Temporarily removing a privilege for abusing
that privilege

Holding students accountable for cleaning up their
own messes

Chapter Summary

A CLEAR MESSAGE begins with your words, and most often, that's where communication breaks down. Anger, drama, and strong emotion can easily sabotage the clarity and meaning of your message. A clear message is not harsh, and it's not a lecture. You don't need a lot of words, and you don't need drama or strong emotion to show that you mean what you say. You only need to be clear.

Your guidance message should focus on behavior, not on attitude or feelings. It should be specific and direct, stated in a matter-of-fact manner, and it should specify the consequences for noncompliance so the student has all the information he or she needs to make an acceptable choice to cooperate. Clear guidance messages reduce testing and dances and set up instructive learning experiences.

7

Stopping Power Struggles Before They Begin

I F TUNING OUT were an Olympic event, nine-year-old Travis would be a gold medal contender. He knows how to ignore directions better than any student in his class, and he can hook almost any teacher into a power struggle. Once he hooks them, he's a master at wearing them down with arguments and debates. Travis has perfected his skills with years of practice at home.

What Travis doesn't realize is that his current teacher has figured out his game. She read a book about classroom dances and recognizes his tactics for what they are. She's ready to stop his dances before they begin. She gets her chance the next day.

When Travis is supposed to be working at his seat, he gets up, walks to the back of the room, and turns on the computer. Then, he begins playing a game.

"Travis, you need to finish your paragraphs before you're ready for computer time," says his teacher. Travis doesn't respond. He continues playing.

"She'll remind me a few more times," he says to himself, "then she'll get upset and give me a final warning before I have to return to my seat. I'll probably get a full game in."

Not this time. His teacher walks over to the computer. "Travis, what did I ask you to do?" she inquires matter-of-factly.

Travis is dumbfounded. "What is going on?" he wonders. "No reminders or upset? No final warnings or instructions?" He can't believe it. She places her hand on the keyboard and waits for his response.

"You said I need to finish my paragraphs before any computer time," he replies.

"Right," she says, with her hand still on the keyboard. "Now do it, please."

But Travis isn't ready to give up so easily. He tries a different tactic. "I don't see why I can't finish the game I've already started," he says, looking for a little bargaining room. He presents the bait skillfully, but his teacher doesn't bite.

"We're finished talking about it, Travis," she says matter-of-factly. "If you bring it up again, the computer won't be available to you for the rest of the day. If you really want to know why you can't use the computer now, we can arrange a time to discuss it after school or during one of your recesses." Travis doesn't want to know why *that* bad. He heads back to his seat to finish up.

As the example illustrates, the best way to stop a classroom dance is not to start one. We need to begin with a clear verbal message, avoid the bait students use to hook us, and be prepared to move quickly to our action step if needed. Travis's teacher does this effectively. You can, too, but if you've danced in the past, don't expect your students to give up their testing quickly.

Your aggressive researchers will likely challenge even your clearest verbal messages and do everything they can to get you back out on the dance floor. You'll probably be tempted to go along with it, too. This chapter will help you resist the urge. You'll learn how to recognize the bait, avoid the hook, and stay off the dance floor. Let's begin with the typical bait we encounter in the classroom and how best to avoid them.

When Students Tune Out, Check In

ONE OF THE best ways to hook teachers into power struggles is to tune out and ignore their requests. When this happens, teachers wonder, "Did my message get across? Am I being ignored? Is it time to move on to my action step?"

The check-in procedure is a simple way to answer these questions without getting hooked into the old repeating-and-reminding routine. When in doubt, check in with the child by saying one of the following:

"What did I ask you to do?"

"Did you understand what I said?"

"Were my directions clear?"

"Tell me, in your words, what you heard me say."

For example, morning snack is over, and it's time for Mrs. Jansen's preschoolers to get ready to go out to the playground. "Put your napkins, wrappers, and other garbage in the waste can," she says. Most of them do, except for Stacey, who just looks at her blankly and then heads to the door with her classmates.

"Did she hear what I said?" wonders Mrs. Jansen. "She doesn't act like she did." Mrs. Jansen is tempted to ask Stacey a second time, when she remembers the technique she learned in the book—when in doubt, use the check-in procedure. She gives it a try.

"Stacey, what did I ask you to do before you go outside?" asks Mrs. Jansen.

"Pick up my mess," replies Stacey.

"Then do it, please," says Mrs. Jansen matter-of-factly. Stacey goes back to pick up her mess.

In this case, Stacey was limit testing. She had the information she needed but chose to ignore it. She fully expected to hear a lot of repeating and reminding before she would actually have to pick up her mess, if she would have to pick it up at all. The check-in procedure (see figure 7.1) helped her teacher

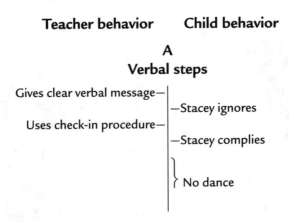

Figure 7.1   The Check-In Procedure

clarify their communication, avoid a dance, and eliminate the payoffs for tuning out all at the same time.

Now, let's consider another scenario. Let's say that when Mrs. Jansen checks in with Stacey, she responds with the same blank stare, because she really was tuned out completely. What should Mrs. Jansen do?

She should give Stacey the information that Stacey missed the first time and preview her action step. Mrs. Jansen's message might sound like this: "Put your napkins, wrappers, and other garbage away before you go outside. You won't be ready to leave until that job is finished." Now, Stacey has all the information she needs to make an acceptable choice. All Mrs. Jansen needs to do is follow through.

The check-in procedure also can be used in situations where children respond to our requests with mixed messages; that is, they give us the right words but the wrong behavior. Sam, a high school senior, is an expert at this. He sits in his seventh-period literature class and doodles when he's supposed to be writing a short plot summary. There are thirty minutes left in the period. The teacher notices his lack of progress.

"Sam, you have thirty minutes to finish up," he says as he passes by Sam's desk.

"I will," says Sam, but ten minutes go by, and he hasn't written a sentence. He hopes to avoid the assignment altogether or talk his way out of it when the bell rings. His teacher suspects this also and decides to check in.

"Sam, what did I ask you to do?" inquires his teacher.

"I'll finish up," says Sam in a reassuring voice.

The teacher clarifies Sam's message. "Your words say that you will, but your actions say you won't. Let me be clearer. You won't be ready to leave until you finish your plot summary. I'll be happy to stay with you after school if you need more time to finish up." Now, his teacher's message is very clear.

"Darn! It didn't work," Sam says to himself. He gets out a clean piece of paper and hurries to complete the assignment before the bell rings.

When Students Argue, Cut It Off

THE TIME FOR arguing and debating is not when your rules are being tested or violated. That's the time for action. If you take the bait and engage students in arguments or debates over your rules, what you're really saying is that your rules are negotiable.

To strong-willed students, in particular, negotiable feels a lot like optional, and optional rules invite testing. Teachers who engage students in verbal sparring matches over classroom rules are opening themselves up for power struggles. How do you avoid the power struggle?

The cutoff procedure is a respectful method for ending an argument or discussion before it develops into a power struggle. When students try to hook you into arguing or debating over your rules, end the discussion by saying one of the following:

"We're finished talking about it. If you bring it up again, then . . ." (Follow through with your action step.)

"Discussion time is over. You can do what you were asked, or you can spend some quiet time by yourself getting ready to do it. What would you like to do?" (Follow through with a time-out consequence.)

For example, a group of sixth-grade boys plays catch with a football on the blacktop area. Their errant passes barely miss younger children playing nearby. The yard duty teacher intervenes.

"Guys, it's not okay to play catch on the blacktop," says the teacher matter-of-factly. "You can play on the grass away from the younger children."

"We're not hurting anybody," says one boy.

"Why can't they move if they don't want to get hurt?" asks another.

The teacher isn't sure his message got across. He decides to check in. "Did you guys understand what I asked you to do?" he inquires.

"Yeah, but I don't see why we should," says one boy. The others nod in agreement.

"I'm not going to debate with them about why they should follow the rules," the teacher thinks. He decides to end this potential power struggle before it begins. "We're finished talking about it," he says. "If you pass the ball on the blacktop again, I'll have to take it away, and you'll spend the rest of the recess on the bench."

Now, his message is really clear. The boys know their options. They have all the information they need to make an acceptable decision. Either way, whether they cooperate or test, they will learn the rule he's trying to teach. No dances this time (see figure 7.2).

Emily's first-period teacher also uses the cutoff technique effectively when Emily arrives late to class and tries to talk her way out of a tardy slip.

"I was only a couple of minutes late, Miss Stevens," pleads Emily. "It won't happen again. I promise."

"I hope not," replies Miss Stevens, "but you still need to pick up a tardy slip before I can let you back in class."

"It's not fair!" insists Emily, hoping for a little bargaining room. It nearly works. Miss Stevens is about to argue the issue of fairness when she remembers the technique she read about in the book.

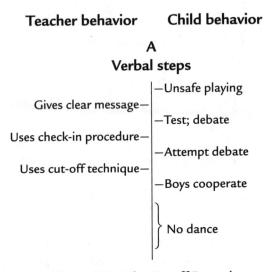

Figure 7.2   The Cutoff Procedure

"We're finished talking about it, Emily," says Miss Stevens matter-of-factly. "If you want to discuss it further, we can arrange a time with your counselor after you pick up your tardy slip." That wasn't what Emily wanted to hear. Reluctantly, she heads to the attendance office.

When Students Get Hot, Cool Them Down

EFFECTIVE PROBLEM SOLVING is difficult for anyone to do, adults or children, in an atmosphere of anger and frustration. The cooldown is an excellent method for restoring self-control and keeping both sides off the dance floor until the time is right for problem solving. The procedure is easy to carry out. In situations of anger or upset, separate yourself from the child by saying one of the following:

When both sides are upset: "I think we both need a little time to cool down. Have a seat at the back table. We'll talk about it during our next break."

When the child is upset: "You look angry to me. You can cool down at the back table or in Mrs. Kenner's classroom next door. What would you like to do?"

When the teacher is upset: "I'm feeling angry, and I need some time to cool down. You can read quietly at your desk while I get myself under control, or you can put your head down for five minutes."

Be sure to allow sufficient time for all parties to restore control before attempting further problem solving. People recover at different rates. Don't assume the child has calmed down because you have. If communication breaks down a second time, use the procedure again. Use it as often as you need it. The following example illustrates how it works.

Brett, age nine, lives in a home where discipline involves a lot of yelling, name-calling, threats, and angry accusations. Often he arrives at school upset and on the defensive. Even minor corrections can set him off. That's what happened when his teacher tried to refocus him during a math exercise.

> The cooldown is an excellent method for restoring self-control and keeping both sides off the dance floor until the time is right for problem solving.

"Brett, turn around in your seat, please," says the teacher matter-of-factly. "You only have ten minutes to finish the worksheet."

"Why don't you say something to Greg!" shouts Brett. "He talked to me first. Why do I always get blamed?" Brett's face is flushed with anger, but his teacher knows what to do.

"Brett, you look pretty angry," she says in a calm voice. "I'll set the timer for five minutes. Take some time to cool down."

Brett picks up his pencil and worksheet and heads to their prearranged cooldown area at the back table. He grumbles and complains the whole way there, but the five minutes helps. When the timer goes off, he's under control and ready to rejoin the class. No angry dances this time. Brett is learning a tool for managing his angry feelings.

Sometimes, teachers need time to cool down more than their students. That's what Mr. Conner discovered when he became a junior high school teacher. His quick temper caused of a lot of angry dances. He was wearing down, when one of his colleagues suggested he give me a call.

"The kids know my buttons," Mr. Conner confessed. "They push the hardest when they know I'm close to losing it. I think they enjoy watching me blow up."

I asked him to describe what his students did to push his buttons. Then I asked him to describe, from beginning to end, what he did in response to their behavior. As he spoke, I diagrammed the interaction on the board (see figure 7.3).

Mr. Conner's diagram revealed an angry, punitive dance. The dance usually began with a minor disruption, and Mr. Conner usually responded with blaming and accusations. When his students denied their guilt or attempted to argue, which they usually did, he became angry and raised his voice. The more they argued, the angrier he became. Before he knew it, he was shouting and threatening to send them to the office. It was clear from Mr. Conner's diagram that he didn't know how to stop his dances short of an angry explosion. He needed a way to restore self-control before things went too far.

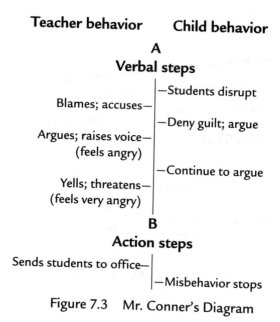

Figure 7.3   Mr. Conner's Diagram

I showed him how to start off with a clear message and how to use the cutoff technique and time-out procedure when students tried to hook him into arguments. Now he was prepared to interrupt his dances, but he still needed a tool to restore his self-control. I introduced the cooldown and encouraged him to use it whenever he felt hot. We arranged a follow-up conference two weeks later.

"How did it go?" I asked when Mr. Conner arrived for our follow-up. He looked more relaxed.

"The methods worked!" he said. "When my students try to hook me into arguments, I tell them we're finished talking about it and send them to the classroom next door for a time-out if they persist. If I feel hot, I take out a book and read quietly for five minutes, and I ask my students to do the same. No yelling. No threats. No shouting. The kids know things are different. They don't try to push my buttons as often." Mr.

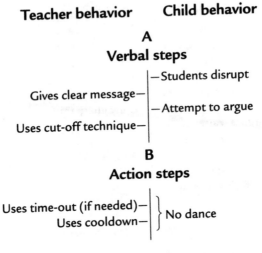

Figure 7.4   The Cooldown

Conner had some new tools for stopping his dances and staying under control. His new diagram looked like figure 7.4.

When Students Challenge, Give Limited Choices

Bev and Sandy, both high school seniors, sit next to each other in their second-period class. They're good students, but they also like to talk, which has become a problem. Their teacher gives them some choices.

"Bev and Sandy, you can sit together quietly, or you can sit apart quietly. What would you like to do?"

"We'd like to sit together," says Sandy. Bev nods in agreement. They made their choices. Now, all their teacher has to do is follow through.

Bev and Sandy's teacher is using *limited choices,* a highly effective method for handling testing and avoiding power struggles while teaching responsibility and problem solving. The way this teacher sets the situation up, the girls cannot avoid being responsible for their choices and behavior. The rule is clear, and so is the consequence for noncompliance. The girls have all the information they need to make an acceptable choice to cooperate.

Let's say, for the sake of argument, that the girls make a poor choice and continue talking. What should the teacher do? She should follow through with a logical consequence and move the girls apart. Either way, the girls will learn the intended lesson. Both choices, acceptable or unacceptable, lead to effective learning.

Guidelines for Using Limited Choices

The following guidelines will help you use limited choices most effectively.

1. Restrict the number of choices you present.

Limit the options to two or three, and be sure the desired corrective step is one of them. For example, if you don't want your students to wear hats in the classroom, you might say, "You can

wear hats in the corridors or anywhere on the school grounds, but not in the classroom. If you wear them in the classroom, they're going to remain in my desk for the rest of the week. You can take them home on Friday."

If the student attempts to introduce other choices that are not acceptable, you should respond, "These are your choices and your only choices. What would you like to do?" Strong-willed students often try to turn limited choices into one of their favorite games, Let's Make a Deal. Hold firm with the choices you offer.

2. Remember, the choices are your limits.
State them firmly with no wiggle room, or you may invite limit testing. For example, if you don't want students to tilt backward in their chairs, you should say, "You can sit the right way, with all four legs on the floor; or we can put the chair up for the next ten minutes, and you can sit on the floor or stand next to your desk. What would you like to do?"

3. Make the student responsible for the decision.
After presenting limited choices, ask the student, "What would you like to do?" This question places the hot potato of responsibility in the student's lap, not yours.

4. When students state their intention to comply but fail to do so, follow through with the stated consequence.
For example, if you say, "You can play tetherball by the rules or find another game to play," and the student continues to play unfairly, you simply follow through and restrict the student from playing tetherball.

Examples of Limited Choices

The following examples illustrate some of the many ways limited choices can be used. Often, this guidance procedure leads to an acceptable choice, but I've also included examples where students respond with testing or defiance so you can see how to follow up with an instructive logical consequence.

It's lunchtime, and Harry, a preschooler, tries to amuse his friends by taking bites of his peanut butter and jelly sandwich and opening his mouth to reveal the contents. His teacher asks him to stop, and he does for a while but then starts again. His teacher gives him some choices.

"Harry, you can sit with the group if you eat your lunch the right way. If you don't, you'll have to eat by yourself at the back table. What would you like to do?" she asks. Eating alone is no fun. Harry decides to cooperate.

Jessica, a third grader, is a talented jump roper, but she isn't very tolerant of others with less skill. Sometimes, when others attempt difficult tricks, Jessica swings the rope extrafast to end their turn. When the yard duty teacher sees what Jessica is doing, she intervenes.

"Jessica, you can play the right way or find another game to play," says the teacher. "What would you like to do?"

"I'll play the right way," says Jessica, but a few minutes later, she's back to her old tricks. This time the teacher follows through with logical consequences.

"You'll have to find another game to play for today," says the teacher matter-of-factly. "You can try jump rope again tomorrow." Jessica will probably think carefully next time she decides to end someone's turn.

Maria, a sixth grader, refuses to go to the time-out area after being disruptive. Her teacher gives her some choices.

"Maria, you can spend ten quiet minutes at the back table or twenty minutes in Mr. Dickson's class next door. What would you like to do?"

"Ten is better than twenty," Maria thinks. Reluctantly, she heads to the back table.

It's the third week of school, and Manny, a seventh grader, continues to disrupt his science class every day. His teacher has used time-out consistently, but the pattern continues. She suspects she may need assistance from Manny's parents. After class, she presents Manny with some choices.

"Manny, I've tried to help you stop disrupting for three weeks, but we haven't made much progress. Can we work this out between the two of us, or do we need some help from your parents?" Manny is sure he doesn't want his parents involved.

"I think we can work it out," he says.

"I hope so," says the teacher, "but if we can't, I'll have to schedule a conference with your parents." Now, the consequence for continued disruption is clear. All the teacher needs to do is follow through.

Sid, a tenth grader, knows it's not okay to wear a bandanna in class but does it anyway. When his teacher asks him to take it off, he refuses. She gives him some choices.

"You can put the bandanna away, or you can work it out with Mr. Clayborn, our vice principal," she says matter-of-factly. "What would you like to do?" Sid knows what will happen if he has to deal with Mr. Clayborn. Reluctantly, he removes the bandanna.

When Students Dawdle, Use a Timer

THERE ARE TWENTY minutes until recess, and Karen, a fourth grader, still has thirty math problems left on her worksheet. When the teacher passes by Karen's desk, he sees her doodling on her workbook. He's been through this dawdle drill before.

"Karen, you need to finish your worksheet before you go out to recess," says her teacher.

"I will," says Karen, who pretends to get busy but, as soon as her teacher leaves, resumes doodling. She hopes to avoid the assignment altogether. There are fifteen minutes left until recess. Her teacher suspects what she's up to. When he cruises by to check on her progress, his suspicions are confirmed. He places a timer on her desk and sets it for fifteen minutes.

"If the worksheet is not complete when the timer goes off," says the teacher matter-of-factly, "I'll find you a comfortable spot on a bench so you can finish it during recess."

"Darn!" Karen grumbles to herself. She can't see any way out of it. She scrambles to finish the worksheet before recess.

Ignore Attitude, Not Misbehavior

GRUMBLING, MUMBLING, EYE rolling, door slamming, looks of impatience, and stomping off in a huff are tempting baits that are hard for most teachers to resist. If you bite and respond on the child's level, then you're back in the dance, and what have you taught?

A lesson in disrespect? They already know that. When your students try to hook you with their disrespectful attitude, remember Anthony's teacher in the next example.

Anthony, a sixth grader, knows he's not supposed to read comic books during class time, but when his teacher isn't looking, he decides to do it anyway. She sees him and intervenes.

"Anthony, hand over the comic book, please," she says in a firm, matter-of-fact voice.

Anthony gives his teacher a look of disgust, rolls his eyes, mumbles something under his breath, and starts to complain.

"It's not fair!" he says. "Last year, Mr. Rosen allowed us to read comic books in class after our work was done. I don't see why I have to follow your stupid rule."

Anthony's teacher holds firm and waits. "I'm the adult. He's the kid," she reminds herself. "I'm not going to get hooked by his bad attitude."

When Anthony sees she isn't going to budge or dance, reluctantly he makes the right choice and hands over the comic book.

"Thank you, Anthony," says the teacher.

Anthony did his best to hook his teacher with his disrespectful attitude, but she didn't take the bait. Instead, she held her ground, maintained her composure, and remained focused on getting what she wanted—his cooperation.

Does ignoring a disrespectful attitude mean that it's okay? No, it's not okay. It doesn't feel good, and we don't like it. But, if you reward a disrespectful attitude by responding to it, you'll likely see a lot more of it. Avoid the reinforcement error. Be the adult. Don't bite.

When does attitude cross the line and become misbehavior that shouldn't be ignored? This is a judgment call every teacher must make at the time. I can offer some guidelines to keep you on track. Mumbling, grumbling, eye rolling, looks of disgust, and even sticking out the tongue are baits I generally ignore. Profanity, name-calling, insults, hurtful statements, or rude gestures cross the line. I respond to these with time-outs.

When Students Cross the Line, Hold Firm

DO YOUR STUDENTS sometimes try to evade your consequences by pleading for a second chance or by promising not to do it again after they have misbehaved? If so, do you go along with it? Teachers who do are setting themselves up for further testing and power struggles. When children give you the right words but the wrong behavior, hold firm and stay focused on the behavior. Let's look at how Dean's teacher does this.

Dean, a third grader, sits at his table group and gives another student a kick under the table. The student lets out a loud "Oww!" The teacher comes over to investigate.

"Dean kicked me," the student complains. He lifts up his trouser cuff to reveal a visible red mark.

> When children give you the right words but the wrong behavior, hold firm and stay focused on the behavior.

"I barely touched him," says Dean. "It didn't hurt. Besides, he had his legs spread out on my side of the table."

"It's not okay to kick others," says his teacher, matter-of-factly. She sends him to the back table for a time-out. "You can return to your desk in fifteen minutes."

"I won't do it again," Dean says contritely. "Can I have another chance?"

His teacher holds firm. "That's a good choice for next time," she says. "This time you need to go to the back table."

Alexis, a high school junior, had a similar experience when she tried to stretch a five-minute bathroom trip into a twenty-five-minute excursion. After class, her teacher takes Alexis aside.

"Alexis, you know the rule. Bathroom passes are five minutes," says the teacher. "Unless you have a note from your parents, you're going to have to take your bathroom trips before or after class. Your five-minute bathroom privilege will be restored next quarter."

"Come on, Mrs. Donaldson," says Alexis contritely. "I forgot. I won't do it again. I promise."

Her teacher holds firm. "That's a good choice for next quarter," she replies. No second chances and no dances. Alexis will probably think carefully before she tries to take advantage of that privilege.

When Teachers Cross the Line, Apologize

MR. TIMMONS'S DAY starts off bad and gets worse. He wakes up with a sore throat that isn't bad enough to call in sick. When he arrives at school, his usual parking spot is taken, and he has to park in the reserve lot across the street. It's raining. When he arrives at his classroom, he finds a note on his desk informing him that the film on Egypt he planned to show after lunch didn't arrive from the media center. He has to revise his lesson plan. To top things off, Curtis, his most challenging student, acts out most of the morning, and after lunch, provokes others in his table group. Mr. Timmons loses control.

"What's wrong with you, Curtis?" he shouts. "I'm sick and tired of your bratty attitude day after day. You act like a two-year-old." Mr. Timmons was about to say something even more hurtful when he realized what he was doing and stopped himself.

"Have a seat at the back table, Curtis," Mr. Timmons says. "I need some time to cool down."

After a five-minute cooldown, Mr. Timmons goes to the back table to apologize.

"I'm sorry for the hurtful things I said," he begins. "I lost my temper, but that's no excuse for treating you disrespectfully. Will you accept my apology?" Curtis nods and returns to his seat.

Providing guidance for strong-willed children is challenging and exhausting work. From time to time, we all lose our patience, react in frustration, and say or do things we later regret. How should we handle this when it happens?

An apology is the best way to begin. The gesture conveys all the right messages. It shows children how to be respectful of other's feelings. It teaches them how to heal the little hurts in relationships that often lead to resentment and power struggles. Most important, an apology from a caring adult gives children permission to be human and the courage to try harder.

> An apology from a caring adult gives children permission to be human and the courage to try harder.

Some teachers believe that apologizing to students is a sign of weakness that diminishes the child's respect for adult authority. My years of counseling have shown just the opposite to be true. To children, an apology is not a sign of weakness. It's a sign of strength that inspires them to try harder. Children respect adults who have the courage to be human and take responsibility for their own imperfections and mistakes.

Don't Personalize Misbehavior

WHEN YOUR STUDENTS misbehave, do you sometimes ask yourself, "Why is he doing this to me?" If so, you're probably personalizing the testing and setting both of you up for power struggles. Aggressive research is wearing, but most of the time, it's not intended to be a personal attack. Tyrone, a seventh grader, is a good example.

Tyrone's first period teacher has asked him repeatedly not to wear his Rollerblades into the classroom. The wheels leave scuffmarks on the floor, which makes extra work for the custodian. Sometimes, when Tyrone is running late and thinks his teacher isn't looking, he sneaks into the classroom with his

Rollerblades on to avoid a tardy slip. On this occasion, he gets caught.

"Tyrone!" Why are you deliberately disobeying me?" asks his annoyed teacher. "You know I don't allow Rollerblades in the classroom. They leave marks that are hard to clean up."

"I was being careful," Tyrone replies. "I didn't think you'd mind if I didn't leave any marks."

"Well, I do mind," says his teacher. "It's not considerate. The custodian has enough work to do without cleaning up your messes. Do you understand? Now take them off and give them to me. You can have them back on Friday."

"That's not fair!" protests Tyrone. "I won't do it again. Can't I have one more chance?" he pleads.

"You can next week," replies his teacher. "Hand them over, please."

"You're mean!" grumbles Tyrone as he passes over his Rollerblades.

Tyrone's testing is not intended to be an attack on his teacher's authority. In fact, his testing is not about her at all. It's about him and how he learns. Tyrone needs to collect a lot of evidence in the form of experience before he's convinced that her rules are mandatory, not optional. Persistent testing is part of his normal learning process.

Tyrone's teacher was on the right track when she took away his Rollerblades for violating her rule, but she turned an instructive guidance experience into a power struggle when she personalized his testing.

If you tend to personalize your students' misbehavior, try to hold on to the bigger picture. Aggressive research is a normal learning process for strong-willed kids. Teachers set themselves up for power struggles when they take their students' testing personally.

Chapter Summary

LET'S REFLECT ON the new tools you've added to your guidance toolbox thus far. In the last chapter, you learned how to be clear with your words, but sometimes even the clearest message isn't enough to prevent students from hooking us into power struggles. In this chapter, you learned some practical strategies for stopping power struggles and classroom dances by not allowing them to begin. You learned how to check in when kids tune out, how to cut it off when kids try to argue or debate, how to cool kids down when they get angry or upset, how to give limited choices when children test or challenge, and how to use timers when children dawdle and procrastinate. You know how to ignore the tempting attitude bait students use to hook you, how to hold firm when kids cross the line, and how not to personalize your students' misbehavior.

You're as prepared as you can be to use your words effectively, but your words are only the first part of your overall message. If your students continue to test, then it's time to act. Consequences are the second part of your overall message. They speak louder than your words. It's time to get acquainted with your next set of tools.

8

How to Support
Your Rules with
Consequences

So far, you've learned how to give clear signals with
your words and how to stop power struggles before they
begin. These steps provide all the verbal information children
need to behave acceptably, but as you know, your words are
only the first part of your total message.

Children may still decide to test, and when they do, the
time for talking is over. It's time to act. You must answer their
research questions with concrete action messages that they really understand. Consequences are the second part of your
limit-setting message. They speak louder than words.

This chapter will show you how to use these instructive
guidance tools in the clearest and most understandable way. If
you've relied on permissiveness in the past, you'll discover how
to use consequences to regain your credibility and authority
and to teach your students to tune back in to your words. If
you've relied on punishment in the past, you'll discover how to

build cooperative relationships with your students based on mutual respect rather than fear and intimidation. For anyone recovering from a bad case of soft limits, the consequences in this chapter will be a big step in the direction of effective communication and problem solving. Get to know them. Make friends with them. You'll need to use them frequently with your aggressive researchers. They are your ticket to credibility.

Why Consequences Are Important

CONSEQUENCES ARE LIKE walls. They stop misbehavior. They provide clear and definitive answers to children's research questions about what's acceptable and who's in charge, and they teach responsibility by holding children accountable for their choices and behavior. When used consistently, consequences define the path you want your students to stay on and teach them to tune in to your words.

If you've relied on permissive or punitive methods in the past, you will probably need to use consequences often during the first four to eight weeks that you implement the guidance strategies in this book. Why? Because your aggressive researchers will probably test you frequently to determine whether things are really different. This is the only way they will know that your rules have changed and that your walls are really solid. You are likely to hear comments such as "You're not fair!" or "You're mean!" as they attempt to break down your walls and get you to revert back to your old behavior.

> Consequences teach responsibility by holding children accountable for their choices and behavior.

This is what Mr. Harvey discovered when he attended one of my workshops looking for more effective ways to handle the daily testing, resistance, and arguments he was encountering in the classroom. It didn't take him long to recognize that his permissive approach was part of the problem. His limits were soft, and his consequences, if he used them at all, were late and ineffective. His kids were taking advantage of him, and he was eager to put an end to it. After he completed my workshop, he made an announcement to his class.

"I'll be running the classroom differently from now on," Mr. Harvey began. "I'm not going to repeat my directions anymore or remind you to do the things you're supposed to do. I'm not going to argue or debate if you don't want to do it. I will only ask you once. If you decide not to cooperate, then I will use consequences to hold you accountable." He explained logical consequences and the time-out procedure.

"He doesn't mean it," whispered one student. "Yeah, he knows who's really in charge here," chuckled another. Their reaction was understandable. Their previous experiences gave them little cause to regard his words seriously.

But, Mr. Harvey kept his word. When he gave directions or requested their cooperation, he said it only once. No more repeating or reminding. When the kids ignored him or tuned out, he used the check-in procedure. When they tried to argue or debate, he used the cutoff technique. If they persisted, he followed through quickly with logical consequences or time-out.

"What got into him?" wondered several students at the end of the first week. "Yeah, we liked him better the old way."

The methods worked. For the first time, Mr. Harvey's students were accountable for their poor choices and behavior. They were learning to be responsible, but their testing didn't let up for a while.

In fact, their testing intensified during the first few weeks. His aggressive researchers did everything they could to wear him down and get him to revert back to his old ways. It didn't work. He didn't give in or compromise, even when they told him he was mean or unfair. He was prepared for their resistance.

An initial increase in testing during the first four weeks is a normal and expected part of the learning and change process. After all, Mr. Harvey told his students things were going to be different. How could they know for sure that he really meant what he said? Of course, they had to test and see for themselves. When they did, Mr. Harvey answered their questions with instructive consequences.

Four weeks after he started, Mr. Harvey noticed a change. The change was subtle at first, not dramatic. There was less testing and more cooperation. The kids were tuning back in to his words. They were beginning to change their beliefs about his rules.

Your consequences will accomplish your immediate goal of stopping your students' misbehavior when it occurs, but teaching them to tune back in to your words will take time. How much time? This depends on your consistency, the length of time you've been using soft limits, and the amount of training your students need to be convinced that your rules have changed.

As you accumulate hours of consistency between your words and actions, you will notice less testing and less need for consequences. This will be your signal that your students are tuning back in. They are beginning to change their beliefs about your rules.

How You Use Consequences Determines Their Effectiveness

THE EFFECTIVENESS OF your consequences depends largely on how you apply them. If you apply them in a punitive or permissive manner, your consequences will have limited training value. You'll be teaching different lessons than you intend, and you, not your students, will be responsible for most of the problem solving. If you apply consequences in a democratic manner, however, your signals will be clear, and so will the lessons you're trying to teach. Consequences are most effective when used democratically.

Let me illustrate this point by showing how three teachers can use the same consequence for the same misbehavior with varying degrees of effectiveness. Mr. Wallace uses the permissive approach. When he sees Kenny cheating at tetherball, he gives Kenny a lecture on the importance of honesty and fair play and asks him to sit out his next turn. "What a joke!" Kenny says to himself. Within minutes, he's back to his old tricks.

Mrs. Hunter uses the punitive approach. When she sees Kenny cheating at tetherball, she singles him out for humiliation. "Nobody likes to play with a cheater!" she says in a loud, accusatory voice. "If you can't play fair, you won't play at all. No more tetherball for a week."

"A week!" exclaims Kenny. "That's not fair!" He walks off feeling angry and resentful and considers ways to get back.

Miss Vallas uses the democratic approach. When she sees Kenny cheating, she calls him aside respectfully. "Kenny, you can't play tetherball if you don't play by the rules," she says matter-of-factly. "You need to find another game to play for the rest of this recess. You can try tetherball again next recess." No lectures. No humiliation. No long or drawn-out consequences. Next recess, Kenny plays by the rules.

Each of the teachers in these examples decided to limit Kenny's tetherball time as a consequence for not playing by the rules. Mr. Wallace applied the consequence permissively. His message was respectful, but his consequence lacked firmness. It was too brief. Kenny continued testing.

Mrs. Hunter applied the consequence punitively. Her message was more than firm. It was harsh and not very respectful. Kenny understood the rule she was trying to teach, but he didn't feel good about the way her message was delivered. He left their encounter feeling angry and resentful with no greater desire to cooperate.

Miss Vallas applied the consequence in a democratic manner. Her message was both firm and respectful. Her consequence achieved the right balance between the two extremes. It wasn't too long, and it wasn't too brief. It was instructive. No feelings were injured. No relationships were damaged. Kenny received the information he needed to make a better choice. He didn't need a week to show that he could cooperate.

Miss Vallas was effective because she understands how to use consequences. You can too. Let's look at the properties of effective consequences.

Immediacy

It's snack time, and Ricky, age four, decides to blow bubbles in his carton of milk. His classmates are amused, but not his teacher. She gives him some choices. "Ricky, it's not okay to blow bubbles in your milk. You can drink it the right way, or you'll have to put it away. What would you like to do?"

"I'll drink it the right way," says Ricky. He does, too, for a while, but as soon as his teacher leaves, he decides to test. He puts the carton to his lips and blows some more big bubbles. Without any further words, his teacher removes the milk carton. Ricky will have another chance to drink the right way next time they have snacks.

Consequences are most effective when they are applied immediately after the unacceptable behavior. The immediacy of the consequence helped Ricky make the cause-and-effect connection between his misbehavior and the consequence he experienced. The lesson was instructive. If his teacher had chosen instead to overlook his misbehavior and withhold his milk during the next snack period, her consequence would have had much less impact.

> Consequences are most effective when they are applied immediately after the unacceptable behavior.

Consequences that are administered late have less guidance value and may set up the teacher and student for further problems. Consider the following.

Will, a sixth grader, decides to amuse his friends by making bathroom sounds during instruction. His annoyed teacher intervenes.

"I don't appreciate that, Will," she says. She writes his name under the frown face on the blackboard.

Will stops his disruption for the moment, but a few minutes later, he makes another rude noise. His peers laugh. Will's teacher intervenes a second time.

"I've had enough from you!" she says. Then, she writes a check after his name on the blackboard. "You'll be sitting out your next recess."

"Big deal!" Will thinks to himself. He got two good rounds of laughter from his peers, and there are still forty minutes left before recess. What's to prevent him from continuing his antics? Not much. He does it again.

"Okay, Will," says his exasperated teacher. "You just lost your next recess, too. Want to try for another?" she taunts. He might, but even if he does and she follows through, what will she accomplish? Delayed consequences give students opportunities for more acting out and prolong power struggles.

From a teaching-and-learning perspective, delayed consequences are less effective because they violate learning theory. Kids hear the word *stop,* but they don't associate the word with the experience of stopping. The message lacks clarity and firmness. Worse yet, it provides opportunities for continued testing and power struggles.

Consistency

Tina, an eighth grader, loves to visit with friends between classes, but her next class is PE, and she doesn't want to be late. Last time she arrived late to PE, she had to go to the office for a tardy slip and lost points for missing calisthenics.

"I'll be careful," Tina says to herself. She keeps an eye on her watch and continues to visit. With one minute to go, she sprints for class and nearly makes it. Her teacher greets her at the door.

"Hi, Tina," says Mrs. Perles, as she points in the direction of the attendance office. "I'll see you after you pick up a tardy slip."

"Not again!" says Tina remorsefully. She searches for a good excuse. "I had trouble with my locker," she says convincingly. "Can't this be an exception, please?"

Mrs. Perles holds firm. "Sorry, Tina," she says. "You can explain your situation to Mr. Harris, our vice principal, if you wish, but there's nothing more I can do."

Tina is determined to avoid consequences if she can. When she appeals her case to Mr. Harris, he also holds firm. "Ten minutes is plenty of time to get to class," he says. "I'm sure you'll be more careful next time."

"Shoot! Tina says to herself. "He's as uptight as Mrs. Perles." She picks up her tardy slip and heads back to class.

Consistent consequences are vital to effective guidance. Your consistency helps children collect the data they need to arrive at the conclusions you intend. Some students, like Tina, need to collect a lot of data before they are convinced, but the process is the same for all. Tina will learn that she is expected and required to show up for class on time.

As the example illustrates, consistency has many dimensions. There's consistency between our words and our actions. There's consistency among staff and between the classroom and the office, and there's consistency between the ways consequences are applied from one time to the next. All are important. Tina experienced consistency in all of these areas. She received the clearest possible signal about her school's rule.

Let's say, for the sake of argument, that Tina's PE teacher is only 60 percent consistent about enforcing her rule about showing up for class on time. What can she expect from Tina and others? More testing? Of course. In reality, the rule is only in effect 60 percent of the time. How will the kids know when it is and is not in effect? They will have to test. Inconsistency is an invitation for testing.

Logically Related

When we fail to pay our phone bills for several months, does the phone company respond by disconnecting our cable TV service? No. That would not stop us from using our phone without paying. Instead, they use a consequence that is logically related to the behavior they want to change. They shut off our phone service and charge us a reinstallation fee when they hook us back up. This teaches us to be more responsible about paying for our phone service.

Children also learn best when the consequences they experience are logically related to their behavior. It makes little sense to take away a child's recess privileges or an upcoming field trip because that child decides to bother a classmate during instruction. What does annoying others have to do with recesses or field trips? The consequences and the offending behavior are not logically related.

A more instructive consequence would be to temporarily separate the student from others and provide him with some time to get back under control. The message might sound like this: "Jimmy, you need to move your desk about five feet away from Ben. You can move back to your old spot after lunch." Jimmy hears *stop* and experiences stopping. The consequence is both immediate and logically related to the behavior we want to change. No feelings are hurt. No one is humiliated. Jimmy simply gets a clear message. He has the data he needs to make a better choice next time.

Logical consequences are highly effective guidance tools because they place the focus where it belongs—on behavior, not on the child. The child is less likely to personalize the message. Logical consequences inspire cooperation and positive learning. They are seldom perceived as a personal attack.

> Logical consequences are highly effective guidance tools because they place the focus where it belongs—on behavior, not on the child.

Punitive thinking, on the other hand, is not logical thinking. When students misbehave, punitive teachers ask themselves, "What do they like? What do they care about? I'll show them! I'll take it away!" Punitive consequences are intended to hurt, humiliate, overpower, or shame students into cooperating. They may stop misbehavior, but they're often perceived as a personal attack rather than an instructive guidance lesson.

Punitive consequences most often inspire anger, resentment, and retaliation.

Proportional

Consequences are most effective when they are proportional to the behavior—that is, not too much, not too little, not too long, and not too short. This concept is difficult to grasp for those who use the punitive and permissive models. Consider the following.

Stephanie, a second grader, makes disruptive noises while her classmates work quietly at their seats. The teacher tries to ignore the noise, but it gets louder. Finally, she walks over and asks Stephanie to stop. Stephanie does, for a while, and then starts up again a few minutes later.

"I've had enough of your rudeness!" says the teacher angrily. She sends Stephanie to the office and tells her not to return until after lunch. It's only 9:30.

Sure, the consequence stopped Stephanie's disruptive behavior, but it also eliminated all her opportunities to demonstrate that she could cooperate and behave acceptably during the remainder of the morning. A brief five- or ten-minute time-out would have accomplished the teacher's purpose adequately.

When it comes to applying consequences, more is not necessarily better. Consequences of brief duration often achieve our training goals more effectively than long-term consequences, particularly with preschool and elementary school children. Why? Because brief consequences, applied consistently, give children more opportunities to collect data and make acceptable choices. More teaching and learning occur.

This principle is difficult for many teachers who operate from the punitive model to accept. From their perspective, if a little is good, then a lot must be wonderful. They tend to go overboard with the length or severity of their consequences; then they add to their own frustration by expecting change to happen rapidly. They don't realize that long, drawn-out consequences actually slow down the training process by providing fewer opportunities for learning. Worse yet, teachers must endure the resentment their consequences cause.

Consequences of unclear duration also create problems. Byron, a third grader, is a good example. When he disrupts class, his teacher asks him to go to the time-out area until she feels he's ready to return to his seat.

"How long is that?" Byron wonders. "Five minutes? Ten? Twenty? Possibly all morning?" Byron isn't sure, but he knows one way to find out. Every few minutes he calls out, "Is it time yet?" His annoyed teacher considers adding more time.

> Effective consequences have a beginning and an end that are clear and well defined.

Effective consequences have a beginning and an end that are clear and well defined. Unclear or open-ended consequences invite the type of testing Byron did. If his teacher had specified five minutes as the amount of time Byron needed to spend in time-out, her consequence would have been clear. Byron probably wouldn't have persisted with his disruptive questioning.

Respectful

Drake, a sixth grader, enjoys negative attention, and he has discovered a good way to get it. When it's his turn to be blackboard monitor, he runs his fingernails down the center of the board and gets the intended response. His teacher isn't amused.

"Drake, you can erase the board quietly, or we can find someone else to do the job. What would you like to do?"

"Okay," says Drake with a mischievous smile. "I'll do it the right way." He does, too, for the rest of the morning, but when he's finishing up a job later that afternoon, he runs his fingernail down the board once again.

"Take your seat please, Drake," says his teacher matter-of-factly. She turns to the class. "Who would like to be Drake's replacement for the rest of the week?" A half dozen hands shoot up.

Drake received a clear message about his teacher's rules and expectations. He also received an important object lesson in respectful problem solving. No one was blamed or criticized. No feelings were hurt, and no relationships were damaged.

> The method we use is the method we teach. The method itself communicates a message about acceptable behavior.

Now, consider how another teacher who uses the punitive approach might have handled this situation. When Drake runs his fingernail down the board the first time, this teacher explodes.

"I knew I couldn't trust you with even a simple task," she says angrily. "You obviously need a few years to grow up before you're ready for this type of responsibility. Now take your seat!" Sure, her consequence stops Drake's misbehavior, but what does he learn in the process?

The method we use is the method we teach. The method itself communicates a message about acceptable behavior. When we apply consequences in hurtful ways, we teach hurtful problem solving.

Followed by a Clean Slate

It's been three weeks since Kyle, a seventh grader, was suspended from school for instigating a food fight in the cafeteria. He threw a carton of milk and hit another student in the head. Although Kyle has been well behaved in the cafeteria ever since, his fourth-period teacher continues to remind him almost daily about the poor choice he made and the consequence he experienced.

Kyle's teacher can't seem to let go of the consequence. Her focus is stuck on stopping the unacceptable behavior when it should be directed to encouraging Kyle's present cooperation. Kyle needs a clean slate and a fresh opportunity to show that he can make an acceptable choice and behave responsibly.

When a consequence is over, it should really be over. No debriefing. No lecture. No "I told you so." Your words and your actions have taught the lesson you're trying to teach. Now, it's time to let the lesson sink in. If you say more than is needed or add new consequences, you may undermine or sabotage the guidance lesson altogether. It's time to let go. If the child has not mastered the lesson you're trying to teach, you may need to go through the teaching and learning steps again. That's fine, but stick to the steps that work and avoid the ones that don't.

What You Can Expect

WHEN YOU BEGIN holding your students accountable with effective consequences, you are likely to encounter an initial increase in testing and resistance. Don't be alarmed. This is temporary. It's a normal part of the learning and retraining process.

Your students have already formed beliefs about how you are supposed to behave based on months and sometimes years of experience. They are not likely to change these well-established beliefs overnight just because you said things are going to be different. They will need to experience more than your words to be convinced.

Imagine how you would react if a close friend told you he was going to behave differently. Let's say this person had always been critical and judgmental of others in the past, and now he claims that he's going to be more tolerant and accepting. Wouldn't you want to see the change for yourself over time before you believed it? Most of us would. Students are the same.

Telling students that you've changed may not be enough to change their beliefs or their behavior. They will want to experience the change for themselves over time before they are likely to revise their beliefs and accept the fact that you are different. You will have to show them with your consistent behavior.

In the meantime, you should expect them to test your new methods and do everything they can to get you to behave "the way you are supposed to." If you've been doing a permissive dance in the past, they will probably continue to ignore you, tune you out, challenge your requests, and dangle delicious bait to get you back out on the dance floor. If you've been punitive, they will probably continue to annoy you and provoke your anger.

Consequences will play an important role during this retraining period. You will probably need to use them frequently. The more hours of consistency you achieve between your words and actions, the quicker your students will learn to tune back in, reduce their testing, and cooperate without the need for consequences.

How long will this take? This depends on a number of factors—the age of your students, your consistency, temperaments, and how much history you and your students need to overcome. Most teachers who apply the methods with good consistency report a significant reduction in testing during the first eight weeks. Younger children, ages three to seven, respond more quickly. Older children and teens require longer. Your consistency will accelerate the learning process for children of all ages.

The notion of a quick fix is very appealing. We all want our students' behavior to improve as quickly as possible, but we also need to recognize that these patterns did not develop overnight. Retraining takes time. Expectations of a quick fix will only set you and your students up for unnecessary frustration and disappointment. Allow the teaching and learning process the time it needs to do its part.

What About My Students with Special Needs?

STUDENTS WITH ADD or similar special needs do not require different behavior management; they just require more of it. The methods we cover in this book will be effective, but you should expect to use consequences more frequently. Why? Because students with ADD miss many of your verbal signals. They require more action signals to stay on course.

Chapter Summary

CONSEQUENCES CAN BE powerful training tools when used in appropriate ways. They can stop misbehavior. They can teach your rules, and they can promote responsibility by holding children accountable for poor choices and behavior. When applied consistently, consequences define the path you want your students to stay on.

The key to using consequences effectively is the manner in which we apply them. When we apply them in permissive or punitive ways, consequences have limited instructional value. They teach different lessons than we intend, and we end up being responsible for most of the problem solving. When we apply consequences in a democratic manner, however, we can stop misbehavior and teach our rules in the clearest and most understandable way.

Effective consequences share certain properties or characteristics that contribute to their effectiveness. Your consequences will have their greatest impact when they are immediate, consistent, logically related, proportional, respectful, and followed by a clean slate. Now that you understand how to get the most guidance value from your consequences, let's move on and examine the different types of consequences available to you.

9

Natural Consequences
Natural Learning Experiences

I T'S SNACK TIME in Mrs. Clarey's kindergarten class. She passes out small paper cups filled with nuts and raisins to her students, and they all go outside to eat their snacks on the lawn. Two of her students, Dustin and Max, decide to play a game with their food. They toss their snacks into the air and try to catch them in their mouths. Most ends up on the ground.

"Their snacks won't last long like that," Mrs. Clarey thinks. She's right. Within minutes, the boys come up and ask for more.

"Sorry," she replies. "One cup each is all we get."

Mrs. Clarey let the natural consequence of losing snacks teach the lesson her hard-way learners needed to learn. Like many of us, she was probably tempted to say, "I told you so," or to provide a lecture on the poor choice of playing with their food. She also knew that any further words or actions on her part would take responsibility away from the boys and sabotage their real-life learning experience. Dustin and Max will probably think carefully next time they decide to play that game.

Natural consequences, as the name implies, follow naturally from an event or situation. They are nature's version of the "hard way." Natural consequences send the right action messages to children because they place responsibility where it belongs—on the child. Natural consequences require little or no involvement from teachers. We can easily sabotage the training value of this guidance strategy when we become over-involved, try to fix the problem, add more consequences, give lectures, or add an "I told you so."

Some teachers find natural consequences easy to use and welcome opportunities to let children learn from their own mistakes. For others, particularly those who operate from the punitive model, natural consequences are not easy to use. When something happens, they have to fight their desire to take charge and control the lesson. Doing nothing when you want to do something can be frustrating.

If you find yourself wanting to take charge and control the lesson, practice limiting your involvement to restating the obvious facts of the situation. For example, if your students kick the soccer ball onto the roof after you asked them to play away from the building, you might say, "When the ball is on the roof, it's not available to play with." No further words or actions are needed.

Situations for Using Natural Consequences

HERE ARE SOME of the many situations where you can use natural consequences.

1. When playground equipment or learning materials are lost, damaged, or stolen due to carelessness, misuse, or lack of responsibility.

Natural consequence: Don't repair or replace the lost or damaged items until enough time has passed for students to experience the loss.

Mr. Ackers, a principal at an inner-city elementary school, loves basketball. He'll do almost anything to encourage his students to play. When the kids ask him to lower the rims on one of the courts so they can stuff the ball through the basket, he is happy to help out.

But, Mr. Ackers soon notices a problem. Some kids continue to hang on the rims after they dunk the ball. "The rims won't last long if they keep that up," Mr. Ackers says to himself. When he explains his concern to the kids, they promise to

be careful, but many continue to hang on the rims. By the end of the week, one rim is so badly damaged it is unusable. So, the kids play half-court games with the remaining lowered rim. It's not long before that one is damaged, too.

"We need new rims to practice dunking," the kids say the next time they see Mr. Ackers. He recognizes his opportunity to use a natural consequence.

"Rims are expensive," he says. "They don't last long when people hang on them. It will be a while before we can replace them." He wants the kids to experience the loss for several weeks or perhaps a month before he replaces the rims. Next time, they'll probably think twice before hanging on them.

2. When children make a habit out of forgetting.
Natural consequence: Don't remind them or take away their responsibility by doing for them what they should do for themselves.

Nine-year-old Kendra has a habit of forgetting her homework and lunch money in the morning. Each time this occurs, one of her parents drops the forgotten item off at school. Noticing that this had become a pattern, Kendra's teacher suggests that the parents not make any extra trips for a two-week period.

"Kendra is a good student," says the teacher. "If she misses one or two lunches or assignments, it's not going to hurt her." Her parents agree.

On Tuesday of the first week, Kendra forgets her lunch money. When lunchtime arrives, she asks her teacher if her parents dropped off her lunch money. "Not yet," says her teacher.

That night, Kendra complains to her parents. "You forgot my lunch money! I couldn't eat lunch today."

"I'm sure you'll remember it tomorrow," says her father matter-of-factly. Nothing further was said.

Kendra did remember her lunch money, but on Thursday she left without her homework. Around midmorning she asks her teacher whether her parents dropped it off. "Not yet," says her teacher. Kendra received a zero on the assignment.

Once again, she complains to her parents. "You forgot to bring my homework. I got a zero on that assignment!"

"You're a very good student," says her mother. "I'm sure you'll remember it tomorrow." She did.

3. When children fail to do their part.
Natural consequence: Let them experience the result.

Austin, a ninth grader, knows he's supposed to take his dirty gym clothes home on Fridays to be washed, but when he opens his locker Monday morning, he sees the bag of dirty clothes. The aroma is unmistakable.

"Oh, no!" he says to himself. "What am I going to do?" He decides to present his dilemma to his gym teacher.

"May I be excused from gym class today, Mr. Paik? I left my gym clothes in my locker over the weekend. They really stink."

Mr. Paik understands the situation. He also recognizes his opportunity to let the natural consequence teach Austin the lesson he needs to learn.

"Sorry, Austin," says Mr. Paik matter-of-factly. "There's nothing I can do. You can wear them the way they are or lose half a grade for not dressing. It's up to you."

Austin decides to wear them. His classmates give him plenty of room to do his calisthenics. Austin took his gym clothes home that evening. He didn't forget again.

4. When kids dawdle or procrastinate.
Natural consequence: When possible, let them experience the consequence of their procrastination.

Michelle, a tenth grader, is a pro at procrastination. Each morning, Monday through Friday, she waits until the last possible moment to get ready for school. After she misses her bus, which she does most of the time, she pleads with her parents for a ride. Reluctantly, one of them bails her out then lectures her about responsibility all the way to school.

"This is crazy!" complains Michelle's mom to her daughter's guidance counselor. "She makes it to school on time, but we end up late."

"What would happen if you and your husband left for work on time without prodding, reminding, or offering Michelle a ride after she misses her bus?" asks the counselor.

"She would miss her bus and have to walk about a mile and a half to school," replies Michelle's mom. "I'm sure she would be late."

"Right," agrees the counselor, "and she would have to pick up a tardy slip at the attendance office before she could be admitted to class. After three tardy slips, she would have to put in an hour of detention. Maybe you should let the natural consequences of her procrastination teach the lesson Michelle needs to learn."

That evening, her parents sat down with Michelle and explained that things were going to be different. "We're not going to prod or remind you anymore in the morning," said her mom, "and we're not going to bail you out with rides if you miss the bus."

"I'll believe it when I see it," Michelle thinks.

She became a believer the next morning. Not a word was said when she went into her usual stall, not even when she missed her bus at 7:30. Her parents left for work on time. At 7:45, Michelle wasn't even dressed. She walked to school and picked up a tardy slip. The second day followed the same pattern, but that's all it took for her to get the message. The third day, she caught her bus and arrived at school on time. Natural consequences helped her make a better choice.

Questions and Answers About Natural Consequences

Q Are poor grades on report cards an effective natural consequence for children who fail to complete their assignments or homework?

A The answer depends on how much the child values grades. When children value the grades they receive, then low marks can be an instructive natural consequence. When children don't value grades, however, low marks have little impact. You will need to use logical consequences to get the message across.

Q Several of my students regularly forget to bring their lunches or lunch money to school, and I end up bailing them out by lending them money or calling their parents to arrange a drop-off. This has become a problem. Should I politely refuse to help them the next time they ask, or are there some preparatory steps I should take to ensure the success of the natural consequence?

A There are several preparatory steps I recommend for handling this type of problem. First, contact the parents, explain the problem, suggest natural consequences as a solution, and request their support. This reduces the likelihood that your natural consequences will be misunderstood or perceived as a punitive measure. Most parents will be happy to support your plan when they understand what you're trying to achieve.

Second, inform the students that you can't help them out any longer. Now the hot potato is in their lap. All you need to do is allow the consequence to teach its lesson the next time they forget.

Q : I have been consistent about not bailing my students out when they forget homework or lunch money, but some continue to forget. Does this mean natural consequences are ineffective?

A : No. Natural consequences are training tools. Use them as often as necessary to teach the lesson your students need to learn. Some children need to collect a lot of data by learning things the hard way before they arrive at the desired conclusion and change their behavior.

Chapter Summary

NATURAL CONSEQUENCES FOLLOW naturally from an event or situation. They send the right messages to children because they place responsibility where it belongs—on the child. This is learning the hard way. The child is simply allowed the opportunity to experience the outcome of his or her own poor choice or behavior. The process requires little or no involvement from teachers other than not trying to fix the problem. Overinvolvement by adults is one of the surest ways to sabotage the training value of the natural lesson.

10

Logical Consequences

Structured Learning Experiences

I T'S MUSIC TIME in Mrs. Kellerman's third-grade class. The kids have been practicing the song "Hot Cross Buns" with their recorders all week. They've nearly mastered it. The practice goes well until Lisa decides to prolong the rehearsal. Each time she reaches a certain point in the song, she blasts away with a high note.

The first time, everyone laughs, even Mrs. Kellerman. They think it's an accident. The second time, only Lisa laughs. Mrs. Kellerman gives her some choices.

"Lisa, you can practice the right way, or you'll have to put away your recorder and sit quietly while the rest of us practice. What would you like to do?"

"I'll practice the right way," says Lisa. The practice resumes. When the class reaches that familiar point in the song, Lisa can't resist. She lets out another high note.

"Put your recorder away, Lisa," says Mrs. Kellerman matter-of-factly. "You can join us for music again tomorrow."

Lisa's teacher is using a logical consequence to support her rule about cooperating during music. Because Lisa chose not to cooperate with her teacher's request, she temporarily lost the privilege of practicing recorder with the class. Her teacher's message is clear: Use the recorder the right way, or put it away. The consequence is directly related to Lisa's choice and her behavior. In effect, she chose the consequence she experienced.

Logical consequences are a highly effective guidance procedure popularized by Rudolf Dreikurs and proponents of Adlerian psychology. Unlike natural consequences that follow naturally from an event or situation, logical consequences are structured learning opportunities. They are arranged by an adult, experienced by the child, and logically related to the situation or misbehavior.

> Logical consequences are structured learning opportunities. They are arranged by an adult, experienced by the child, and logically related to the situation or misbehavior.

These wonderful guidance tools accomplish all of our guidance goals. They stop misbehavior. They teach responsibility, and they are effective with the full spectrum of students: compliant or easy-way learners, strong-willed or hard-way learners, and those in between. When used in a firm but respectful manner, logical consequences set the gold standard for effective classroom guidance.

What makes these tools so effective? They teach, but they don't hurt. The focus is where it belongs—on behavior, not on the child. No shaming. No blaming. No long, drawn-out, unrelated consequences that cause anger and resentment. Logical consequences are designed to teach, not to coerce or force compliance. The learning process is cooperative, not adversarial.

Some teachers have difficulty using logical consequences because they're unsure when to use them or how to set them up. This chapter will show you how to do that. You'll find that logical consequences are easy to use when you think in simple terms and follow a few general guidelines.

Guidelines for Using Logical Consequences

LOGICAL CONSEQUENCES HAVE their greatest impact when they are immediate, consistent, temporary, and followed with a clean slate. The following guidelines should be helpful.

Use Your Normal Voice

Logical consequences are most effective when carried out in a matter-of-fact manner with your normal voice. Angry, dramatic, or emotionally loaded tones convey overinvolvement on your part. The message is more likely to be perceived as a personal attack. When this occurs, an instructive lesson can backfire into a power struggle and generate resentment. Remember, our goal is to discourage the unwanted behavior, not the child performing the behavior.

Think Simply and Logically

Some adults have difficulty with logical consequences because they think too hard and try to come up with the perfect consequence for the situation, or they don't think at all, react in anger, and use a punitive consequence that causes anger and resentment.

Punitive thinking is not logical thinking. The intent is to over-power and force compliance, which is not an effective approach with aggressive researchers.

When you think in simple, logical terms, an appropriate logical consequence usually jumps out at you. For example, most misbehavior involves at least one of the following circumstances: children with other children, children with adults, children with objects, children with activities, or children with privileges. In most cases, you can apply a logical consequence by temporarily separating one child from another, a child from an adult, a child from an object such as a jump rope, a child from an activity such as a game, or a child from a privilege such as recess or computer use. Take a moment and ask yourself, "What's happening here?" Then follow through. It's easier than you might think.

Follow Through Directly

Thad and Byron, two sixth graders, are supposed to be working on a science experiment. Instead, they pinch each other with tweezers from their dissection kits. Their teacher intervenes directly with logical consequences.

"Put away the tweezers," she says matter-of-factly. "Thad, please sit at the back table for the next ten minutes, and Byron, you can sit in the empty chair next to my desk. You both can have your tweezers back in ten minutes if you use them the right way."

By separating them from their dissecting tools and each other, the teacher succeeds in stopping their misbehavior and teaching the intended lesson.

Use Timers for Dawdlers and Procrastinators

Timers are useful in situations when children test and resist limits by dawdling or procrastinating. Liz and Becky are good exam-

ples. These two fourth graders live for recess. They're usually the first ones out the door when the bell rings and the last ones to return when recess ends. It's the last part that has become a problem, but their teacher has a plan for holding them accountable.

The next time the girls arrive late from recess, their teacher greets them at the door with a stopwatch. She clicks the watch as they walk through the door and announces, "You both owe me forty seconds from your next recess. You can leave forty seconds after everyone else."

Forty seconds may not sound like much of a consequence, but it can be an eternity to two fourth graders who want to be the first ones out the door. After several of these experiences, Liz and Becky started returning to class on time.

Use Logical Consequences As Often As Needed

Logical consequences are training tools. Use them as often as needed to stop misbehavior and support your rules. If you need to repeat the same consequence three or more times a day for the same misbehavior, don't be too quick to assume that the consequence is ineffective. More likely, you're dealing with an aggressive researcher who needs to collect a lot of data before he or she will be convinced you mean business. Well-established beliefs and behavior patterns don't change overnight. Let the teaching and learning process run its course.

When to Use Logical Consequences

LOGICAL CONSEQUENCES HAVE instructive applications in a wide variety of situations. The following are just a few of the many possibilities.

1. When children misuse school equipment.
Logical consequence: Separate the child from the item temporarily.

Derek, a third grader, knows it's not okay to swing on the tetherball rope but does it anyway and gets caught.

"Stop swinging on the tetherball rope, Derek," says the yard duty teacher. "You need to find another game to play today. You can try tetherball again tomorrow."

2. When students arrive to class unprepared.
Logical consequence: Teach responsibility with a classroom rental center.

Miles, a ninth grader, arrives at his third-period class without his textbook, writing paper, or a pencil. When it's time to begin an assignment, Miles raises his hand.

"Mrs. Thomas, I don't have a book, paper, or anything to write with," he says.

She signals him to come over to a table provisioned with class supplies.

"Welcome to my rental center," she says. "Collect what you need and take it back to your desk. The rent today will be wiping off the blackboard and emptying the pencil sharpener before you leave for your fourth-period class. Remove one of your shoes and leave it under the table for collateral." Miles won't leave without paying rent.

Miles's teacher could have given him the items he needed, but who would have been responsible for solving the problem? Classroom rental centers are an effective strategy for holding students responsible for arriving to class prepared.

3. When students make messes.

Logical consequence: Have them clean it up.

Todd and Kirk, two seventh graders, write graffiti in the boy's bathroom and get caught. Graffiti has been a serious problem at their school. A lot of money has been spent on cleaning it up. The staff is concerned, but they are divided about the best way to deal with the problem.

The principal wants to send a strong message to other students. He suggests suspending the boys for a week and turning the matter over to the police.

The dean of boys thinks the principal's plan is too harsh. "They need to understand the seriousness of what they did," he says. He recommends eight weeks of mandatory counseling.

The vice principal has another idea. He proposes a logical consequence. "Todd and Kirk helped make the mess. Shouldn't they clean it up?" He suggests giving them some choices. "They can put in forty hours of their own time cleaning up graffiti, or they can be suspended, and the matter can be turned over to the police." Everyone liked the plan.

When the choices were presented to the boys, they decided to avoid the police and put in forty hours of clean up. The lesson wasn't lost on others.

4. When students are destructive.

Logical consequence: When possible, have them repair, replace, or pay for the damaged items.

Sondra, a fifth grader, is a determined campaign manager. She'll do almost anything to get her candidate elected, including tearing up posters of a rival candidate. She does this and gets caught. The principal calls her to the office.

"I know you want to help your friend, but destroying posters of other candidates isn't the best way to go about it," says the principal. "Nadia is missing fourteen posters. I asked her to give me one to use as a model. You need to bring in fourteen more just like it tomorrow and help her put them up before class."

5. When students misuse or abuse privileges.

Logical consequence: Remove or modify the privilege temporarily.

Mr. Peters, a tenth-grade biology teacher, has a liberal policy on giving hall passes—that is, until students take advantage of him. Garrett is one of those students. When he takes nearly fifteen minutes to retrieve something from his locker, Mr. Peters meets him at the door.

"No more hall passes this quarter," says Mr. Peters. "We'll try it again next quarter."

6. When students behave aggressively.

Logical consequence: Separate the aggressive student from others temporarily.

Cleve, a first grader, throws sand at others in the sandbox. When his classmates complain, the yard duty teacher uses a logical consequence.

"We don't throw sand," says the teacher. "You need to find somewhere else to play this recess. You can play in the sandbox again next recess if you don't throw sand."

7. When students try to hook you into arguments.

Logical consequence: Separate yourself from the child temporarily.

Roberta, a ninth grader, wants to leave class early to get a good seat at a spirit rally. When her teacher denies the request, Roberta does her best to turn a no into a yes.

"Come on, Mr. Richards," pleads Roberta. "Be fair!"

"You'll have plenty of time to get a seat if you leave with everyone else," he replies.

"Yeah, but not a good seat," argues Roberta. "I don't want to sit in the very back. What's the big deal, anyway?" Her voice has a sarcastic tone. Mr. Richards decides to cut off the discussion.

"We're finished talking about it," he says. "If you bring it up again, you'll have to spend some time by yourself."

"Why?" Roberta protests. "Are you afraid you might be wrong?"

"Take your books and have a seat at the back table," says Mr. Richards. "I'll let you know when it's time to rejoin the group." He said the discussion was over, and he backed up his words with a time-out.

8. When students waste or misuse instructional time.

Logical consequence: Have them make up the wasted time.

Kendall, a third grader, has twenty minutes to complete a page of math problems before recess. Fifteen minutes go by. He hasn't done a single one. He hopes to avoid the assignment altogether.

"Put your worksheets on my desk when you're finished and line up for recess," says the teacher. Kendall is the first to turn in his assignment. He hopes she won't check his work. She does.

"You're not ready, Kendall," says his teacher matter-of-factly. "Your work isn't finished."

"I'll finish it at home tonight," he says, hoping she'll go for it. She doesn't.

"The assignment is due now," she says. "Since you've chosen not to finish it during class time, you'll have to finish it during recess." Kendall spends his recess completing his worksheet. He'll probably think carefully next time he wants to avoid an assignment.

9. When students fail to master basic skills.
Logical consequence: Have them practice the skill during recess academy.

Lining up for recess, entering and exiting the classroom, raising a hand to be called on before speaking, or just sitting quietly during instruction are examples of basic social skills students must master to be successful at school. When students fail to demonstrate mastery of basic skills, a practice session on their own time can be a highly effective logical consequence. Even a brief session can have a huge impact. Consider the following.

> When students fail to demonstrate mastery of basic skills, a practice session on their own time can be a highly effective logical consequence.

Students in Mr. Carroll's fourth-grade class are expected to walk, not run, down the corridor when dismissed for recess, but Parker and Michael are determined to be the first to arrive at the tetherball poles. Several students have complained about the boys running and bumping into others. Mr. Carroll knows it time for a practice session. He takes the boys aside before the next recess.

"Parker and Michael, you'll be joining me for recess academy," he announces. "We need to practice walking the corridors. Running is dangerous." The boys spend the first five minutes of their recess walking up and down the corridor while Mr. Carroll supervises.

"Good job!" he says after five successful round trips. "If you do that each time, we won't need to practice again." He gives the boys an appreciative smile and sends them out to the playground.

10. When students disrupt activities.

Logical consequence: Separate the disruptive child from the activity temporarily.

Roy, a fifth grader, knows he's supposed to sit quietly at school assemblies but decides to show off for his friends. His teacher takes him aside.

"Roy, you can sit with your friends if you're quiet. If you're not, I'll have to move you. What would you like to do?"

"I'll be quiet," says Roy, but within minutes, he's talking loudly and being disruptive. His teacher intervenes a second time.

"Roy, you need to sit next to me," she says matter-of-factly.

11. When students bring unacceptable items to class.

Logical consequence: Separate the student from the item temporarily.

The students in Miss Lowe's tenth-grade literature class know they're not supposed to bring magazines, comic books, pocket video games, or a variety of other items to class, but Yasmine sits in the back row and thinks she won't get caught. She pulls out a teen magazine, conceals it under her notebook, and tries to read it while Miss Lowe teaches. Yasmine gets caught.

"Yasmine, please put the magazine on my desk," says Miss Lowe. "You can have it back at the end of the quarter."

Logical Consequences with a Price Tag

IMAGINE A LINE that separates two types of consequences: those that place a minimal drain on your time, energy, and resources and those that are costly and require considerable time, planning, and assistance to carry out. Most of the consequences we've examined thus far have been inexpensive. Now, we will cross the line and look at a group of consequences that carries a higher price tag. Most are familiar procedures used to address extreme or persistent misbehaviors. All can be used as logical consequences, and all require more time, planning, and assistance from others to carry out.

Before using costly procedures, there are some questions we should ask ourselves. First, is the misbehavior severe enough to warrant an expensive consequence? Second, have we exhausted all the less expensive options to resolve the problem? Third, are the people we need to assist us willing and available to help?

If the answer to any of these questions is no, then we should continue our guidance efforts at the least expensive level. When we involve administrators, counselors, or others in the guidance process before they are needed, we drain valuable school resources and risk alienating parents and our colleagues in the process. Expensive consequences should be used judiciously. With this in mind, let's look at some of these expensive, but potentially effective, procedures.

Parent Conferences As a Logical Consequence

Parent conferences can be an effective logical consequence when efforts to resolve problems with students individually fail. Notice how the teacher sets up the consequence in the following example.

It's the fourth week of school, and Adam, a sixth grader, continues to clown around daily. His teacher has exhausted all of his usual steps to resolve the problem, but the clowning continues. He thinks it's time to arrange a parent conference, but before he does, he discusses the consequence with Adam.

"I try to work out problems with my students before I involve their parents," the teacher begins, "but we haven't made much progress. Do we need some help from your parents?"

Adam wants to avoid this step if possible. He promises things will improve, but the next day, he picks up where he left off. It's as though their conversation never took place. So Adam's teacher follows through and schedules a twenty-minute conference for the following morning before school.

The teacher begins the conference by commenting on Adam's strengths and positive qualities. Then he shares his concerns and the steps he has taken to deal with them.

"How can we help?" asks Adam's father.

"When Adam arrives home with a notice because he spent time outside the classroom for disrupting, please make sure he completes the work he misses. I'll write his missed assignments on the notice."

"We can do more than that," replies Adam's mother. "On the days that Adam has difficulty cooperating, we will set aside an hour after school to practice cooperation. I can think of lots of things I would like some cooperation with." Adam doesn't like the sound of this remedy.

With a solution in place, Adam's teacher thanks the parents and arranges a follow-up conference four weeks later to evaluate Adam's progress. But, Adam's behavior improves right away. The conference provided the wake-up call and accountability he needed.

In Adam's case, the conference was effective because his parents were willing to take responsibility for resolving the problem and willing to follow through. Their support made the difference. Adam's teacher also helped his own cause by following some general guidelines for effective conferencing. You can, too. The following tips should help.

Guidelines for Conducting Parent Conferences

- *Be proactive.* Schedule the conference promptly after you've exhausted your options to resolve the problem at a lower level. No parent likes to hear that a problem has been allowed to continue for a long period of time before he or she is notified or involved. Parents will appreciate your responsiveness.

- *Include the child in the conference.* The fact that the parents and teacher are working together sends a strong message to the child: "We care, and we will work together to hold you accountable." Sometimes the message is lost when the child is excluded from the conference.

- *Be positive.* You can create the right climate for problem solving by beginning the conference with a positive statement or anecdote about the child, such as "Miguel is a real helper in the classroom" or "I know I can count on Greg's leadership on the playground." A positive start helps parents relax and become more receptive to what follows.

- *Keep the conference focused.* Sometimes conferences ramble or lose their focus because the parents and teacher do not share the same agenda. The best way to tackle the problem of hidden or competing agendas is to state the purpose and goals for the conference at the outset as well as your time constraints. Ask the parents whether they have any additional issues they would like to discuss, and, if needed, schedule a follow-up call or conference. When parents realize that their concerns will be addressed, they're less likely to interrupt or steer the conference in other directions.

- *Come prepared to offer solutions.* No parent likes to have a problem dumped in his or her lap or to be put on the spot to come up with a quick solution. Come to the conference prepared to offer a solution or a back-up plan in the event your solution is not feasible. If the solution to the problem is not clear, be prepared to direct the parents to the appropriate resources for assistance such as counseling, a professional evaluation, helpful books, or parenting classes.

- *Schedule a follow-up conference to evaluate progress.* Follow-up conferences demonstrate commitment and build accountability into the process. Don't assume parents will follow through and take all the corrective steps you suggest. Build some accountability into the process by scheduling a follow-up conference to review progress and to discuss any remaining steps that need to be taken. Don't bring closure to the problem-solving process until the problem is solved.

On-Campus Suspension (OCS) As a Logical Consequence

Some misbehaviors such as extreme defiance, disruption, or injurious behavior require removing students from the classroom for more than brief periods. In these situations, on-campus suspension can be an effective logical consequence.

Darrell, an eighth grader, knows it's not okay to wear hats in the classroom but decides to challenge the school rule and do it anyway. He arrives at his first-period class with his hat on and waits for the teacher to ask him to take it off. When she does, he explodes.

"Buzz off!" he shouts. "I don't have to follow your stupid rules or take any crap from you or anybody else." He slumps back in his chair defiantly.

"Pick up your books and take them with you to OCS, Darrell," says the teacher matter-of-factly. "You can join us again tomorrow." She hands him a slip with the time on it and sends him to the on-campus suspension center for the rest of the period.

Darrell was hoping his protest would be his ticket home for the day. When he arrives at OCS, he decides to stick with his original plan and keeps his hat on.

"You know the rules, Darrell," says the OCS supervisor. "If you don't take it off, I'll have to send you to the vice principal's office. He'll probably send you home for the day."

"Go ahead. Make my day," Darrell says to himself. He knows his parents can't afford to take any time away from work. He'd love to spend his day hanging out at the mall. He leaves his hat on.

When Darrell arrives at the office, the vice principal has a good idea about what's going on. He gives Darrell some choices. "You can spend the rest of the period in OCS with your hat off, or you can spend the rest of the day in OCS with it on. What would you like to do?"

These were not the choices Darrell expected. He takes a moment to consider what his day would be like in OCS. No visiting with friends between classes or during lunch. None of his usual privileges. He would eat lunch by himself, take periodic bathroom breaks, and spend most of his day catching up on assignments from his various classes. Reluctantly, Darrell takes off his hat and heads to OCS for the rest of first period.

> On-campus suspension removes the audience and payoffs for misbehavior.

As the example illustrates, on-campus suspension has many advantages. It stops the immediate misbehavior. It removes the audience and payoffs for misbehavior. And it maintains the student in an instructional setting to the greatest extent possible. The message to Darrell was clear: You will stay at school. You can cooperate in class and enjoy your usual privileges and the company of your peers, or you can work quietly by yourself without your peers or privileges. The best option was not difficult to figure out.

Although OCS is best suited for larger schools with a high incidence of misbehavior, the procedure can be adapted for smaller schools. The procedure is flexible. Some schools use OCS as a second-stage time-out area.

The primary disadvantage of OCS is cost. An on-campus suspension center is expensive to operate. It requires a full-time staff position to supervise students, an available classroom, and a set of record-keeping procedures to track referrals, arrivals, departures, and no-shows. The following guidelines will help you set up an on-campus suspension program.

Guidelines for Operating OCS

- *Select an appropriate place for OCS.* The room should be large enough for students to sit well apart from one another.

- *Provide work folders.* OCS should be a quiet place for students to work. Referring teachers should send work folders along with their students.

- *Adapt the procedure if necessary.* Elementary schools or schools with a low incidence of extreme misbehavior can adapt the procedure by using it as the second stage of a two-stage time-out procedure described in the following chapter.

- *Hold no-shows accountable.* Students who fail to show up for OCS should make up the missed time in after-school detention, Saturday school, or experience a similar consequence.

- *Hold referring teachers accountable.* OCS referral forms should include a section for the teacher to complete indicating all prior steps taken to resolve the problem. The referral should clearly indicate that OCS is an appropriate consequence for the student's misbehavior.

Saturday School As a Logical Consequence

Saturday school is an effective logical consequence at the secondary level for handling problems with tardies, cuts, or truancy. The message is clear: Make up the time you missed. Although the program requires costly supervision, room space, and record keeping, much of the costs can be recovered through the additional aid generated by student attendance.

The biggest disadvantage of Saturday school is that the consequence cannot be enforced without parent support. When parents are willing to hold their children accountable, a day or two of Saturday school can be very instructive. Consider the following.

Julie and Miranda, both ninth graders, decide to hang out at the mall during the first three periods of their day. When they arrive at their fourth-period classes, they are called to the attendance office.

"May I see the excuse notes from your parents so I can admit you to class?" asks the attendance clerk. Neither girl has a note or a good excuse. The clerk alerts the vice principal, who gives the girls some choices.

"You both will have to make up your truancies with half a day of Saturday school. There are two Saturdays left in the month. Which one would you like?" Julie and Miranda both know their parents will support the consequence. They'll probably think carefully next time they consider spending class time at the mall.

After-School Detention As a Logical Consequence

After-school detention is another logical consequence for handling problems such as tardies or wasted time. As Nick discovers in the following example, the procedure provides accountability for those students who want to move on to more pleasurable activities at the end of their day.

Nick, a seventh grader, arrives late for class for the third time during the semester. When he goes to the attendance office to pick up a tardy slip, he's informed that he must put in one hour of after-school detention that afternoon as a consequence.

"What a drag!" Nick says to himself. "I was planning to go skateboarding with my friends." After-school detention gave Nick a new reason for arriving at class on time.

Off-Campus Suspension As a Logical Consequence

Off-campus suspensions share the same limitation as parent conferences. The success of the procedure depends on cooperation between home and school. The school can exclude a student from campus, but it has no control over what happens when the student leaves. Enforcing the consequence is the parents' job. The parents must be willing to enforce the consequence for it to be effective.

When parents aren't willing to enforce the consequence, many students view the suspension as a vacation day and welcome opportunities for more. In effect, the consequence becomes a reward for continued misbehavior. When parents are willing to enforce the consequence, such as the parents in the following example, off-campus suspension can be instructive.

Chase, a third grader, decides to play a joke on the girl sitting in front of him. As she begins to sit down, he pulls out her chair, and she falls backward. The joke isn't funny. She has a gash on the back of her head that will probably require stitches.

The teacher asks Chase to collect his books and assignments and sends him to the office with a note. The principal promptly calls his parents and informs them that Chase has been suspended from school for the rest of the day.

"How can we help him learn from this experience?" asks Chase's mom. The principal offers some helpful tips.

"Suspensions are most effective when children spend a quiet day in the house without the privileges they would normally enjoy. No TV, video games, riding bikes, playing in the neighborhood, or hanging out with friends, at least not during school hours. They should spend their time catching up on missed schoolwork, reading, or doing other quiet activities. Tomorrow, Chase can return to school with a clean slate."

In this case, cooperation between home and school ensured the success of the procedure. The off-campus suspension provided Chase with the instructive lesson he needed.

Chapter Summary

LOGICAL CONSEQUENCES ARE structured learning experiences. They are arranged by the adult, experienced by the child, and logically related to the event or misbehavior. Logical consequences set the gold standard for school guidance. They accomplish all of our guidance goals. They stop misbehavior. They teach responsibility, and they promote cooperative relationships in the classroom. Get to know them. Make friends with them. They are your ticket to credibility in the classroom.

Logical consequences are easy to use if we think in simple, logical terms and follow some general guidelines. Most incidents of misbehavior involve at least one of the following circumstances: children with other children, children with adults, children with objects, children with activities, or children with privileges. In most cases, we can apply a logical consequence by temporarily separating one child from another, a child from an adult, a child from an object (such as a toy), a child from an activity (such as a game), or a child from a privilege (such as recess). For best results, apply logical consequences immediately and use them as often as needed.

11

Two-Stage Time-Out

A Stop Signal That Works

CASSIE, AGE THREE, sits on the floor building a tower with blocks, when the boy sitting next to her accidentally bumps her. "Move!" shouts Cassie angrily. "You almost knocked over my tower." When the boy doesn't move, Cassie gets up and kicks him in the back. He screams. The teacher intervenes.

"Cassie, please sit by yourself at the back table for a while," says her teacher matter-of-factly. "I'll set the timer for three minutes." When the time is over, Cassie and her teacher explore other ways to get people to move without kicking.

In another classroom, Mitch, a sixth grader, tries to spice up a social studies lesson with some live entertainment. While his teacher writes at the board, Mitch pretends to conduct an orchestra. He gets a few laughs. The teacher catches a glimpse of what's going on.

"Have a seat please, Mitch," says the teacher matter-of-factly. Mitch sits down, but he isn't finished yet. He got a few laughs earlier, and he's hungry for more. When the teacher returns to the board, Mitch jumps up once again and begins conducting. More laughter. This time, the teacher decides to put a little distance between Mitch and his audience.

"Take your books and have a seat at the back table, Mitch," says the teacher. "You can join us again in ten minutes." He sets the timer. Mitch heads to the back table.

Mitch is quiet for a few minutes and then renews his quest for attention. He drums on the table loud enough to distract others. This time, the teacher decides to separate Mitch completely from his audience.

"Pick up your books and take them with you to Mrs. Currier's class," says the teacher. "You can join us again in twenty minutes." Mitch heads off to Mrs. Currier's room. He won't find a receptive audience there. She teaches second grade.

Both teachers in the previous examples are using time-out. Cassie's teacher used a one-stage procedure to support her rule about kicking. Mitch's teacher needed a two-stage procedure to stop Mitch's persistent disruptiveness. In this chapter, you'll learn how to use both of these procedures to handle a variety of challenging misbehaviors. You'll learn how to set up time-outs, how to carry them out, and how to overcome the obstacles teachers confront with these procedures.

Effective Use of Time-Out

TIME-OUT IS A highly effective guidance tool when used as it was intended—as a logical consequence. The consequence sends all the right signals to children. It stops their misbehavior. It removes them from their audience and payoffs for disruption, and it helps children restore self-control quickly so they can return to instruction.

Teachers like time-out because they can stop disruptive behavior quickly and effectively without losing valuable time for instruction. Administrators like time-out because it keeps disruptive students out of the office and allows teachers to manage disruptive behavior at the classroom level. The procedure is easy to carry out and can be used at all grade levels—preschool, elementary, even secondary school.

Unfortunately, time-out has received some unfavorable press because the procedure has been so widely misused and misunderstood. Those who operate from the punitive model have used it as a jail sentence to force children into submission. The punitive version of time-out sounds something like this: "You sit in the corner and don't leave until I tell you to. I don't want to hear a peep out of you." Punitive time-outs can be quite lengthy, several hours or even days, and they are often carried out in an atmosphere of anger or upset. The goal is to humiliate or shame students into cooperating.

On the other extreme, those who operate from the permissive model view time-out as a tool for the child to use at his or her discretion. The child decides when it starts, when it ends, or whether it even happens at all. The permissive version of time-out sounds something like this: "I think it would be a good idea if you take some quiet time by yourself for a while at the back table, okay? You can rejoin the group when you're ready." The child decides the length of time, which is usually quite brief. The goal is to persuade students into cooperating.

Actually, neither of those methods is really time-out. Time-out is not jail, nor is it an optional consequence for students to

> Teachers like time-out because they can stop disruptive behavior quickly and effectively without losing valuable time for instruction.

use at their own discretion. When time-out is used in either of these ways, responsibility shifts in the wrong direction, and most of the training value of the consequence is lost.

Time-out is really time away from reinforcement or temporary loss of the "good stuff." In most classrooms, the good stuff consists of the many rewards of daily routines such as being a member of the group, enjoying full privileges, participating in group activities, getting recognition and attention from others, and enjoying the freedom that goes with cooperation. The goals are to stop the misbehavior, restore self-control, and reintegrate the student into instruction as quickly as possible.

Does time-out still sound like jail? The two are similar to the extent that both provide a solid set of walls to stop misbehavior and remove reinforcement. There are also some major differences.

Time-outs are generally brief (three to twenty minutes) and are designed to keep students in instruction as much as they can be. The procedure can be used repetitively, which provides many opportunities for teaching and learning corrective behavior. Jail sentences, on the other hand, tend to be lengthy (hours or days) and are designed to exclude students from instruction and learning. There are few, if any, opportunities for students to practice responsible corrective behavior in jail.

Guidelines for Using Time-Out

TIME-OUT IS A quick, simple, and easy-to-carry-out procedure that can be used with students of all grade levels (preschool through secondary) and in many different situations. The procedure is most effective when presented as a logical consequence and carried out in a firm, respectful, and matter-of-fact manner. The following guidelines should be helpful.

1. Select an appropriate time-out area.

Selection of an appropriate place or places for time-out is critical to the success of the procedure. The best places for time-out within the classroom is an unoccupied desk, table, or three-sided study carrel positioned away from others near the periphery of the classroom. These areas separate disruptive students from their stage and audience temporarily.

What should we do when students persist with their disruption while in time-out? We have to become creative and select a second time-out area or stage 2 outside the classroom. Use a buddy teacher's classroom as the second-stage time-out area.

Why not use the school office? The school office is one of the least suitable places for time-out. It's the hub of school activity, with busy people and lots of interesting things going on. For many students, time-out in the office is like watching their own personal soap opera. The consequence is actually a reward, a big reinforcement error. Remember, time-out should be time away from reinforcement. You won't accomplish your purpose if you send a disruptive child to an entertaining area.

Some teachers send students outside the classroom to sit in the hallway for time-out. Is this a recommended practice? Time-outs in the hallway have several disadvantages. The procedure removes students from instruction, often needlessly, and the hallway creates problems with supervision. Most students can take time-out in the classroom without isolating them from instruction and without compromising your duty to keep them supervised. For those students who need more, the two-stage procedure is a better way to go.

> You won't accomplish your purpose if you send a disruptive child to an entertaining area.

Can time-out be used outside the classroom in settings such as the cafeteria, library, or playground? Yes. Select a chair, a bench, or some comfortable spot away from other children. Then keep track of the time.

2. Use a two-stage procedure for persistent disruption.

What should you do when students continue to disrupt while in time-out? I recommend using a two-stage time-out procedure such as the one Mitch's teacher used in the opening example. A two-stage procedure is ideal for aggressive researchers like Mitch, because it provides escalating consequences for escalating misbehavior. Each stage further separates the disruptive child from his or her audience and from the payoffs for misbehavior. Each stage also provides more time for the child to restore self-control.

The procedure is very simple. Stage 1 time-outs take place in the child's immediate classroom for a predetermined period of time. Most students will decide to cooperate at this point. A few, like Mitch, may decide to test, and when they do, you'll need a back-up area outside your classroom for time-out. Stage 2 time-outs should take place in a buddy teacher's classroom for twice the usual period of time. If your school has a supervised on-campus suspension center (OCS), that location is an excellent choice as a second-stage time-out area.

When choosing a buddy teacher, select someone who is familiar with the procedure and who is willing to carry it out in a firm, matter-of-fact manner. The ideal buddy teacher is someone with older or younger students, eliminating the possibility of a receptive audience. Generally, older students do not like to be in classrooms with younger students and vice versa. If you are a middle school or high school teacher, you may want to select a buddy teacher with advanced placement or accelerated students who do not appreciate clowning around or disruption. The buddy teacher's job is to provide a place for the child to sit during time-out, to supervise the child, and to keep track of time. This is not a time for interrogation ("What did you do this time?") or shaming ("Oh, no, not you again!"), nor should it be a rewarding or pleasurable experience. If the child cooperates during the time-out, the usual outcome, then he or she returns to class when the time is over.

3. Introduce time-out to your students before using it.

You can prevent a lot of testing, resistance, and confusion if you introduce the time-out procedure to your students before using it, preferably during the first few days of school. Pose some hypothetical situations and walk your students through the complete procedure so they can see how it works. Consider the following sample introduction from an intermediate teacher to the class.

"I use the time-out procedure when someone disrupts class. Here's how it works. If I think you are unaware of your behavior, I will usually give you a warning such as, 'Jimmy, you need to work quietly now,' so you can stop what you are doing. If you continue to disrupt, or if I'm sure you are aware of what you are doing, I will ask you to go to the time-out area. You can take your books and follow along with the lesson or just sit quietly. When the time-out is over, I will ask you to return to your seat. If you leave the area before the time-out is over, you'll have to go back, and the time will start over.

"If you continue to disrupt while in time-out, I will ask you to go to Mrs. Smith's class [buddy teacher] for twice the time. You can take your books and work quietly when you're there or just sit quietly. She will let you know when the time-out is over and you can return to class. Any questions about how time-out works?"

4. Use a timer.

Time-outs should always have a beginning and an end that is clear to all involved. Open-ended, vague, or arbitrary time limits such as "You can return when I think you're ready" or "Go to the time-out area for a while" set up both teacher and students for further testing and power struggles.

The best way to keep track of time is to use a time-out timer available through educational supply catalogues. A kitchen timer with an inoffensive chime also works fine. I don't recommend relying on wrist watches, wall clocks, or other imprecise measures or permitting your students to set the timer or control the time. Teachers who use this practice discover that time-outs in their classroom are very brief. Once you set the timer, you effectively take yourself out of the picture. The remaining part is between the child and the timer.

How long should time-outs be? One minute per each year of age is a good rule of thumb for preschoolers (for example, four minutes for a four-year-old). Stage 1 time-outs should be five to ten minutes for primary level students (kindergarten through grade 3) and ten to fifteen minutes for intermediate (grades 3 through 6) and secondary students (grades 7 through

12). Stage 2 time-outs should be twice as long as stage 1 time-outs for each respective group.

Keep one additional factor in mind when determining the appropriate length of time for time-out. In all cases, time-outs should be long enough for the child to restore self-control. For example, if a five-year-old continues to tantrum for twenty minutes before he regains self-control, then that's how long he needs to spend in time-out.

5. For limit testing, set up time-out with limited choices.

Lindsey, a second grader, knows she's supposed to keep her hands to herself in the classroom but decides to tickle her neighbor. Her teacher notices and gives Lindsey some choices.

"Lindsey, you can keep your hands to yourself, or you can take five minutes at the back table to get yourself under control. What would you like to do?" Her choices are clear. Lindsey decides to cooperate.

Brad, a seventh grader, whistles while he's supposed to be working quietly on a writing assignment. The noise disturbs others. His teacher asks him to stop, and he does briefly, but starts up again a short time later.

"Brad, you need to work on your assignment quietly at the back table," says his teacher matter-of-factly. Brad picks up his papers and heads to the back table for a ten-minute time-out, but within a minute, he whistles again. This time, his teacher gives him some choices.

"Brad, you can work quietly for ten minutes at the back table, or you can go next door to Mr. Jacob's room for twenty minutes. What would you like to do?"

"I'll finish up here," replies Brad. He doesn't have any friends in Mr. Jacob's class.

Brad was testing. When he found the wall he was looking for, he made the right choice and cooperated. When you encounter limit testing, you can usually set up a first- or second-stage time-out consequence with limited choices, as Brad's teacher did.

6. When rules have been violated, apply time-out directly.
Evan, a kindergartner, wants to play with the new hula hoop his teacher brought to class. When the bell rings for morning recess, he races out to find it, but Carly is already playing with it.

"Hey, I was going to play with that!" shouts Evan when he sees Carly with the toy. He tries to wrestle it away from her, but Carly holds on tight. The struggle continues until Evan decides to bite her on the arm. She screams.

"He bit me," sobs Carly when the teacher comes to investigate. Evan looks remorseful.

"She wouldn't give me the hula hoop," Evan replies.

"We don't bite," says the teacher matter-of-factly. "You need to sit down next to the wall for five minutes. We'll talk about other ways to share the hula hoop when the time is over."

When Evan's teacher arrived on the scene, her rule about biting had already been violated. The time for limited choices had passed. Evan needed to experience the consequence associated with his poor choice. Time-out achieved this purpose effectively.

7. After the time-out, provide a clean slate.
When the timer goes off, the consequence should be over, provided the child has stopped misbehaving and is under control. If the child throws a tantrum or is not under control, then he or she is not ready to come out. You can say, "The timer went off. You can leave the time-out area when you're calmed down but not before that time."

When the child is ready to come out, invite him or her back in a friendly voice. Try to resist the temptation to add an "I told you so" or a lecture that personalizes the lesson and sabotages the effectiveness of the consequence.

8. Hold children accountable for time missed from class.

When children disrupt to the point that they need to be removed from class, their behavior should be seen as a red flag. Parents should be alerted. If the behavior develops into a pattern, you'll need parental assistance.

The notification form shown in figure 11.1 is one simple method to keep parents informed. Send the form home with students after school on the days that they require a second-stage time-out. Parents are asked to sign the form and return it with their child the next day. Inform your students that you will follow up with a phone call if the signed notice is not returned.

Mrs. Deaver

Date: _____

Room #22   Notice # _____

This is to inform you that _____ missed _____ minutes of class time today because he/she continued to disrupt the class after being asked to stop. The problem was handled at school and no further assistance is required at this time.

Please indicate that you received this notice by signing and returning it with your child tomorrow. If you have any questions, please call. Thank you.

_____

Parent signature   Date

Figure 11.1   Parent Notification Form

9. Use time-out as often as you need it.

Time-out is a training tool that promotes children's learning when used consistently and appropriately. Don't assume the procedure is ineffective when students persist in their testing or continue to violate your rules. More likely, they need to collect more data to arrive at the conclusions you intend. Consistent repeated exposure to your consequences should lead to the learning you desire.

When to Use Time-Out

TIME-OUT CAN BE used in a variety of settings, such as the classroom, playground, library, or cafeteria to address a variety of misbehaviors referred to as "target behaviors." In classroom settings, most target behaviors fall under the general category of disruptive behavior or those behaviors that interfere with your classroom routines, procedures, or the teaching and learning of others. The following are some of the many target behaviors you can address with time-out.

Attention-Seeking Behavior

Alejandro, age four, loves attention—any kind of attention. While his teacher reads a story about farm animals, Alejandro makes the sound for each animal in the story. His teacher asks him to stop, and he does, for a while, until she comes to the part about pigs. Then he lets out a series of grunts and snorts.

"Take a seat at the back table, Alejandro," says his teacher matter-of-factly. "It's not okay to interrupt while I'm reading." She sets the timer for five minutes. Alejandro loses his audience.

Limit-Testing Behavior

Buz, a fifth grader, is told he cannot use his skateboard on the playground during school hours, but he tries his best to wear his teacher down and turn a no into a yes. "Come on, Mr. Easton," Buz pleads. "I'm not going to get hurt. I know how to use it safely."

"You know the rules, Buz," replies Mr. Easton. "No skateboards on the playground during school hours."

"Well, they're stupid rules," says Buz, "and I don't see why I have to follow them."

"We're finished talking about it," says Mr. Easton, realizing the futility of further discussion. "If you bring it up again, you'll have to spend some time by yourself." Buz won't let go.

"Why can't we make an exception, just this once?" asks Buz, looking for a little bargaining room. "I'll even wear my bike helmet and elbow pads." Mr. Easton doesn't take the bait. He's done as much as he can with his words. Now it's time for Buz to experience stopping.

"Have a seat at the back table, Buz. I'll let you know when ten minutes are over."

Disrespectful Behavior

Rita, a tenth grader, is unhappy with her teacher for not granting her a deadline extension on a term paper. "You're so unfair!" complains Rita. "Other teachers help students out when they are in a bind. Why can't you?"

"Sorry, Rita," says Mr. Simmons. "You've had a month. I can't give you any more time. It's not fair to the others."

"You are so uptight!" says Rita with a biting tone to her voice. "What do you care, anyway? You probably get your thrills making life miserable for your students."

"Have a seat at the back table, Rita," says Mr. Simmons matter-of-factly. "I'll let you know when fifteen minutes are up."

"Oh, that really hurts," says Rita sarcastically. "What happens if I don't go to the back table?" she taunts.

Mr. Simmons gives her some choices. "You can go to the back table for fifteen minutes, or you can spend the rest of the period at the on-campus suspension center. What would you like to do?"

Rita lets out a big huff. Reluctantly, she heads to the back table.

Defiant Behavior

The kids are lined up to go out for recess when Mrs. Lopez notices that one of her second graders has left his art materials all over his desk. "Gregory, you need to put away your art materials before you can go out for recess," says Mrs. Lopez.

"I'll do it when I get back," he says insistently.

"No," she replies. "You can't leave until it's done."

"Well, I'm not going to do it!" says Gregory, crossing his arms. Mrs. Lopez gives him some choices.

"You can pick up the items on your desk, or you can spend the next five minutes at the back table getting ready to do it. What would you like to do?" Gregory glares at her and marches to the back table to sit down. After five minutes, the buzzer rings.

"The time is over," Mrs. Lopez announces. "Are you ready to clean up your desk so you can go outside?"

"I'm still not doing it!" says Gregory as defiantly as before.

"That's up to you," says Mrs. Lopez. She gets up to reset the timer, but Gregory has a sudden change of heart.

"Okay," he says, realizing the firmness of her resolve. He picks up quickly and tries to salvage what's left of his recess.

Antagonistic or Hurtful Behavior

Olivia, an eighth grader, goes to the board to write out a solution to a math problem. She seems unsure. When it's time to go over her work, the teacher finds an error. Olivia looks embarrassed. A classmate does his best to make her feel even worse.

"Nice try, Olivia," says Marco sarcastically. "You only missed it by a hundred." The teacher intervenes.

"Have a seat at the back table, Marco," says the teacher matter-of-factly. "It's not okay to treat anybody like that in this classroom." Marco heads to the back table for a fifteen-minute time-out.

Violent and Aggressive Behavior

Logan and George, both sixth graders, get into a heated argument as they head out to the playground. They yell at each other and call each other names. When the yard duty teacher arrives on the scene, the boys are wrestling on the blacktop with a crowd of students cheering them on. Logan's shirt is ripped, and George has a scratch on his forehead. Both are upset.

"Get up, guys," says the teacher.

"He pushed me first," says George.

"But you called me an asshole," counters Logan.

"You both need to spend fifteen minutes by yourselves," says the teacher, "then we'll talk about other ways to handle the situation." She directs the boys to separate benches at opposite ends of the playground. When the fifteen minutes are up, she calls them over to discuss other ways to resolve their differences without fighting.

Tantrums

Samantha, age five, is accustomed to getting her own way at home. When she hears no, Samantha has a proven strategy for turning it into yes. She throws a tantrum. Her parents usually give in. Things are different in Samantha's kindergarten class.

"Recess is over," announces Samantha's teacher. "It's time to come inside." One by one, the kids file back into the classroom—that is, everyone except Samantha. She continues to play on the monkey bars.

"Samantha, you need to come in, too," says the teacher.

"But I'm not ready to come in," says Samantha insistently. "I want to play some more."

"You can play next recess, but now you need to join the class," replies her teacher. Samantha doesn't move. So her teacher takes Samantha's hand, and together, they begin to walk back to class.

"What's going on?" Samantha thinks to herself. This isn't how it's supposed to work." As they near the classroom, she decides to play her trump card. She throws a tantrum. She plops herself down outside the door and begins to cry. "I won't do it!" she sobs.

"That's up to you," says her teacher. "You can join us in five minutes if you're done crying." She sets the timer and asks a parent volunteer to watch Samantha during the time-out.

Samantha is still crying when the buzzer goes off. Fifteen minutes go by, and Samantha is still crying. Finally, twenty minutes after the tantrum began, Samantha walks back into the classroom.

"Hi, Samantha," says the teacher in a friendly voice. "Have a seat." The tantrum didn't work. Next recess, Samantha returns to class with everyone else.

Questions and Answers About Time-Out

Q : **What should I do when students refuse to go to the time-out area?**

A : This is probably further limit testing to determine whether you will really follow through or an extreme act of defiance. In either event, you should set up the next consequence by giving the student some limited choices. For example, you might say, "You can go to the time-out area as you were asked, or you can go to the office and work it out with the principal or your parents. What would you like to do?" Give the child twenty to thirty seconds to think it over, and then follow through based on his or her decision. If this is an extreme act of defiance, you will probably need assistance from others.

Q : **What should I do when students leave the time-out area before their time-out is over?**

A : Again, this is probably further limit testing. State firmly that they must stay in the time-out area until the full time elapses. If they leave before the time-out is over, ask them to return to the time-out area and start the time over again.

Q : **What should I do when students yell and scream while in time-out?**

A : This sounds like a tantrum, or it may be a discharge of pent-up anger and frustration. Do not reward the tantrum by giving in to it or by resorting to threats, lectures, or other forms of coercion. It's time to move on to a second-stage time-out outside the classroom.

Q : **What should I do when students knock over chairs or other items while in time-out?**

A : When you introduce the time-out procedure to your class at the beginning of the year, inform them that if they make a mess while in time-out, they will have to clean it up before they leave. A little prevention goes a long way. Remove breakable items from your time-out area.

Q : **When I ask some students to go to the time-out area, they mumble, grumble, or talk back disrespectfully as they go there. Should I add five minutes each time they do this?**

A : No. That's probably what they want you to do, and if you play it out to the fullest extent, your time-outs will become jail. These students are doing their best to incite a power struggle and get you back out on the dance floor. As tempting as the bait might be, don't bite. If they go to the time-out area and stay there the full time without further disruption, then your time-out procedure is working. If they use obscenities or disrupt during stage 1, then move on to stage 2. Your students will realize there are no advantages to escalation.

Q : **What are students supposed to do while in time-out?**

A : The purpose of time-out is to stop the immediate misbehavior and help children restore self-control. Children can do a number of things in the time-out area to achieve this purpose. You may want to present these options as choices. For example, you might say, "You can bring your book and assignment and follow along with the lesson, or you can just sit there quietly." Some teachers set out *Weekly*

Readers or other reading material in the time-out area to help disruptive children settle down and restore self-control. If you provide nothing for an angry or upset child to do while in time-out, you increase the likelihood of further disruption.

Q : **What should I do when I ask a student to go to my buddy teacher's classroom for a second-stage time-out, and I suspect he or she may not go there directly, if at all?**

A : Select a responsible student in your classroom to be an escort. Escorts are an effective way to ensure that children arrive at their destination. Or, if they don't, the escort can inform you quickly so you can notify the office or take other steps to intervene.

Q : **Secondary students sometimes try to defeat the two-stage procedure by not showing up at the buddy teacher's class or on-campus suspension center (OCS). How should we deal with this problem?**

A : Referring teachers should routinely follow up with their buddy teacher or OCS supervisor to verify compliance. No-shows should be held accountable for making up the time in after-school detention or Saturday school. It doesn't take too many of these experiences to increase compliance with the two-stage procedure.

Q : **How much disruption is too much? When is it time to use more than time-out as a consequence?**

A : Tolerance for disruption varies from teacher to teacher. Some teachers consider two or three disruptive incidents a week to be excessive for any student. Others can tolerate ten or more incidents a week if they see a general pattern of improvement. If you use the two-stage time-out procedure consistently for four to six weeks and experience only minimal reduction in disruptive behavior, then it's time to investigate the underlying causes for the behavior and consider other guidance steps. In the next chapter, we'll examine guidance strategies for your most disruptive students.

Chapter Summary

THE TWO-STAGE TIME-OUT procedure is a stop signal disruptive children really understand. It stops their misbehavior. It removes them from their audience and payoffs for misbehavior, and it helps them restore self-control quickly so they can rejoin instruction. Best of all, the procedure allows teachers to manage disruptive behavior at the classroom level without involving administrators or support staff. The two-stage time-out is an inexpensive solution for costly behavior problems.

Time-out also is a versatile guidance tool. It can be used in a variety of situations with children of nearly all ages, preschool through secondary. For most students, a one-stage procedure is sufficient to stop their misbehavior and restore their self-control. Your aggressive researchers may require a two-stage procedure that provides escalating consequences for escalating misbehavior. Each stage further separates the disruptive child from his or her audience and from the payoffs for misbehavior.

12

Managing Extreme Behavior

MOST SCHOOLS HAVE procedures for handling emergencies such as fires, power failures, and natural disasters, but few schools adequately prepare teachers for the types of emergencies they're most likely to encounter in the classroom. I'm talking about extreme acts of defiance or disruption, destructive behavior, and violent or assaultive behavior. In these situations, we cannot afford to fly by the seat of our pants and operate without a plan. The cost to our personal safety, the safety and welfare of our students, and to our careers is too great. We need effective plans and procedures to protect us. This chapter will attempt to fill the gap and provide you with the procedures you need to manage the extreme behavior you're most likely to face.

Legal and Safety Considerations

IMAGINE YOURSELF IN the following situation. You're writing instructions on the board when one of your students suddenly becomes enraged and throws a chair across the classroom, narrowly missing several of his classmates. Do you have a plan for handling this crisis? What would you do? Would you shout at him to stop? Would you plead with him? Would you run to the nearest classroom or to the office for help? Would you risk injury and use physical force to restrain him from throwing more chairs? Would you send an emergency call to the office? What would you do until help arrived?

Without a carefully thought-out plan, you and your students are vulnerable because each intervention involves an element of risk. If you leave the classroom to summon help, you place your job in jeopardy because you have a legal obligation to keep your students supervised. If you fail to take appropriate action to protect your students, you could be liable for their injuries because you have a legal obligation to protect their safety and welfare. If you attempt to restrain an enraged student and injure him in the process, you could be liable for his injuries. If you become injured, a bad situation just became worse because now the situation is even more out of control.

Legal and safety considerations should be paramount when deciding how to manage extreme situations. Your overriding concerns should be to:

1. Keep your students supervised.

2. Keep your students safe.

3. Minimize risk to your students and to yourself.

You should always have a plan for back-up support from your school administrator or some other staff member designated to handle emergencies. Physical restraint and hands-on procedures should be interventions of last resort and should be carried out by those trained to use them. With these guidelines in mind, let's look at some of the extreme situations you're most likely to confront and effective ways to intervene.

Extreme Defiant Behavior

ROSS, A FIFTH GRADER, started his day with a chip on his shoulder. He bothered and provoked other students in desk group throughout the morning and was sent to time-out twice before the morning recess. After recess, he starts up where he left off before. He hums to himself as he works on an assignment and disturbs his classmates. When they complain, the teacher asks Ross to take his paper and pencil and finish his assignment at the back table.

> Physical restraint and hands-on procedures should be interventions of last resort and should be carried out by those trained to use them.

"Forget it!" he shouts. "I'm not going, and you can't make me. I don't have to follow your stupid rules or do anything you say if I don't want to." He stands next to his desk with his arms folded and continues humming, defiantly.

All eyes are on Ross. The tension is extreme. Teaching and learning have come to a screeching halt. All of his classmates are wondering, "What's she going to do?" Her credibility and authority are on the line.

But this teacher has a plan. She takes a couple of deep breaths and then calmly asks her students to line up at the door, leaving Ross standing alone next to his desk. She joins her class at the door and makes an announcement.

"Ross needs to make a decision about whether or not he wants to be part of our class today. Let's give him three minutes of silence to help him make up his mind." She looks at her watch and turns to Ross.

"Would you like to join us and cooperate, or would you prefer to work it out with our principal, Mrs. Donnelly, in the office? I'd be happy to call her if that's what you prefer. I'll give you a few minutes to think about it." She looks at her watch again and waits in silence with the rest of her class. She's prepared to act when the three minutes are over.

The spotlight is squarely on Ross and so is the hot potato of responsibility. It's up to him to decide what he wants to do. He is responsible for the outcome. Ross looks around the room, hums defiantly for about thirty seconds, and then begins to feel self-conscious and stops. He realizes there is no way out and squirms uncomfortably.

"Okay," he says, "I'll join the class."

"Good choice," says his teacher. "Have a seat." She asks the rest of the class to return to their desks and continue with their writing assignment.

This teacher is effective because she's prepared and operates with a plan. She fulfills all of her basic responsibilities. She keeps all of her students supervised. She keeps them safe, and she minimizes risk. She remains in control of the situation the whole time.

Her first step is to separate the parties involved. Since Ross is defiant, the easiest thing to do is to separate others from him. She asks her class to line up at the door and joins them. Everyone is supervised. Everyone is safe. She minimizes the risk by creating a safe distance between Ross and others.

Her next step is to give Ross some time to cool down and a way out of the situation he put himself in. She offers him some choices. He can cooperate and rejoin the class, or she will call the office, where he can resolve the matter with the principal. The choice is his and so is the responsibility for the outcome. She's prepared to follow through with the consequence based on his choice.

In this case, Ross chooses to cooperate and rejoin the class, but let's consider the other possible scenario. Let's say that Ross remains defiant at the end of the three minutes. What should his teacher do? She should follow through, call the office, and have Ross escorted out of class. All of her students are watching. Her credibility and authority are on the line. In situations like this, teachers need back-up support.

Dangerous or Destructive Behavior

BRENT, AN EIGHTH grader, disrupts his social studies class by throwing pencils and wads of paper at his classmates. He gets caught, and his teacher, Mr. Jeffries, asks him to go to the back table for a fifteen-minute time-out. Things are quiet for a few minutes, and then someone shouts, "Watch out!" When Mr. Jeffries turns around, he sees a chair flying across the room narrowly missing several students. Brent is standing at the back table with a second chair in his hands. Mr. Jeffries asks his students to put their heads on their desks and cover them with their arms, and then he turns to Brent.

"Put the chair down, please," says Mr. Jeffries, but Brent lets it fly. This one bounces off a counter and shatters a large window. As Brent reaches for another chair, Mr. Jeffries orders his students to quickly exit the classroom and line up outside the door. He joins them at the door and calls the office for help. His kids are safe, but Brent continues his rampage.

"Put the chair down, Brent," Mr. Jeffries says again. His words have little effect.

"You're all a bunch of shitheads!" Brent shouts and lets the third chair fly that crashes into a desk. Moments later, the vice principal arrives with the campus security officer, who escorts Brent from the classroom.

This scene sounds like an educator's nightmare, but Mr. Jeffries had a plan. He knew his first duty was to protect his students from danger, so he mobilized the biggest part of his classroom that was still under his control—his cooperative students. He moved them outside the classroom as quickly as possible; then he sent for back-up support from the office. A simple two-step plan was enough to fulfill all of his obligations. He kept his students supervised. He kept them safe, and he took the appropriate steps to minimize risk. He didn't put himself or his students in needless danger by attempting to restrain Brent physically.

Violent or Assaultive Behavior

WHILE MR. TAMORI prepares for his fifth-period biology class, he hears a commotion in the hallway outside his classroom. He looks out his door and sees two students wrestling on the ground and punching each other while a group of students shouts and encourages them on.

Mr. Tamori approaches the boys and asks them to stop, but there's so much shouting, the boys can't hear him. "Time to get rid of the crowd," Mr. Tamori says to himself. He asks all but one student to leave and sends that student to the office for help. Then, Mr. Tamori asks the boys to stop a second time.

This time, they hear him. The fight is over, but the boys are still very upset.

"He started it!" shouts one of the boys as he gets up off the pavement.

"You're the biggest liar!" shouts the other, pointing an accusing finger.

"Both of you need a few minutes to calm down," says Mr. Tamori matter-of-factly. "This isn't a good time for talking." He understands the futility of problem solving while the boys are upset. His first step is to cool them down. He asks one of them to have a seat in his classroom and the other to sit outside the door in the corridor.

The boys are separated. Now they can cool down. Mr. Tamori stands at the door and waits for back-up from the office. Within minutes, the vice principal arrives and escorts the boys to the office, where they can resolve the matter.

Mr. Tamori managed this assaultive incident effectively by following his simple three-step plan:

1. Separate the parties.

2. Cool them down.

3. Call for help.

In this case, separating the parties meant separating the crowd from the two boys and the two boys from each other. Mr. Tamori fulfilled all of his duties. He kept them supervised. He kept them safe, and he took the appropriate steps to minimize risk.

Chapter Summary

MANAGING EXTREME BEHAVIOR is not something we should undertake without a plan. The cost to our safety, the safety of others, and our careers is too great. We need a set of procedures to protect us. Our overriding consideration should be to fulfill our basic safety and legal obligations to our students—that is, to keep them supervised, to keep them safe, and to take appropriate steps to minimize risk.

Your basic crisis management plan should involve at least the following three steps: (1) separate the students from the source of danger, (2) provide cooldown time to deescalate the situation and restore control, and (3) summon help. Back-up support should always be part of your plan. Physical restraint or other hands-on procedures increases the level of risk and should be used only by staff trained to carry out such procedures. Most teachers report that it's safer and easier to separate an entire class from one defiant or assaultive student than it is to separate that student from the class.

13

Using the
Office for
Back-Up Support

I F YOU ASK students and parents what teachers should do with misbehaving students, you're likely to hear, "Send them to the office." If you ask teachers the same question, you're likely to hear the same answer. In most schools, the office is regarded as the pinnacle of school authority and the best place to send misbehaving students. This thinking is deeply ingrained in the culture of the school.

In actuality, the office is one of the worst places to send misbehaving students. This chapter will show you why. We'll examine the administrator's role in the guidance process, the many challenges administrators face, and the consequences of their effective and ineffective guidance practices.

Reinforcement Errors in the Office

FROM A STUDENT'S point of view, the office is an inherently interesting place. It's staffed with the busiest and most friendly people in the whole school who are not available to drop everything and deal with misbehaving kids, much less supervise them. So what happens when misbehaving kids are sent to the office? Most of the time, they sit, and what do they see? They see sick kids; upset kids; late kids; kids who have forgotten lunch money, homework, and permission slips; kids with bumps and scrapes; and kids like themselves who are in trouble. They hear complaints about teachers who are late to report attendance or the lunch count, and they hear about all the messes the custodian has to clean up. To students, the office is one big soap opera.

Some kids want more than entertainment. They want to be part of the action. What do they do? They do the same things they do in the classroom. They clown around and disrupt the office while the secretaries tell them to settle down, be quiet, stay in their seats, and warn them they'll be in even bigger trouble when the principal arrives.

What happens in the meantime? They get live entertainment, negative attention from the secretaries, power and control over the whole office. This is a pretty good deal for disruptive, attention-seeking students. Can the office be any more rewarding? Unfortunately, it can. In some schools, the next round begins when the principal arrives. The following is a typical example.

Mr. Winters, an elementary principal, arrives at his office pressed for time. He has a meeting in thirty minutes. There's a stack of phone messages on his desk, and three students are waiting outside his door for disrupting class.

He calls the first student into his office. Vincent, a sixth grader, slumps into his chair and gives the principal a surly look while he reads a note from the teacher. "Vincent used profanity and called me insulting names when I asked him to stop disrupting class," the note reads. The principal picks up the phone, calls Vincent's mother at work, and informs her that Vincent is suspended from school for the rest of the day for using profanity in the classroom.

"He will be waiting for you to pick him up in the office," says the principal. "He can return to school tomorrow."

"Great!" Vincent says to himself. "Now, I have a free day to do anything I want! I can play video games, ride my skateboard, or hang out in the mall." He knows his mom will drop him off at home and return to work.

The principal calls the next student into his office. Celia, a fifth grader, was referred for passing notes and talking during instruction. The principal gives Celia a ten-minute lecture on cooperation and sends her back to class.

"Wow! I really like our principal," Celia thinks. "He's nice. All he does is talk." Do you think this intervention will cause Celia to think carefully next time she decides to pass notes or talk during instruction? Not likely. She'll be back.

The principal checks his watch and then calls the third student into his office. Patrick, a fourth grader, is a regular. This time he was sent for talking back to his teacher.

"I didn't do it," says Patrick. "I tried to explain why I wasn't in my seat, but she wouldn't listen. It's not fair!" The principal assigns Patrick trash detail during lunch recess and gives him one hour of after-school detention. He returns to class angrier and more resentful than when he arrived. He's bent on revenge. Everyone knows Patrick will be back.

For students like Patrick, Celia, and Vincent, the office is a revolving door that reinforces and perpetuates their behavior problems. The reinforcement errors begin the moment they arrive, and sometimes, the problem is compounded by ineffective guidance. The combination of an entertaining setting and ineffective guidance keeps everyone stuck on a discipline treadmill.

The Administrator's Role in the Guidance Process

SCHOOL SITE ADMINISTRATORS play the most important role in the school's guidance and discipline program. They carry out school policy; provide back-up support for classroom teachers; coordinate supervision for the playground, cafeteria, library, and hallways; and arrange in-service training for staff. They face the toughest cases. They make the toughest decisions, and they bear the greatest burden of responsibility. The buck stops at their door.

Site administrators must be experts in effective guidance and discipline. They can't afford not to be. Their leadership role requires it, and their credibility depends on it. Staff confidence and school morale hang in the balance. Everyone in the system looks to them for leadership and effectiveness. The guidance practices site administrators use set the standard and the tone for the entire school.

As the leader of the school's guidance system, site administrators spend much of their time with two types of duties: (1) carrying out the school's discipline policy, and (2) providing back-up support for classroom teachers. Let's look at each of these duties.

School Discipline Policy

The school's discipline policy, also referred to as "school standards for behavior," "discipline code," or "consequences for misbehavior," describes the procedures teachers and administrators use for handling school discipline problems. School discipline policies range from permissive to highly punitive and cover all points in between. Some are clear and effective, but most are simplistic, "one-size-fits-all" production line lists of punitive sanctions for dealing with severe or recurring discipline problems. Not only are these procedures ineffective, but they also become reinforcement errors that perpetuate the cycle of misbehavior and bog the system down. Punitive and permissive discipline policies keep teachers and administrators on the treadmill. The following is a typical list of the types of sanctions or consequences staff are expected to use at the elementary level:

> The guidance practices site administrators use set the standard and the tone for the entire school.

- Warning
- Loss of recess or other school privileges

- Parent notification (a call or a note)
- Detention
- Sent to the office
- Parent conference
- Half-day suspension
- Full-day suspension
- Three-day suspension
- Referral to school expulsion committee
- Referral to special programs

Who are the students with "severe or recurring discipline problems?" That's right. They're the 10 to 15 percent who cause 90 percent of school discipline problems, the ones who don't respond well to punitive or permissive guidance methods. Do you sense a bad match between the guidance policy and the students most in need of effective guidance? You bet! The results are predictable—anger, frustration, alienation, resentment, retaliation, low morale, and recurring behavior problems.

Exclusion and alienation are not effective guidance practices. If we want to get off the discipline treadmill, we need to rethink our discipline policies and find a way to connect with the 10 to 15 percent of students who are high-risk for behavioral problems. We need to use limit-setting practices that are respectful and motivational strategies that promote positive relationships, and we need to direct more of our time and energy into teaching them the skills they need to be successful.

Providing Back-Up Support for Classroom Teachers

The most time-consuming aspect of the site administrator's role in the school guidance system is providing back-up support for classroom teachers. What is back-up support? The answer depends entirely on the school's discipline policy, because back-up support takes place within the context of the school's discipline policy. The two work hand in hand. You can't discuss one without a clear understanding of the other. In many cases, the administrator's back-up support role has already been defined by the school's discipline policy.

When the school's discipline policy is clear, carefully thought out, and based on effective practices, everyone understands his or her role and responsibilities in the guidance process. The office is less likely to be misused and abused as a place for guidance and discipline. When the policy is unclear, poorly conceived, or based on ineffective practices, the office becomes a dumping ground for inappropriate referrals.

As we untangle the issues of policy and back-up support, the more important questions come into focus: What is the administrator backing up? Are the guidance practices in the classroom effective or ineffective? Is back-up support an appropriate use of administrative time? Lastly, we have to consider the quality of the back-up support the administrator offers. Is it effective or ineffective? Let's look at the range of scenarios.

> When the school's discipline policy is clear, carefully thought out, and based on effective practices, everyone understands his or her role and responsibilities in the guidance process.

When ineffective practices in the classroom are supported by ineffective practices in the office, we have a worst-case scenario. Problems don't get resolved. School morale declines. Everyone remains stuck on the treadmill. When ineffective practices in the classroom are supported by effective practices in the office, problems get resolved, but site administrators remain stuck on the treadmill. When effective practices in the classroom are supported by ineffective practices in the office, parents and teachers lose confidence in the administrator, staff morale declines, and the office becomes a revolving door for the same misbehaving students.

The best-case scenario is the only scenario that makes any sense. When effective practices in the office are used to support effective practices in the classroom, teachers and administrators can work in synchrony and enjoy a mutually supportive relationship. Teachers handle as much as they can in the classroom, and administrators step in only when needed. Everyone's time is respected.

Challenges Administrators Face

SITE ADMINISTRATORS FACE the greatest challenges of anyone in the guidance system. They work with the most difficult students, respond to the widest range of guidance practices, and struggle with the serious problem of inappropriate referrals on a daily basis. Let's look more closely at each of these challenges.

Working with Challenging Students

Who are the students lined up outside the principal's door on any given day? They're not the compliant ones who cooperate for the asking, the ones who are eager to please and permit a wide margin for ineffectiveness. These students rarely end up in the office.

No, the students lined up outside the principal's office are the 10 to 15 percent who cause 90 percent of school behavior problems, the hard-way learners, the ones who have to experience the consequences of their unacceptable behavior repeatedly before they're convinced that cooperation is the better route to go. Site administrators work almost exclusively with this group. Call them challenging, difficult, strong-willed, or aggressive researchers. Whatever you call them, the fact remains that they don't respond well to ineffective guidance. Punitive or permissive guidance methods don't work with these students. There's no margin for ineffectiveness. Site administrators must be experts in effective guidance and discipline.

The democratic approach is the only way off the treadmill. Site administrators must be skilled at diffusing power struggles, deescalating a crisis, using natural and logical consequences, conducting problem-solving conferences, using incentives and positive forms of motivation, and teaching social skills. Teachers and parents are counting on them to be effective.

Inconsistency Among Staff

When schools lack a clear guidance policy or a uniform set of effective guidance procedures, inconsistency among staff is the rule. The range of guidance practices in many schools spans the full spectrum of approaches. Some teachers are permissive. Some are punitive. Some use a mixed approach and flip-flop back and forth between punishment and permissiveness. Still others take a democratic approach and are very effective. When it comes to teaching our rules and standards for acceptable behavior, the methods we use are all over the map.

We wouldn't consider teaching academic subjects in this manner. The practice runs counter to everything we know about effective teaching and learning. Instead, we use the methods we know are effective and produce the best learning outcomes. We train staff to use these methods in a consistent manner, and we strive to reach as many students as possible. Why should it be any different in the important area of guidance and discipline?

What lesson do students learn when teachers vary in the way they define and enforce classroom rules? That's the point. There is no single, cohesive lesson. Instead, students receive a series of mixed messages and mixed lessons about our rules and expectations that sets everyone up for testing and conflict.

How does inconsistency affect school administrators? It keeps them on the treadmill. Inconsistency among staff creates confusion and fragmentation in the guidance process. When students arrive at the office, administrators are unsure what they're backing up. Often, back-up becomes damage control.

Passing the Hot Potato

Sending students to the office or involving administrators in the guidance process should be interventions of last resort reserved for emergencies or when all steps taken to resolve problems at the classroom level have failed. Unfortunately, this is not the practice in many schools where the office is used as a dumping ground for discipline problems and administrative assistance is requested too early in the guidance process. Passing discipline problems to others is one of the biggest and most costly abuses of the school guidance system.

> Sending students to the office or involving administrators in the guidance process should be interventions of last resort.

The game is called "passing the hot potato," and the object of the game is to shift the discipline problem, and the responsibility for resolving it, from the teacher's lap onto someone else's lap, preferably the administrator's, as quickly as possible. At the middle school and high school levels, vice principals and guidance counselors usually end up with the most hot potatoes in their laps. In busy schools, the same potato can be passed back and forth between the classroom and the office many times in the same day, compounding opportunities for reinforcement errors.

In most cases, the cause of the problem can be traced back to one or more of the following factors:

1. An ineffective discipline policy

2. Burned-out teachers

3. Inadequate training in classroom management

4. Confusion about the teacher's role and responsibilities in the guidance process

In some cases, administrators invite the game of hot potato by involving themselves too early in the guidance process. Sometimes, classroom teachers sincerely believe that guidance and discipline is not part of their job description. Whatever the cause, the destructive consequences of this practice are clear. Hot potato creates division and resentment among staff, wastes valuable time and school resources, and keeps everyone stuck on a treadmill. Site administrators and office staff feel resentful toward teachers who use the office as a dumping ground. Classroom teachers feel unsupported and resentful toward administrators and office staff who don't respond quickly to their referrals. Hot potato is a divisive game that wastes valuable time and school resources.

What is the remedy? The problem should be addressed at two levels: the symptom level and the causal level. At the symptom level, site administrators can discourage the practice of hot potato by having staff complete an incident report prior to sending students to the office. The incident report should document the steps teachers take to resolve problems at the classroom level prior to passing them on to the office. In short, the incident report defines what an appropriate referral is and details the steps staff should take to resolve the problem at the classroom level before passing it up the system.

Incident reports are a step in the right direction, but they're not a long-term solution to the problem. A long-term solution requires that we address the problem at the causal level and remedy the conditions that create it. To stop the game of hot potato and the damage it causes, site administrators need to develop a clear and effective guidance policy, establish a uniform set of effective guidance practices for all staff, and provide effective in-service training for all members of the guidance process.

Chapter Summary

CONTRARY TO POPULAR belief, the school office is not a good place to send misbehaving students. In fact, it's one of the worst places. The office is a soap opera that provides live entertainment for misbehaving students and reinforces their unacceptable behavior. The practice of using the office as a dumping ground for behavior problems is one of the most costly and divisive practices in the school. It creates resentment among staff and wastes valuable time and school resources.

As the leader of the school's guidance system, site administrators play the most important and the most challenging role. They carry out school policy, provide back-up support for teachers, and are responsible for coordinating and managing guidance services throughout the school. Site administrators must be experts in effective guidance and discipline. They can't afford not to be. Their leadership role requires it, and their credibility depends on it. They work with the most challenging students, make the toughest decisions, and bear the greatest responsibility for the successes and failures of their school's guidance system.

The best way off the discipline treadmill is to develop a clear and effective guidance policy, establish a uniform set of effective guidance procedures, and provide in-service training so all members of the guidance system can work together from the same page.

14

Inspiring Cooperation with Positive Motivation

LIMITS DEFINE THE path we want students to stay on, but limits alone may not motivate them to head in the intended direction. Cooperation is still a voluntary act. Short of using consequences, what can we do to inspire their cooperation? How can we tip the scales in our favor?

This chapter and the next will show you how to do that. In this chapter, you'll learn how to inspire children's cooperation through the power of encouragement and positive motivation. No shaming. No blaming. No humiliating children into cooperating. No bribes or special rewards for getting them to do what they should be doing anyway. The methods are quick, effective, easy to use, and inexpensive in terms of the drain they place on your time and energy. You'll find them a refreshing alternative to punishment and coercion.

Motivation and Limit Setting

IMAGINE TWO DIFFERENT paths in front of you. One involves only work, and the teacher uses a lot of criticism, threats, and coercion to keep you on it. The other mixes work with pleasure, and the teacher uses a lot of encouragement and respectful guidance to keep you on it. Which path would you choose? Of course, the choice is clear.

The question illustrates a basic truth that applies to all of us, children included. The more positives we see in our path, the more likely we are to head in the intended direction. A path with positives is always most inviting.

When it comes to motivating children, most teachers head in one of two directions. They take a positive approach and use generous helpings of encouragement and rewards to inspire the behavior they want. Or they take a negative approach and rely primarily on threats, punishment, and coercion to force children into cooperating. There isn't much in between.

The approach teachers use has a lot to do with the type of limits they set. Teachers who are ineffective in their limit setting are accustomed to encountering resistance. They get angry and frustrated, and often they end up saying discouraging things to their students. They assume that the problem is their students' lack of cooperation, not the way cooperation is being requested. Discouraging messages and ineffective limits go hand in hand.

Teachers who use firm limits, on the other hand, expect cooperation, but they recognize that children are most likely to cooperate when asked in a respectful manner. Encouraging messages inspire cooperation. Firm limits and encouraging messages also go hand in hand.

Encouraging and discouraging messages have different effects on children's behavior. One leads to cooperation. The other leads predictably to resistance. If our goal is to inspire cooperation, then discouraging messages are one of the surest ways not to achieve our objective.

Negative Messages Inspire Resistance

IT'S NINE O'CLOCK in the morning, and Tyler, a fifth grader, has already disrupted the class three times. Number 4 is about to happen. He chips a piece off the end of his eraser and flicks it at the girl sitting across from him. He gets the expected response.

"Cut it out, Tyler!" she complains, loud enough for the teacher to hear.

"What does it take to get through to you, Tyler?" says his exasperated teacher. "Can't you see others don't appreciate your clowning around? I expect your behavior from a first grader, but not a fifth grader. Why don't you act your age for a change?"

"Why don't you try to be an interesting teacher for a change?" says Tyler. He knows she's hooked. Things are about to escalate.

"Nobody talks to me like that!" his teacher explodes. "I've had enough of your disrespect. You may think that you can treat people like dirt, but you'll end up getting a taste of your own medicine." She hands Tyler two sheets of paper and directs him to the back table. "You can return to your desk after you write one hundred times, 'I will not be disrespectful to my teacher.'"

"No way!" says Tyler defiantly. "You can't make me if I don't want to."

"You can't go out for any recesses until you do," she threatens.

"Big deal!" says Tyler. "I could care less." He makes no move to begin the writing.

Tyler's teacher did not start off with the intention of provoking an angry power struggle with one of her students. Her goal was to stop Tyler's misbehavior and enlist his cooperation, but she was using one of the surest methods not to achieve that goal.

Discouraging messages frequently have the opposite of their intended effect. They inspire resistance, not cooperation, and lead predictably to escalating misbehavior and power struggles. Discouraging messages are the fuel for hurtful classroom dances.

> Discouraging messages are the fuel for hurtful classroom dances.

Tyler's teacher doesn't realize that she set herself up for a power struggle by starting off with a signal that wasn't clear. When Tyler tests, she becomes frustrated and angry and tries to shame him into cooperation by criticizing and humiliating him in front of his peers. The focus is on Tyler's maturity, not his misbehavior. Her message conveys no confidence in his ability to cooperate or behave acceptably. In effect, she's saying, "You're not capable, I have no confidence in you, and I don't expect you to cooperate." He doesn't.

Would you feel like cooperating with someone who said these things to you? Or would you feel more inclined to retaliate? Tyler responds as many of us would—with resistance and retaliation. He perceives her message as a personal attack. He digs in his heels and launches a counterattack.

Negative messages feel bad. They hurt, humiliate, and are often perceived as a personal attack rather than an attempt to discourage unacceptable behavior. Their focus is misdirected, and that's why they backfire.

Let's not overlook another, more subtle message that accompanies our negative attempts to motivate. What we do is what we teach. The methods themselves teach a lesson about communication and problem solving. By role-modeling hurtful, coercive methods, Tyler's teacher is teaching him that hurtful statements are an acceptable way to motivate others to cooperate. Without realizing it, she is teaching the very behavior she's trying to stop.

Examples of Negative Motivational Messages

Negative messages come in a variety of forms. Some are subtle and result from overinvolvement or helping too much. Others are explicit and direct, such as the messages Tyler's teacher used in the previous example. All discouraging messages convey little confidence in the child's ability to make good choices and behave acceptably. They tend to personalize misbehavior and carry an underlying message of shame and blame. Let's look at the underlying message in each of the following.

1. **Can you cooperate just once in a while?**
Underlying message: "I don't believe you can cooperate." The effect is to blame, diminish, single out, and humiliate.

2. **Show me you have a brain and make a good choice for a change!**
Underlying message: "You're not very bright, and I have little confidence in your ability to make good decisions." The effect is to diminish, shame, and humiliate.

3. **Would it be asking too much to get a little respect?**
Underlying message: "I don't expect you to treat me respectfully." The effect is to blame and diminish.

4. Is that the best you can do?
Underlying message: "You're not very competent. You don't live up to my expectations." The effect is to shame, blame, diminish, embarrass, and humiliate.

5. I don't believe it! You actually did what you were asked for a change.
Underlying message: "I don't expect your cooperation." The effect is to shame, embarrass, diminish, and single out.

6. Try that again. I dare you.
Underlying message: "I don't expect your cooperation, so continue misbehaving so I can show you I'm the boss." The effect is to challenge, provoke, blame, diminish, and intimidate.

7. There's one jerk in every classroom.
Underlying message: "You're not worthwhile or acceptable." The effect is to reject, shame, blame, single out, and humiliate.

8. That's real bright!
Underlying message: "You make poor decisions. I have no confidence in your ability." The effect is to diminish, shame, blame, and humiliate.

9. I knew I couldn't count on you.
Underlying message: "You're not capable or trustworthy. I have no confidence in your ability." The effect is to shame, blame, diminish, and humiliate.

Positive Messages Inspire Cooperation

JACOB, A KINDERGARTNER, is waiting in line to go out to the playground when a classmate accidentally bumps him. Jacob gives him a push, and the boy falls down. The teacher intervenes.

"Jacob, we don't push in line," says the teacher matter-of-factly.

"Tommy bumped into me first," Jacob replies. "He was in my way."

"What are we supposed to do when others are in our way?" the teacher asks.

Jacob just stares at her blankly. "I don't know," he says.

"You're supposed to say 'Excuse me' and wait for them to move," says the teacher.

"Sometimes they won't move," says Jacob.

"You should ask an adult for help when that happens," says the teacher. "Now you have two good choices. What are you going to do next time?"

"I'll say 'Excuse me' and wait for them to move," replies Jacob. "If they don't, I'll ask you for help."

"Good!" says the teacher. "I'm sure you'll handle it fine. Now, what do you need to say to Tommy?"

"Sorry, Tommy," says Jacob.

"Thank you, Jacob," says the teacher. She gives him an appreciative smile.

Jacob's teacher used encouragement effectively. Much of her success, however, is due to the way she starts off. She begins with a limit-setting message that is both firm and respectful. No one is blamed or singled out. In a few brief sentences, she creates a positive atmosphere for problem solving. Now, her encouraging words can have the greatest impact.

The focus of her message is on choices and corrective action, not on Jacob's worth or capabilities. She provides the information and skills he needs to behave acceptably and then expresses her confidence in his ability to handle the situation better next time. Her message is positive and inspiring: "You're capable; I have confidence in you; I expect you to cooperate."

How would you feel if someone said that to you? Would you feel accepted and supported? Would you feel like cooperating? Jacob did, and so would most of us. Positive, encouraging messages feel good and motivate us to cooperate. They meet our need for belonging, reaffirm our feelings of competence and self-worth, and instill confidence in our ability to handle challenging problems. Encouragement can make the difference between co-operation and resistance.

> Positive, encouraging messages feel good and motivate us to cooperate.

Alfred Adler, a major figure in the development of psychiatry, considered encouragement to be a fundamental component in the process of changing human behavior. His writings and those of his leading proponents continue to have a major impact on practices in education, applied psychology, and other related fields. Encouragement is gaining the recognition it deserves as an effective tool for motivating cooperative behavior. The following guidelines will help you use this tool effectively.

Guidelines for Using Positive Messages

Knowing what to encourage is the key to using encouragement effectively. The focus of our message should address our basic training goals: better choices, acceptable actions, cooperation, independence, and improvement. All lead to greater responsibility.

Encouraging Better Choices

Sometimes children misbehave because they are unaware that other, more effective choices are available for handling the situation. Teachers and other guidance providers are in an ideal position to help children explore their choices and make better ones. Consider the following.

Regina, a ninth grader, is suspended from her fourth-period class for being disruptive. She arrives at her counselor's office with a note from her teacher.

"What happened, Regina?" asks the counselor.

"I guess I lost my cool," Regina replies. "Sherri Mullins has been spreading rumors about me all week. I think she's jealous because we both like the same boy, but Scott has been calling me, not her. Sherri sits right behind me in my fourth-period class and whispers lies about Scott while we're supposed to be working. I turned around and told her to shut up. Then I called her a bitch. I guess I was kinda loud. Mrs. Swain sent me here. I'm really embarrassed."

"What do you think Sherri was trying to do?" asks her counselor.

"Make me upset," Regina replies.

"It sounds like she succeeded, too," observes her counselor. "How could you handle this differently the next time it happens?"

"I could confront her outside class and tell her I know what she's doing," says Regina.

"Do you think she would stop if you did?" asks the counselor.

"Probably not," replies Regina upon reflection. "It would just show her that she was getting to me."

"What else could you do?" inquires the counselor.

"I could ignore her," says Regina, "but that's really hard to do, especially when she bugs me in class."

"You're right," the counselor replies. "Ignoring someone is hard to do when they sit directly behind you, but ignoring her is a good choice. She would probably stop if she saw it wasn't working. What else could you do?"

"I could ask Mrs. Swain to move me," suggests Regina.

"That's a good choice," says the counselor. "I'm sure that would help. Can you think of anything else?" Regina thought for a moment.

"Well, I guess I could ask Mrs. Swain to tell Sherri to leave me alone, but I'd prefer to leave Mrs. Swain out of it," says Regina.

"I understand," says the counselor. "You've got some good choices to use next time. I'm confident you'll handle it just fine."

Regina left her counselor's office feeling supported and encouraged. She was aware of her options, and she was prepared to make a different choice next time the situation arose.

Encouraging Acceptable Actions

Making an acceptable choice is an important first step, but getting kids to act on that choice is our larger training goal. Sometimes our encouraging words are most effective when we focus directly on actions.

For example, Cynthia, a sixth grader, knows she's not supposed to interrupt when her teacher talks to others, but she is eager to leave class for a student council meeting. She decides to interrupt anyway.

> Sometimes our encouraging words are most effective when we focus directly on actions.

"May I go to the library, Mr. Perrin?" Cynthia asks excitedly. "My student council meeting is about to start." Mr. Perrin does not look pleased.

"Cynthia, what are you supposed to do when you want to talk to me while I'm in the middle of a conversation?" he asks.

"Wait for you to finish," replies Cynthia.

"Right," says Mr. Perrin. "Now go back to your desk and come back and try it again."

Cynthia returns to her desk and then approaches Mr. Perrin a second time. He's still talking. She waits patiently. When there's a pause in the conversation, she interjects her question. "May I go to the library for the student council meeting?"

"Sure, Cynthia," he replies, "and thank you for asking me the way you did." He gives her an appreciative smile. No feelings were hurt in this lesson. Mr. Perrin got his message across in a positive and respectful way.

Zach, a preschooler, received some instructive guidance when he used a commanding tone to get a classmate to pass some crayons.

"Give me the crayons, Jared," demands Zach. "You can't keep them all." The teacher hears him and intervenes.

"Zach, how are we supposed to ask?" Zach remembers. "Let's try it again," says his teacher.

"May I have the tray of crayons, please?" says Zach. Jared hands them over.

"Good job Zach!" says the teacher. "That's the way we like to be asked."

No shaming. No blaming. No angry words or looks of disapproval. All Zach needed was a little encouragement and an opportunity to show he could behave acceptably.

Encouraging Cooperation

We don't need misbehavior to cue us to the need for encouragement. Any time a child helps out, cooperates, or makes a contribution, we have an opportunity to use encouraging messages. Our encouragement increases the likelihood children's cooperation will continue. Consider the following.

Trent, age four, notices his teacher walking toward the door with a tray full of snacks. Her hands are full. He opens the door and holds it open while she walks in.

"Thanks, Trent," says the teacher. "You're a great helper!" Trent beams with pride. The lesson wasn't lost on others.

Mr. Flores, a third-grade teacher, is called out of the classroom briefly when a parent arrives at his door. The kids have a great opportunity to clown around, but they don't. When he steps back into the room, everyone is working quietly at their seats. He appreciates their cooperation and lets them know it.

"Thanks for handling things so well while I was called out," he says. "You guys are great. I knew I could count on you."

A word or two of encouragement at the right time can have a big impact. The following are just a few of the many possibilities:

"I like the way you handled that."

"Your desk looks great today."

"Good job!"

"Your helping out makes a big difference."

"I knew I could count on you."

"Thanks, I appreciate your thoughtfulness."

Encouraging Independence

One of our larger guidance goals is to assist children to handle problems on their own. We do this by teaching effective problem-solving skills and by limiting our involvement so children have opportunities to practice those skills independently. Encouragement plays an important role in the process. It gives children the confidence to take risks and act independently. Consider the following.

Joey, a fifth grader, runs to tattle on a classmate. "Mr. Kilmer, Damen was copying from my paper."

"Did you ask him to stop or cover up your paper so he couldn't?" asks Mr. Kilmer.

"Well, no," replies Joey, expecting the teacher to handle it.

"Then that's what you need to do if it happens again," says Mr. Kilmer, with a smile. "I'm sure you'll handle it fine."

Randy and Carla, two kindergartners, quarrel over a scooter. "Give it to me," screams Carla, loud enough to attract her teacher's attention. It works. As the teacher approaches, both kids clutch the scooter tightly.

"I think you guys can work this out," says the teacher confidently. "Do you remember our plan for sharing?"

Randy does. He runs back into the classroom and returns a few moments later with a timer. He sets it for five minutes. "I get to use it first," he announces.

"Okay," says Carla reluctantly, "but I get to use it next."

"You sure do," says the teacher. "Good job, guys! You handled it just fine. I knew you could."

Mrs. Ehlers, a seventh-grade science teacher, passes out an assignment to the class. Less than a minute goes by before Barry comes up for his own personal set of instructions. "I don't understand what I'm supposed to do," he says.

"Did you read the directions carefully and think about what you're supposed to do?" the teacher asks.

"I think so," Barry replies, hoping she will do the thinking for him.

"Well, try it again," says his teacher in an encouraging voice. "I'm confident you can figure it out on your own. If you still aren't sure after five minutes, I'll be happy to help."

"Rats!" Barry says to himself. "She didn't go for it." He heads back to his seat to figure it out on his own.

Five minutes later, Barry is busy with his assignment. He may not realize it, but he just received a lesson in independence. His teacher's encouragement and reluctance to rescue him made it possible.

Encouraging Improvement

Some skills, such as taking turns or learning not to interrupt, require repeated effort and practice before they can be mastered. The process is gradual. Adult impatience or expectations of immediate mastery can be very discouraging. Our energy is best directed toward encouraging improvement. The focus should be on effort, not outcome; process, not product.

> The focus should be on effort, not outcome; process, not product.

Trey, a third grader, lives in a home where interrupting is okay. Whenever he has something to say, he just says it. His parents usually stop whatever they're doing and give him their undivided attention.

At school, things are different. Interrupting is not okay. When Trey interrupts, his teacher asks him to raise his hand and wait to be called. They've been practicing this skill for months, but progress has been slow. Trey's teacher feels frustrated.

"Maybe I should make him sit at the back table for five minutes each time he interrupts," Trey's teacher suggests to a colleague. "Maybe that will help him remember." The colleague has another suggestion.

"Try using encouragement first and see what happens," she suggests. "Each time he remembers to raise his hand, let him know how much you appreciate it. When he needs prompts, thank him after he does it the right way."

The next morning, Trey wants to ask a question and remembers to raise his hand without prompts. "Thank you, Trey," says his teacher. "I really appreciate it when you raise your hand." He looks pleased.

Later in the day, Trey starts to blurt out an answer without being called on. "What are you supposed to do when you want to be called on, Trey?" asks his teacher. Trey remembers and raises his hand. "Thank you, Trey," she says with an appreciative smile. His teacher decides to continue the plan for a full month.

Several weeks later, the same colleague inquires about Trey's progress. "How's he doing?" she asks.

"Much better," replies Trey's teacher. "He remembers more than he forgets. In fact, he hasn't interrupted for several days." Encouragement is making a difference.

Involving Parents in the Encouragement Process

ONE OF THE best ways to increase the motivational power of encouragement is to involve parents in the process. When parents and teachers combine their encouraging efforts, children feel even more inspired to make good choices and cooperate.

At the preschool and elementary levels, it's an effective practice to send home special commendations, awards, or certificates of merit acknowledging student effort, cooperation, or achievement. The commendations can be included with other materials in the student's Friday folder. At the secondary level, a personal note to the parents or a phone call has the same effect.

The gesture is rewarding for everybody. Parents like to hear the good news and enjoy sharing that news with their child. The child feels good about having his or her efforts publicly acknowledged. Teachers gain a lot of cooperation and respect from parents and students by simply acknowledging what has taken place. The small investment yields big returns in cooperation.

Chapter Summary

IN THIS CHAPTER, we examined two contrasting approaches to motivating children. We saw how negative and discouraging messages, which often accompany soft limits, achieve the opposite of their intended effect. They inspire resistance, not cooperation, and fuel power struggles and classroom dances.

Positive and encouraging messages, on the other hand, are highly effective motivational tools, particularly when used with firm limits. Encouraging messages meet children's needs for belonging, reaffirm feelings of competence and self-worth, and inspire children to tackle challenging tasks and problems on their own. Encouraging messages can make the difference between cooperation and resistance (see table 5).

Knowing what to encourage is the key to using encouragement effectively. Our messages have their greatest impact when they focus on better choices, acceptable actions, cooperation, independence, and improvement.

Table 5. Encouraging Versus Discouraging Messages

Encouraging Messages	Discouraging Messages
Inspire cooperation.	Inspire resistance, retaliation.
Motivate and empower.	Discourage and humiliate.
Convey respect, confidence, support.	Diminish, blame, reject.
Create cooperative relationships.	Create adversarial relationships.
Meet needs for belonging, confidence, self-worth.	Perceived as personal attack.
Focus on choices and behavior.	Focus on child's worth and capabilities.

15

....

PAT

*A Motivational Gift That
Keeps on Giving*

I F A MOTIVATIONAL tool were available that was easy to use, enjoyable for you and your students, and kept your students on task and cooperating throughout the full instructional day, would you use it? Of course. Most teachers would pay handsomely for such a tool. Well, here's the good news. The tool is available, and it's absolutely free! It's called PAT, or *preferred activity time,* and you can use it with students at all grade levels.

PAT is hardly a newcomer on the educational scene. The practice has been around a long time, and there are many variations to the basic model. One of the most thorough descriptions of PAT and its many variations is provided in Fredric Jones's excellent book, *Positive Classroom Discipline.*

PAT is a group incentive system that uses the most valuable commodity in the instructional day—time—as the treasured resource. Students want it and will work hard for it, and you'll be happy to give it away when they do. PAT is a win-win for everybody.

The genius of PAT is that accountability and team building are built-in components of the system. Your students, not you, are responsible for how they use their class time. They can earn bonus time for on-task behavior or incur penalties for off-task behavior. The choice is theirs. The more they cooperate, the more rewards they share and enjoy. Your job is simply to give PAT away as a group reward for on-task behavior, keep track of time earned or lost, and structure the PAT sessions. Consider the following.

> The genius of PAT is that accountability and team building are built-in components of the system.

It's Monday morning. The eight o'clock bell rings, and students begin to file into Mr. Janzen's sixth-grade class. This year, he has a mature class. They take their seats and settle down. No time is wasted. Mr. Janzen looks around the class and smiles. He gives everyone a warm "Thank you and good morning," and then he walks over to the blackboard and writes a "1" under the bonus column of his PAT chart. His first act each day is to reward his students with a PAT bonus for entering the classroom appropriately, settling down, and getting ready for instruction.

In the top right corner of Mr. Janzen's blackboard is a simple chart for recording PAT with one horizontal column and two vertical columns below that. The horizontal column reads "Time in the bank" and notes the twenty-minute PAT gift Mr. Janzen makes to his class at the beginning of each week. The two vertical columns below that are marked with a plus sign

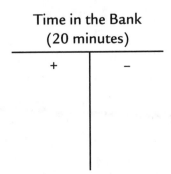

Figure 15.1   PAT Chart

and a minus sign for recording bonus time and penalties (see figure 15.1).

After taking attendance and lunch count, Mr. Janzen asks his class to take out their books and finish the writing exercise they started the previous day. While his students work at their desks, Mr. Janzen roves around the classroom to check on their progress and assist anyone who needs help. As students finish the assignment, the classroom begins to get a little loud and distracting.

"How many think it's too loud in here?" asks Mr. Janzen with his stopwatch in his hand. Several students raise their hands. The class quiets down. No penalty time is deducted. A short time later, Mr. Janzen notices Ashley, one of his slower learners, trying particularly hard to finish up on time.

"Good job, Ashley!" says Mr. Janzen. "I really appreciate your hard work." He walks over to the blackboard and enters thirty seconds under the bonus column. As he does, he hears several students whisper thanks to Ashley. She feels good about her contribution, and so does everyone else.

Later that morning, the class divides into cooperative work groups. Each group is supposed to pick a topic and prepare a presentation on some aspect of ancient Egypt. All the groups seem to be focused and working well except for one. When Mr. Janzen investigates, he notices Stefen poking and annoying several members of his work group.

"Take your book and your worksheet to the back table, Stefen," says Mr. Janzen matter-of-factly. He sets his timer and sends Stefen for a ten-minute time-out. No PAT penalties or time deductions are given. Why not?

PAT is intended to support your limit-setting practices by rewarding on-task behavior and by discouraging off-task behavior. The system is not intended to replace your limit-setting practices. Disruption and attention-seeking behavior should be handled as usual, with logical consequences and time-outs.

After lunch recess, while the class works on their math worksheets, the principal comes on the intercom to announce results of a recent student body election. The announcement cuts nearly ten minutes from Mr. Janzen's thirty-minute lesson plan. "They'll have to work very fast to finish up on time," he thinks. "How do you get students to hurry rather than dawdle?" He offers the class a hurry-up time bonus if they finish in the next ten minutes. They scramble to get it done.

> PAT is intended to support your limit-setting practices by rewarding on-task behavior and by discouraging off-task behavior.

"Thank you," he says when the activity is complete. He walks to the blackboard and adds two and a half minutes to the bonus column. "That's one lesson I won't have to teach over again," he says to himself.

Near the end of the day, while the class is supposed to be working at their seats on a science lesson, Mr. Janzen notices Saul fumbling through his backpack at the back of the classroom. Mr. Janzen holds up his stopwatch in the ready position.

"I was out of paper," Saul pleads, "and I still can't find a pencil." Mr. Janzen looks at Saul patiently, clicks his stopwatch, and then directs a question to the class in a very matter-of-fact tone.

"Can anyone help Saul find a pencil?" About ten hands shoot up in the air. Saul collects the pencil, and Mr. Janzen clicks off his stopwatch. He walks to the board and adds twenty-five seconds to the penalty column.

As the class lines up to leave at the end of the day, Mr. Janzen passes out permission slips for an upcoming field trip and makes an announcement. "The sooner they're all returned, the more bonus time you'll earn."

On Fridays, Mr. Janzen sets aside time for his class to enjoy the PAT they've earned. He adds the time bonuses to the twenty-minute gift on Monday and deducts the penalties. Voilà! What's left is for the class to spend and use at that time or save and carry over into the following week for something even more fun.

Mr. Janzen uses three simple guidelines to determine which activities make it on the "approved list for PAT" in his classroom. First, the activity must be fun and something his students really want. Second, the activity must involve thinking and learning. Third, the activity must be acceptable to both students and the teacher. During the first week, he and his students brainstorm a list of PAT activities, which can be enjoyed on an individual or whole-group basis. Then, they vote on them. As a back-up, Mr. Janzen maintains a PAT cabinet in his classroom loaded with magazines, comic books, books on sketching and cartooning, and board games such as chess, Monopoly, Boggle, checkers, Stratego, Battleship, and Scrabble. What his students choose to do is up to them, but if some or all want to participate in a large-group activity, he expects to be notified early in the week. Large-group activities may require advance planning.

How PAT Works

AS THE EXAMPLE illustrates, PAT is simple to set up and carry out. At all grade levels (kindergarten through secondary), you start off with a gift of PAT that is given without strings attached. It's in the bank, free and clear. How much time should you give? This depends on the age and maturity level of your students. At the primary level (kindergarten through second), it's a common practice to start each day with a ten-minute gift of PAT. At the intermediate level (grades 3 through 6), a twenty- or thirty-minute gift of PAT given twice a week is common. Some mature classes like Mr. Janzen's do fine with one PAT a week. At the middle school and high school levels (grades 7 through 12), a thirty-minute gift of PAT given once on Monday is a common practice. These time frames are only guidelines. You may want to increase or decrease the frequency of your initial PAT gift based on the maturity of your students.

Once the gift of PAT has been made, the rest of the time is spent catching students being responsible and on-task and rewarding them with bonus points or observing them wasting time or being off-task and giving time penalties. The combination of time bonuses plus time penalties adds power and effectiveness to this motivational system. Students control the penalties by their decisions to cooperate or not cooperate. The teacher just keeps track of time. Time bonuses, on the other hand, are controlled and managed by the teacher, who has the enviable job of catching students being good and rewarding them for it. Generosity on the teacher's part works to everyone's advantage. Students are happy because they have more time for fun. Teachers are happy lessons get completed and instructional time is used wisely. It's a win-win for everyone.

Bonuses come in several forms. Unexpected bonuses are the most fun to give. Any time you catch a student, a group of students, or the whole class being responsible, on-task, or making a special effort to cooperate, you're in a position to reward them an unexpected bonus. Even small awards of ten, fifteen, or twenty seconds, offered generously, can have a big impact. Everyone benefits. In our earlier example, Mr. Janzen awarded the class thirty seconds of bonus time for Ashley's particularly good effort.

Hurry-up bonuses are awarded when you need your students to hustle and complete assigned work in a timely manner. Mr. Janzen awarded his class a hurry-up bonus when his lesson was interrupted by an announcement from the office. He needed his kids to hustle, and they did.

Automatic bonuses are given for handling important transitions in the day such as entering or exiting the class properly, shifting from large group instruction to independent seat work,

> PAT bonuses are an excellent way to improve transitions in the day, the times when fooling around and off-task behavior is most likely to occur.

or cooperating when resource staff comes into the classroom. Since it's nearly impossible to determine how much time is saved by a smooth transition, teachers must arbitrarily select an amount of time to award and give that amount consistently. If you recall, Mr. Janzen gave his students an automatic bonus of one minute for arriving promptly and being in their seats after the first morning bell. PAT bonuses are an excellent way to improve transitions in the day, the times when fooling around and off-task behavior are most likely to occur.

Penalties provide an accountability function in the PAT group incentive system by holding students responsible for their off-task behavior, but penalties should be used judiciously and given in a neutral, matter-of-fact tone. Teachers who award penalties in a blaming manner or assign excessive time penalties for minor off-task behaviors defeat the positive nature of PAT and risk turning it into an exercise in coercion. I strongly recommend that you maintain a neutral tone and use a stopwatch to record time penalties for off-task behavior. The process is fair, accurate, and leads to positive learning, not resentment. Your students will simply perceive the penalty as a logical consequence for their off-task behavior. When the class incurs time penalties, you should always be on the lookout for time bonus opportunities to offset the loss and keep the system positive.

The Teacher's Role

TEACHERS HAVE THREE primary duties in the PAT incentive system: giving PAT, recording PAT, and structuring PAT for the enjoyment of all. The role of giver is fairly straightforward. The teacher makes an initial gift of PAT to the class at the beginning of the instructional day or week depending on the age and maturity of the students. The initial gift represents a "good-faith investment" in cooperation. Then, the real fun begins.

From this point forward, teachers spend most of their time trying to catch students cooperating and using time wisely and reward them with time bonuses.

Be generous with bonuses. Small increments of ten to fifteen seconds awarded throughout the day can have a big impact. Try to maintain a positive, appreciative tone when awarding bonus points and remain matter-of-fact when recording penalties. It's their time they're wasting, not yours.

The role of recorder requires strict attention to accuracy. It's essential that you keep an accurate record of time awarded for bonuses and time consumed by penalties, lest you arouse protests, arguments, and complaints of unfairness. The credibility of the entire PAT system depends on it. When teachers are lax in this area, they invite testing, challenges, and bargaining for time. PAT is not Let's Make a Deal. It's based on behavior and responsible use of time.

What's the best way to record time accurately? Use a stopwatch. It doesn't lie. It's not arbitrary or biased. The practice is beyond reproach. When your students see you hold up your stopwatch and hear it click, they know that they're losing time. There's no point in arguing or debating. The clock is running.

Once time is recorded, it should be entered on the PAT chart on the blackboard for all to see. A public record demonstrates your concern for fairness and accuracy and informs your students about where they stand at all times.

The final duty of the teacher is to structure the actual PAT session for the enjoyment of all. How you structure your PAT sessions is limited only by your imagination and creativity. The key point to remember is to make it fun so your students will look forward to it and work hard for it. To get started, put together a PAT cabinet full of high-interest reading material, comics, cartooning or sketching supplies, and table games for students interested in individual or small-group activities. Then, consult with your colleagues and develop a list of fun large-group learning activities that some or all of your students can share. You may want to take a tip from Mr. Janzen and hold a brainstorming session with your students to develop a list of individual and whole-group activities for PAT. Both students and the teacher should agree on the suitability of an activity before it makes it on the approved list of PAT activities.

PAT is a group reward. Everyone gets the same amount, but that doesn't mean they all have to do the same things. Some may want to read or draw. Others may want to play table games. Still others may want to participate in a large-group activity. It's okay if students want to spend their PAT in different ways. All options should be acceptable, but if some or all of your students want a large-group activity, they need to notify you in advance, because some large-group activities require advance planning and preparation.

How often should your students receive PAT sessions? This depends on their age and maturity level. Younger students are very concrete learners, requiring more frequent reinforcement to learn the lessons PAT is designed to teach. Older students are less concrete and need less frequent reinforcement. For primary-level students (kindergarten through grade 2), two PAT sessions daily—one at the end of the morning, the other at the end of the afternoon—is a common practice. Third and fourth graders usually do fine with one PAT daily. Fifth graders, sixth graders, and middle school and high school students usually do fine with one PAT weekly. These frequency levels are only guidelines. You may want to increase or decrease them based on the maturity of your students.

The Students' Role

PAT IS A group incentive system that holds students accountable, individually and collectively, for how they use their time. Time is the resource they all share and have to manage, and accountability and group pressure are built-in components of the system.

All students confront the same set of choices. They can cooperate, use their time wisely, and watch their time bonuses accumulate, or they can dawdle, waste time, and watch their PAT disappear with penalties. The choice is theirs, but they cannot avoid being accountable for their actions, because the time they earn or lose belongs to them as well as to the whole class. Everyone shares equally in the rewards and penalties. Students who goof off and waste time do not have an appreciative audience.

What You Should Expect

WHEN YOU FIRST introduce the PAT system to your class, you may encounter suspicion or reluctance among some of your students, particularly at the secondary level. "This sounds too good to be true," they say to themselves. "What's the catch?" Some will suspect PAT is just another cleverly packaged attempt to manipulate and control students to do more work. Some will scoff at it and reject it before they even try it. That's okay. Encourage them to give it a month and check it out. They'll change their thinking when they see how it works. Even selfish students who are willing to waste PAT at the group's expense will discover that more PAT is better than less PAT. Give them some time to let the lesson sink in. Your aggressive researchers will have to collect the data for themselves before they conclude that PAT really is a good deal.

As your class adapts to this new motivational system, you should begin to notice some curious things happening. First, your students will begin policing each other, reducing your need for limit setting. This translates into smoother transitions, more time for teaching, and less time spent with guidance and discipline. When students are off-task or fooling around, you'll probably hear their classmates say, "Hey, knock it off. We're gonna lose PAT."

Second, you'll begin to notice that your class works better as a group. Team building is a natural outcome of the PAT group incentive system. The system teaches students the benefits of cooperation and responsibility. Once they realize that more cooperation and more re-sponsibility mean more PAT, they'll be happy to cooperate, and they'll become better team players in the process.

> Team building is a natural outcome of the PAT group incentive system.

Third, you should begin to notice that the tone or mood of your classroom has become more positive. Sharing fun with your students on a regular basis provides a great foundation for strong, positive teacher-student relationships. Your students will look forward to their PAT sessions, and so will you.

Chapter Summary

PAT IS A group incentive system that holds students account-able for how they use their time. Time is the medium of ex-change. It serves as an incentive, a reward, and a logical consequence for off-task behavior. But most important, PAT teaches students how to cooperate, be responsible, and use their time wisely.

PAT is a win-win for everyone. Students want it and will work hard to get it when they can have fun with it. Teachers enjoy more time for teaching and learning, less time spent with limit setting, smoother transitions, better cooperation, better relationships, and better achievement. PAT truly is a gift that keeps on giving.

16

Teaching Skills

Showing Them Works Best

How much time do you spend disciplining your students for the predictable misbehaviors they do repeatedly throughout the week? I'm talking about interrupting when others are talking, blurting out during instruction, tilting back in their chairs, talking during instruction, leaving messes around their desks, running in the hallways, and entering and exiting the classroom in a disruptive manner. These are the predictable friction points for most students and their teachers.

You can stop these misbehaviors with natural and logical consequences, but consequences alone won't teach your students the skills they need to behave more appropriately. If you want to get off the discipline treadmill, you have to go to the next step in the guidance process. You have to teach them the skills they need to behave more acceptably. This chapter will show you how to do that. You'll learn some simple but highly effective methods for teaching social skills. Effective skill training is your ticket off the discipline treadmill.

Providing Information Is Sometimes Not Enough

OFTEN, TEACHERS ASSUME that telling students how to handle a situation is equivalent to teaching the skill. For many students, it's not. Providing information is an important first step in the teaching process, but information alone is not enough to help many students master new or unfamiliar skills. They need to be shown what to do, and often they need practice and additional instruction before they can fully master the skills we're trying to teach.

I learned this lesson from one of the strangest referrals I've ever received. Kaley, age six, and her mother arrived at my office with an interesting dilemma. Each day, Kaley left for school with a carefully prepared lunch, but the best items in her lunch box always seemed to end up in some other child's hands. Often, Kaley arrived home in tears.

"I don't understand it," said her frustrated mother. "She knows what to do. I've told her over and over again to say no when older kids ask for her lunch items. Her teacher and principal have done the same thing, but Kaley continues to give them away! Her teacher says there's nothing she can do if Kaley chooses to give her lunch away."

I suspected her mother was right. Kaley probably did know what to do, but I wanted to check this out myself to be sure.

"Kaley, what are you supposed to do when other kids ask for your lunch items?" I asked. She parroted back the words her mother, teacher, and principal told her.

"I'm supposed to say no and tell the teacher if they take them anyway," she said.

Her mother was right. On an intellectual level, Kaley understood what she was supposed to do. But knowing what to do and actually doing it are two different things. I suspected her skill training was incomplete, so I explored the problem a little further.

"Saying no to big kids is sometimes hard to do," I said. Kaley nodded her agreement.

"I get scared," she said.

"Let's practice saying no to big kids for a while," I suggested. "Maybe we can help you feel more comfortable." I wanted Kaley to see, hear, and feel what it is like to do what she was being asked.

I broke the skill down into a few simple steps and then asked her mother to pretend to be one of the big kids. I pretended to be Kaley and used a book for her lunch box. When her mother approached and made a pitch for my chips, I said, "No, they're mine. You can't have them." We went through this procedure several times, and each time I role-modeled different ways to say no. I said no in a loud voice and a soft voice, with eye contact and without eye contact, but each time, I held on tightly to the lunch box and waited until her mother walked away.

"Now it's your turn to practice, Kaley," I said. "This time, I'll pretend to be the big kid, and you can hold the lunch box." I approached her and asked for the chips. She didn't make eye contact, but she did say no very clearly.

"That was a clear no," I said. "That will work just fine. Let's try it again."

We repeated the scenario many times. Each time, I encouraged her to say no a different way to see which way felt most comfortable. She preferred the simple two-word approach,

"No, sorry," and she discovered that she felt more comfortable when she didn't have to look at me while she said it. She was gaining confidence.

"Ready to try this at school?" I asked.

"I guess so," Kaley replied.

I asked her mother to practice the procedure with Kaley a few more times before she left for school the next day. We scheduled a follow-up appointment for later that week.

"How did it go?" I asked when they arrived for the follow-up visit. I could tell from the look on Kaley's face that she had enjoyed some success.

"It went fine," said her mother. "The practice really helped. Her lunch stayed in her hands all week." Kaley had a proud look of accomplishment.

"Congratulations!" I said. She was well on her way to mastering an important skill.

What made the difference? Kaley needed practice and further instruction before she could master the skill her mother and others were trying to teach. The information they provided was a helpful first step, but it didn't go far enough. Kaley knew what to do but not how to do it. Her skill training was incomplete. The simple technique of breaking the skill down into teachable steps, role-modeling each step, and then adding a little encouragement helped Kaley complete the lesson others had begun.

Many children find themselves in situations like Kaley's, where they know what to do but not how to do it. They need more than information. Simply telling them to walk away from a fight, ignore someone who teases, or just say no when peers encourage them to cut class may not be enough. They need our help exploring choices for action, breaking the skill down into teachable pieces, role-modeling the acceptable behavior, giving them opportunities to practice, and catching them being successful. If you follow these simple steps and allow your students to collect the data they need, they will arrive at the desired outcome. Let's look more closely at each step in the skill-training process.

Exploring Choices for Action

SOMETIMES STUDENTS MISBEHAVE because they're simply unaware of other, more effective choices for solving problems or behaving acceptably. Brandon, a kindergartner, is a good example. Brandon completes a five-minute time-out for pushing another child. When the time-out is over, his teacher helps him explore other, more effective choices for handling the situation.

"Brandon, pushing Robert when he teased you was not a good choice. Pushing others will always result in a time-out. What can you do the next time Robert teases you?" she asks.

"I don't know," Brandon replies.

"You could politely ask him not to with your words," suggests the teacher. She role-models how to do it. "Or, you could walk away and try to ignore him. If he continues, you could ask me for help. What are you going to do next time?"

"I'll ask him to stop," says Brandon, "and I'll try to ignore him if he doesn't."

"Good plan!" says his teacher. "That should work, and if it doesn't, I'll be happy to help."

As the example illustrates, *exploring choices for action* is an important first step in the skill-training process. It helps children become aware of their choices. It helps them distinguish between good and poor choices, and it sets the stage for the steps to follow.

From a developmental perspective, exploring choices works best with older children and teens because they have the intellectual capacity to consider hypothetically and think ahead into the future. The method also works with younger children, but you'll probably have to suggest most of the choices. You can use this training step after consequences have been applied or to teach problem-solving skills when no mis-behavior has occurred. Carry out the following steps:

1. Explore with the student, in a question format, other acceptable choices available for handling the situation.
2. Review the consequences for poor choices and non-compliance.
3. Encourage the student to carry out one of the better choices.

Consider the following.

Paula, a sixth grader, is upset because she received partial credit on a late assignment. She appeals her case to her teacher.

"It's not fair!" complains Paula. "I finished the assignment on time. I just forgot to bring it in."

"That is frustrating," acknowledges her teacher. "What can you do to prevent this from happening again?"

"I could ask my mom to remind me," says Paula.

"That's one choice, but whose job is it to keep track of your assignments?" asks the teacher.

"It's mine," Paula replies. "She probably wouldn't do it, anyway."

"What else could you do?" inquires her teacher. "I notice you never forget to bring your backpack. Is that part of the solution?"

"That's a great idea!" says Paula. "I leave my backpack in the front entry when I get home. I'll take it to my room and put my homework inside it when it's done. Then I'll never for-get it."

"You solved that problem!" says the teacher.

Blake, a high school senior, arrives at his counselor's office upset. "I can't stand Mr. Crocker," Blake complains. "He should have become a drill sergeant instead of a teacher. He loves to order people around and make them feel stupid. I want to drop his class."

"It's not too late to drop the class," says the counselor, "but are you sure that's what you want to do?"

"I'm sure!" says Blake emphatically. He sounds determined, but his counselor isn't sure that dropping the class is the best alternative. He helps Blake explore his choices.

"You need two semesters of a foreign language to graduate," says the counselor, "and this is your last semester. It's too late to enroll in another Spanish class. If you drop Mr. Crocker's class, how will you fulfill your language requirement before graduation?"

"I hadn't thought of that," confesses Blake. "If I take Spanish during summer school, could I still graduate with my class?"

"I think so," replies the counselor, "but is that what you really want to do? You have a solid B in Mr. Crocker's class now and six weeks left in the semester. Are you ready to spend four weeks of your summer repeating work you've already completed?"

"Not exactly," says Blake. "My dad expects me to get a job. He would be pretty angry with me if I had to take summer school." Blake's dilemma was coming into perspective.

"Maybe sticking it out in Mr. Crocker's class is worth considering," suggests the counselor. "What can you do to make it more bearable?"

"I guess I'll just have to bite my lip when he tries to humiliate me or order me around," says Blake.

"You have my support if you need someone to talk to," says the counselor.

Blake received a valuable lesson in problem solving. By the time they were done, he understood his choices and the consequences associated with each. No one needed to tell him what to do. The technique of exploring choices helped him arrive at the best solution on his own.

Breaking Skills into Teachable Parts

AN ESSENTIAL PART of teaching social skills is to make the skill understandable to the learner. This involves breaking it down into teachable pieces then teaching the complete skill piece by piece. Let's look at how Sean's teacher uses this approach.

> An essential part of teaching social skills is to make the skill understandable to the learner.

Sean, a third grader, has a habit of interrupting. When he was younger, his parents thought it was just a stage or phase that would pass with time. It didn't. In fact, the problem got worse. Sean's parents decided it was time to do something about it. They tried complaining and criticizing him each time he interrupted. That didn't help. They told him to say, "Excuse me," when he wanted their attention. That didn't help, either. Sean simply prefaced all of his interruptions with the words *excuse me* and continued to interrupt.

When Sean's frustrated parents shared their experiences with their son's teacher, she offered to help because the same problem was occurring at school. The next day after school she called Sean over to her desk.

"Sean, I have a plan to help you stop interrupting," she began. "Here are the steps I want you to follow. When you want my attention, but I'm talking or busy doing something, I want you to raise your hand quietly and make eye contact with me.

Then, I want you to wait for a pause in the conversation; say, 'Excuse me,' once; and wait to be recognized. When I look at you, it's your turn to speak. Do you understand how it works?"

Sean nods.

"Good," says his teacher, "because we're going to practice this skill from now on. When you forget and interrupt, I'll ask you to use the skills I described and try it again. If you interrupt intentionally, I'll ask you to take a time-out. Is this clear?"

Sean nods again.

Sean gets his first practice opportunity the next morning. After recess, he runs into the classroom excitedly and interrupts his teacher, who's talking to the school's speech therapist. The teacher stops Sean before he completes his first sentence.

"What are you supposed to do when you want my attention?" she asks.

Sean remembers.

"Now, go back and try it again," says his teacher.

Sean leaves the classroom and returns a few moments later. He approaches his teacher, who's still talking, makes eye contact, raises his hand, and waits for a pause in the conversation.

"Excuse me," says Sean. His teacher looks at him and smiles.

"Thank you," says the teacher. "What would you like to say?"

Sean and his teacher repeated this drill many times in the days and weeks that followed. No, things didn't always go smoothly. Breaking old habits is not easy. After a few weeks, Sean's successes outnumbered his failures. He was well on his way to mastering an important skill.

Role-Modeling Corrective Behavior

SOMETIMES CHILDREN NEED to see, hear, feel, and experience the skill we want them to learn before they are ready to master it. Role-modeling corrective behavior is a simple but powerful teaching technique that is particularly well suited to younger children and "hard-way" learners. The method is concrete, easy to use, and has varied applications. It can be used to teach problem-solving skills when no misbehavior is involved or to teach acceptable corrective behavior when misbehavior is involved.

When your focus is on teaching skills when no misbehavior is involved, use the following steps:

1. Role-model the corrective behavior you want the student to use.
2. Encourage the student to try it again using the corrective behavior.
3. Catch the student using the skill correctly, and acknowledge the success.

For example, Miss Casey, a preschool teacher, wants her students to get ready to go outside. "It's time to pick up whatever you're using and put it away," she announces. "We need to get ready for recess."

Hilda, age three, hears her teacher and hurriedly throws most of the blocks she's using into their container. Then, she places the container on the shelf. "I'm ready," she says.

"Are you sure you're ready, Hilda?" asks Miss Casey, noticing several blocks are still scattered on the floor and that Hilda's carpet strip hasn't been put away. Hilda nods.

"Well, you're close," says Miss Casey. "Let me show you what your area should look like when you're ready." She places a carpet strip down on the floor and pours out a container of blocks next to the carpet strip. While Hilda watches, Miss Casey picks up all the blocks, puts them in the container, and returns the container to the shelf. Then she puts away the carpet strip.

"Does your area look like this?" asks Miss Casey. Hilda shakes her head. "Then you need to finish the job. I'm sure you'll do fine." Hilda does.

Now, let's look at another application of this technique. When teaching corrective behavior following an incident of misbehavior, use the following steps:

1. Provide a clear, firm, limit-setting message.
2. Role-model the corrective behavior.
3. Encourage the child to try it again using the corrective behavior.
4. Acknowledge effort and improvement.

For example, Joel, a fourth grader, becomes frustrated when the student behind him taps the back of Joel's chair. Joel can't concentrate on his work.

"Cut it out, butthead!" shouts Joel angrily. His teacher intervenes.

"Joel, we don't talk like that in the classroom," says the teacher matter-of-factly. "Do you need some quiet time to cool down?" He shakes his head.

"Chris was tapping the back of my chair, and he has been bugging me all morning," complains Joel. "I'm sick of it!"

"What are you supposed to do when other kids bother or tease you?" asks the teacher. Joel looks at him blankly.

"I don't know," he replies.

"Well, you could ask him politely to stop or ask me to help if he doesn't," says the teacher. "Watch how I do it." He turns to Chris and says, "Chris, please stop tapping my desk." He pauses briefly to let his words sink in, and then looks at Chris.

"Would that work, Chris?" he asks. Chris nods.

"Good!" says the teacher. "That's all there is to it. Now you try it, Joel. Tell Chris what he needs to know." Joel turns to Chris and practices the skill.

"Thanks, guys," says the teacher. "That works much better."

In another example, Mr. Simmons uses role modeling to deal with a disrespectful tenth grader. Mr. Simmons is a popular teacher who runs an informal class. He believes the relaxed atmosphere helps his students feel comfortable. He's probably right, but some students misinterpret his good intentions and push things too far. Dylan is a good example.

"Hey, Simmons," says Dylan in a disrespectful tone. "Give me the hall pass. I need to use the restroom." Mr. Simmons calls Dylan up to his desk.

"I'd be happy to give you a hall pass, Dylan," says Mr. Simmons matter-of-factly, "but not when you ask me like that. Can you think of another way to ask?" Dylan looks at him impatiently and rolls his eyes.

"Come on. Just give it to me," says Dylan with the same impatient tone. He expects Mr. Simmons to become rattled and give in, but Mr. Simmons keeps his cool and remains firm.

"Maybe it would help if I showed you how to ask," Mr. Simmons suggests. "Try this: 'May I use the hall pass for a trip to the restroom?' That will always work."

"Okay. Have it your way," says Dylan, realizing Mr. Simmons's resolve. "May I use the hall pass to go to the bathroom?"

"Sure," replies Mr. Simmons with an appreciative smile. "Thanks for asking the way you did."

Yes, role-modeling corrective behavior even works with teens, but it's not easy to keep our composure when students are as disrespectful as Dylan. Mr. Simmons was very effective. He taught the skill he wanted Dylan to learn and role-modeled the respect he wanted Dylan to show. No one was blamed or singled out. The lesson was a win-win situation for both of them.

Try It Again

TRY IT AGAIN is a simple, concrete, and highly effective guidance procedure that is used almost intuitively by preschool teachers to address minor misbehaviors. The applications of this procedure, however, extend well beyond the preschool level. They can be used with older children and teens as well.

The procedure is easy to carry out. After an incident of minor misbehavior, state a firm limit-setting message and encourage the child to carry out the corrective behavior by saying, "Try it again." The focus is on the corrective action, not the offending behavior. The child is simply given another opportunity to demonstrate that he or she can make a better choice and cooperate. If the child chooses instead to resist, then this procedure leads smoothly to limited choices or logical consequences. Consider the following examples.

> The focus is on the corrective action, not the offending behavior.

A group of preschoolers runs into the classroom yelling and creating a disturbance. Their teacher intervenes.

"Guys, we're supposed to use indoor voices in the classroom." She leads them outside. "Let's try it again the right way." They do.

Ryan, a second grader, is a tattler who capitalizes on every possible opportunity to tattle on his classmates. His teacher wants him to take some responsibility for solving problems on his own. The next day, Ryan approaches her desk during a math activity to tattle on one of the students in his desk group.

"Nikolas is humming while I'm trying to work," Ryan complains. "I can't concentrate. Would you tell him to stop?"

"Did you tell Nikolas his humming was bothering you?" asks the teacher. Ryan shakes his head. "Did you use your words and ask him to stop?" she adds. Ryan shakes his head again. "Well, those are the steps you need to take first before I become involved. I'm confident you guys can work it out." She role-models the message Ryan should give Nikolas and then sends him back to his desk.

Marla, a fifth grader, is working on a writing assignment when her pen runs out of ink. She asks the teacher to lend her another, but all of his pens are blue. She needs a black pen.

"Will someone lend Marla a black pen?" he asks.

"I will," says Dave. He pulls out a black pen and flings it across the room for Marla to catch. He can tell, by the look on his teacher's face, that the aerial display wasn't appreciated.

"Dave, how are we supposed to pass things in the classroom?" asks the teacher.

"Hand them to each other," Dave replies.

"Right," says the teacher. "Please pick up the pen and try it again." Dave picks the pen up off the floor, walks over to Marla, and hands it to her.

"Thanks, Dave," says the teacher. "I appreciate your helping out."

Abby, a ninth grader, is unhappy because she has to go to the attendance office to pick up a tardy slip. When the teacher hands Abby a hall pass, Abby snatches it from her teacher's hand.

"Let's try that again," says her teacher matter-of-factly. She holds out the hall pass for Abby to take once again and waits patiently for her to take it the right way. Abby does.

"Thanks, Abby," says the teacher.

Abby's teacher is effective. She keeps her cool and role-models the respect and cooperation she expects.

Catching Children Being Successful

CHILDREN ARE NATURALLY motivated to learn new skills and to have their successes acknowledged by the important adults in their lives. They don't require treats, toys, and special rewards to become more skillful. They're already motivated to show you what they can do. Skill acquisition is the primary developmental task of early and middle childhood.

One of the most powerful ways to motivate children to learn new skills also is one of the most simple. Catch them being successful and acknowledge it. Let's look at how two teachers do this in the next examples.

It's the first week of school in Mrs. Carter's second-grade class. She notices that one of her students has a bad habit of running to the door to line up for recess. She's afraid someone might get hurt. Each time she sees him run, she asks him to return to his seat and then walk to the door again. They've been through this drill about a half dozen times when Mrs. Carter notices some success. As she announces to the class that it's time to line up for recess, she sees Matt bolt from his seat and then catch himself and walk to the door.

"Thanks, Matt," says Mrs. Carter with an appreciative smile. "I really like the way you handled that." Matt beams. He appreciates having his success acknowledged, and he's eager to show her more.

Mr. Stark, a fifth-grade teacher, has been working with his students all week on entering the classroom quietly in the mornings, putting away their coats and backpacks, and getting in their seats after the bell rings. Each day, he notes improvement, but on Friday morning, everyone gets it right.

"You guys are awesome!" exclaims Mr. Stark. "Thank you." He walks over to the blackboard and adds a minute of PAT under the bonus column. Everyone feels good about it.

Chapter Summary

PROVIDING INFORMATION IS an important first step in the teaching-and-learning process, but information alone may not be enough. Sometimes children need to be shown what to do and given opportunities to practice before they can master the skills we're trying to teach.

In this chapter, we examined five simple and easy-to-use steps that provide students with the information and instructive experiences they need to master the skills we're trying to teach: exploring choices, breaking skills down into teachable parts, role-modeling the corrective behavior, giving opportunities to practice and try it again, and catching them being successful. These steps will help you stay off the discipline treadmill.

17

Solving Problems with Homework

ONE OF THE most familiar dances I see in my counseling work is the dance parents and children do over homework. That's the one where the parents remind, cajole, threaten, and reprimand, and the kids avoid, make excuses, resist, dawdle, or procrastinate. Like most dances, there's a punitive version that's a little louder and a permissive version that's more drawn out. Some parents do a little of both.

Call them "homework battles," "nightly coercion routines," or whatever term you want, but one thing is for sure: There are a lot of parents out there doing it. Most can't say how they got started or what keeps it going, but once it gets started, no one seems to know how to stop. Where can parents turn for help? Hopefully, to you. This chapter will show you how to help parents end their homework dances and put the responsibility for homework back on their child's shoulders, where it belongs.

Many parents don't realize that homework takes place in a system involving three participants: parents, teacher, and child. Each has his or her own set of jobs or responsibilities to carry out if the homework system is to operate smoothly and remain in balance. The system can break down, and often does, when its members do less than or more than their own part.

In this chapter, you'll learn how the homework system operates, why it breaks down, and how to fix it without returning to the nightly coercion routine. You'll see that the key to a successful homework system is helping parents do their own part, and only their part, without taking responsibility away from you or their child.

The Dance

DARREN, A FOURTH grader, and his parents were referred during the middle of the school year. The problem was Darren wouldn't do his homework. He was failing many of his subjects.

Darren's teacher had tried everything—deadline extensions, extra-credit makeup opportunities, stickers, contracts, success charts, pep talks, even a daily note system between school and home. Nothing worked.

Yes, homework sounded like the problem, but was it really? Each year, I see a few kids like Darren for whom homework appears to be the problem but turns out to be only a symptom of something larger, such as a lack of skills, a learning disability, a behavior problem, an emotional or relationship problem, or a problem with drugs or alcohol. I needed to check this out. I interviewed Darren's parents and collected the necessary background information.

From the interview, Darren seemed like a normal, well-adjusted kid. He spent his free time with friends, and he enjoyed skateboarding and bicycling. Other than the power struggles over homework, he enjoyed good relationships with his parents and others. I needed to be sure, however, that Darren was really capable of doing his work.

"Is there any chance that the assignments might be too difficult for him?" I asked.

His parents were prepared for the question. Darren's mother handed me an envelope with copies of past report cards and test scores. I glanced over them briefly. Mostly Bs. Strong test scores. Okay, I was convinced. Darren was capable. Back to homework matters.

Darren's parents had all the familiar complaints: "He tells us he doesn't have any homework, and then we find out later that he does. He knows he's supposed to write down his assignments, but half the time he doesn't do it. When we ask to see them, he says he forgot or lost them or that he doesn't have any that night. So, we get on the phone and call around and find out what's going on. Some nights, it takes us forty-five minutes just to figure out what his assignments are! Fortunately, that has changed. Now his teacher calls me every

Monday and gives me all of Darren's homework assignments for the week."

"Has that helped?" I directed the question to Darren's mother, who was telling most of the story.

"Yes and no," she replied. "At least now we know what he's supposed to do, but getting him to actually do it hasn't gotten any easier. We still go through the same old routine.

"Each night about seven, when dinner is finished and he's enjoyed a half hour of television, we sit down together at the dining room table and go over his assignments. I read the directions, and sometimes I do the first problem with him to make sure he understands how to do it. He just sits there!

"So I begin to prod. 'Come on, get going!' I say. 'Let's get it done tonight before eight for a change.' He may do a problem or two, but then he just sits there again. So I prod some more, and he does a few more. This is how it goes for the first hour until bath time. If we're lucky, he may be half done.

"After the bath, it's more of the same. Sometimes, I get so frustrated I start yelling. This usually brings my husband in, and he has even less patience than I do. He starts yelling, too. Then Darren gets upset. So I console him, and my husband blames me for being too soft. It's crazy! I usually end up lecturing both of them, while Darren sneaks off to watch TV. Most nights, the homework doesn't get done.

"His teacher tells us Darren's homework should take about thirty to forty minutes. In our house it can drag on for hours! He won't do it unless we stand over him and make him do it."

And so it goes, Monday through Thursday, week after week, with his parents devoting a good portion of their evening pushing and prodding, threatening and lecturing, as Darren dawdles, avoids, and works as slowly as possible. Does homework really deserve this much attention? Is the act of getting it done really what's most important?

What Is the Purpose of Homework?

SOMETIMES, PARENTS BECOME so caught up in the task of getting it done that they lose sight of what homework is all about. Let's take a moment to consider why children are asked to do homework in the first place.

Homework teaches children two sets of lessons—one that is immediately apparent and one that requires us to look a little deeper. The most obvious reason for assigning homework is to provide children with opportunities to practice and improve their skills. Practice is essential to skill mastery. A regular homework routine helps children sharpen their skills. This is what Darren's parents were most concerned about. Let's call this lesson 1.

> Homework teaches children how to begin a task on their own, stay with the task, complete it, and be responsible for the outcome.

But, homework also teaches other, more important lessons that can't be measured with letter grades—responsibility, self-discipline, independence, perseverance, and time management. Homework teaches children how to begin a task on their own, stay with the task, complete it, and be responsible for the outcome. In the long run, these skills will have a much greater influence on a child's future success, not only in the classroom but on the job and in life. These lessons are what Darren's parents and teacher were overlooking. Let's call this lesson 2.

How do children learn this second set of lessons? By being allowed opportunities to stand on their own and do their part without interference from parents and teachers. The act alone conveys a powerful set of behavioral messages: "I believe you're capable." "I trust you to do this on your own."

A System Out of Balance

WHEN WE LOOK at all the steps the school and Darren's parents had taken to get Darren to do his homework, one question looms prominently: Whose homework is it, really? Darren's. But who keeps track of his assignments? Mom and the teacher. And who does part of the work? Mom and Dad. And who makes sure it gets turned in on time? Mom. And who experiences the consequences for the homework not getting done? Mom, Dad, and the school. If the homework really belongs to Darren, why, then, is everyone else doing his job for him?

What Darren's parents and teacher didn't realize is that they all had been playing hot potato with responsibility. And guess who ended up holding the potato? Not Darren. The way things were, he had little incentive for changing his behavior. He knew, from experience, that he could count on his teacher and parents to do his part for him.

Darren's parents and the school had fallen into a trap. They had been compensating for Darren's lack of responsibility by doing many of his jobs themselves. The more they compensated, the less Darren did, and the more out of balance their homework system became. Without realizing it, they were actually enabling him to behave the way he was, and he was getting a lot of negative attention in the process.

Sure, all their dancing was getting a little homework done, but at whose initiative? And what about lesson 2? Things were not going to improve until they all got back to doing their rightful jobs.

"I think it's time we take a closer look at your homework system," I suggested to Darren's parents.

"Homework system?" said Darren's father, looking a little puzzled. "I don't think we have one, at least not one I'm aware of."

His response was not unusual. Most parents who become stuck in homework dances are not aware of the roles they play or that they operate within a system.

"Almost every parent has one," I said. "Yours just hasn't been working very well for you." I handed each of them a chart (see table 6) and gave them a few minutes to look it over.

"Look familiar?" I asked. Both parents nodded. "This is what a homework system looks like when parents and teachers end up doing their children's jobs." We reviewed each list.

"How do things get this way?" Darren's father asked.

Some families just start off this way—that is, with their system out of balance. The jobs are not clear from the beginning, or there's too much parent involvement. Parents think they are helping, but as time passes and patterns become established, they begin to notice that they do more and more while their children do less and less.

Other parents become overinvolved when the work is difficult and their children begin to struggle. The parents want to help, and they should up to a point, but when the helping is over and the child knows what to do, it's time to back off and let the child complete the task on his or her own. When parents fail to back off, the rescuing and overinvolvement result in a gradual shifting of jobs.

The problem is gradual and insidious. In many cases, it may go unnoticed entirely until children stop doing their homework altogether, like in Darren's home. By the time parents realize something is wrong, patterns have already become established, and a great deal of compensating has been going on.

Table 6. Homework System Out of Balance

Parents' Jobs	Child's Jobs	Teacher's Job
Make frequent inquiries about assignments.	Provide excuses about assignments (such as "It was lost, stolen; none was assigned; dog ate it.").	Lecture, persuade, or coerce child to do the work.
Remind child to do his or her work.	Listen to reminders, lectures, reprimands from parents and teacher.	Give frequent reminders to do the lessons.
Ask if the work is done.	Wait until the last moment to get started.	Provide deadline extensions and extra-credit and makeup opportunitites.
Make extra trips to school to pick up books or assignments.	Do the work in a busy place where it attracts maximum attention.	Make the work easier in hopes more will get done.
Help out by doing some of the work.	Pretend not to understand so parents will get involved.	Ask parents to become more involved.
Lecture or punish for not doing the work.	Rush through or do it carelessly to get it over with.	Provide special rewards for completed work.
Feel responsible for child's failures.	Blame parents and teacher for poor grades.	Feel responsible for child's failures.

Darren's mother looked confused. "Wait a second!" she said, pointing to the list of Parents' Jobs. "I thought I was supposed to do all these things. Are you saying that I shouldn't help Darren keep track of his assignments each day or remind him to turn in his homework?"

"Exactly right," I replied. "Not if you want to put your system back in balance and help Darren learn responsibility. That's not likely to happen until you stop doing Darren's jobs for him and limit your involvement to the jobs that are rightfully yours. What incentive will he have to do the work himself if he can always count on someone else to step in and bail him out?"

"But I know my son," she countered. "If I don't do those jobs, he won't, either."

"I think you're right," I agreed. "He probably won't until you build some consequences into your homework system to hold him accountable. As it is now, all Darren has to do is endure the prodding and lectures, and he's home free."

I could appreciate her confusion. Darren's mom was getting mixed messages about her appropriate level of involvement. Darren's teachers had asked her to become more involved with Darren's homework, but they gave her no specific plan for going about it. Like most parents, she interpreted the request to mean that she should do more of what she was already doing—more dancing. Now, I was encouraging her to back off.

"How do we get off this treadmill?" asked Darren's father.

"You're right," I said. "It's time we started talking about how to hand the hot potato back to Darren and how to put your homework system in balance."

Putting the System Back in Balance

I HANDED DARREN'S parents a second chart (see table 7). "This is what the homework system looks like when it's in balance," I said. "Notice the distribution of responsibility between the three participants." I gave them a few minutes to look it over, then we reviewed each list of jobs.

In a balanced system, parents limit their involvement and operate as facilitators; they support and promote the home-

Table 7. Homework System In Balance

Parents' Jobs	Child's Jobs	Teacher's Job
Establish a regular time for homework.	Keep track of books and assignments.	Provide instruction.
Establish a regular place for homework.	Start on time and allow time to finish work.	Provide materials.
Provide necessary materials and supplies.	Do own work with only limited assistance.	Provide deadlines.
Provide limited instruction and assistance.	Turn in work on time.	Provide encouragement.
Establish logical consequences for noncompliance and follow through.	Accept responsibility for grades or other consequences.	Provide feedback regarding work returned.

work process but play only a brief role. The key word here is *brief*. Parents set limits on the jobs to be done, and they make sure children have everything they need to carry out their tasks, but that's where their job ends. The rest is up to the child. The child is the one who does the work.

"According to the chart, we should establish a regular time and a regular place for homework," said Darren's mother. "How is that different from what we've been doing?"

"Let's look at some guidelines for establishing times and places for homework in a balanced system," I suggested.

A Time for Homework

When helping parents select a suitable time for homework, keep three considerations in mind. First, they should select a time that can be used regularly. Homework should be a habit, a routine, something the child does on a regular basis. When parents select a stable time, they help their child develop good work habits.

Second, parents should choose a time that is earlier rather than later. Why? Because children are generally fresher and more alert in the late afternoon or early evening than they are later on. They are more motivated to complete their jobs so they can get on to the "good stuff" that awaits them.

Also, there is an accountability issue to consider. When homework is the last task of the day before bed, what consequences are available to use if the child chooses not to comply? None. There's no accountability. The system breaks down. Late homework schedules eliminate opportunities to teach lesson 2 with logical consequences. There is more than a little wisdom to the old axiom "Work before play."

Finally, homework sessions should have a beginning and an end. That is, parents should specify the times they are available to help and times when they are not. For example, if you expect your child to complete his or her homework between 4:30 and 5:00, you might say, "I will be available to help between 4:30 and 5:00, but not after that time." This is one of the surest ways to keep the hot potato in the child's lap and to define how much time parents are willing to devote to homework.

> Parents should specify the times they are available to help and times when they are not.

Time limits have other advantages, too. They teach children to plan and manage their time wisely, and they provide parents and children with time to enjoy each other's company without the intrusion of homework.

Sure, parents can be flexible and extend these deadlines for big exams and special projects, but otherwise, they should specify a regular homework period and do their best to stick to it. If they don't, they may be setting themselves up for long homework sessions or for providing opportunities for children to use homework as a device for garnering negative attention, power, and control over other family members. Again, homework is not worth this much attention.

How much time should parents set aside each day for homework? The guidelines I generally hear from teachers are thirty to forty-five minutes a night for primary-level children (grades 1 and 2), thirty to sixty minutes a night for intermediate levels (grades 3 through 6), and sixty to ninety minutes a night for secondary levels (grades 7 through 12). I recommend that parents consult with their child's teacher before deciding.

What if the child finishes in less than the allotted time? Terrific! If a brief review of the work reveals that it was, in fact, completed and a good effort was made to do it accurately, then there is no point in making him or her stay there to the end of the session. Even if some of the items are wrong? Yes, unless the child specifically asks his or her parents to check the work for accuracy. The emphasis should be on effort, not outcome; process, not product. If the child puts forth a good effort and does the work, that's enough. It doesn't have to be perfect to fulfill lessons 1 and 2.

A Place for Homework

Where should homework be done? The best place for homework is a separate, quiet area away from parents and other family members. A balanced system is difficult to maintain when parents allow children to do homework at the kitchen table or in other busy family areas. Parents risk that homework will receive more attention and parental involvement than it deserves. That's an invitation to dance.

If not the kitchen or dining room, then where? A child's bedroom, a study, or another quiet room works fine for homework provided they are available on a regular basis, away from traffic and distractions such as TV or other family activities, and provisioned with all the right equipment and materials, such as a desk, comfortable chair, lamp, supply of paper, pencils, pens, a dictionary, ruler, tape, stapler, paper clips, and maybe a tray or two to keep things organized.

"How do we get this new system going?" asked Darren's mother, relieved at the prospect that help was on the horizon.

Three Steps to a Balanced System

THE GOOD NEWS for parents who want to end the dance and pass the hot potato back to their child is that the remedy requires less time, energy, and involvement than they are already putting forth. The three steps they will need to follow include (1) clarifying the jobs, (2) building in accountability, and (3) staying off the dance floor.

Step 1: Clarify the Jobs

When I assist parents in repairing a broken system, I always recommend that they sit down with their child and explain the various jobs in a balanced system—the parents' jobs, the teacher's jobs, and the child's jobs. I encourage parents to be very specific about how, when, and where the child should carry out his or her jobs. Some parents find it helpful to post the jobs and time schedules on the refrigerator to eliminate confusion. This is what I encouraged Darren's parents to do.

"Okay," said Darren's father, "the system sounds good in theory, but what happens when Darren chooses not to do his jobs?"

"This is where your accountability measures come in," I replied. In a balanced system, children are accountable for their poor choices because they experience regular and consistent consequences when they choose not to do their part. Consequences provide motivation for making good choices.

Step 2: Build Accountability into the System

When children find a way to avoid homework on a regular basis, often it's because their homework system lacks accountability. They are not likely to change their behavior until their parents build some accountability into the system. How do parents do this? First, they need a procedure for monitoring their child's assignments to make sure the assigned work actually gets home. Second, they need to follow through with logical consequences when their child chooses to do less than his or her part.

Let's begin with procedures for monitoring assignments. There are many creative ways to monitor assignments, but I prefer two methods in particular because they are brief, simple, and require little parental involvement. The monitoring system for elementary students consists of one assignment sheet for the entire week that goes home with the child on Mondays (see figure 17.1). The teacher writes down the assignments and indicates any outstanding assignments in the space at the bottom of the sheet. It's the child's responsibility to get the assignment sheet home. Consequences, such as loss or reduction of that day's privileges, go into effect if that doesn't happen.

The monitoring procedure for secondary students is more complicated because more teachers are involved. Each day, it's

Homework for week of: _____
Monday
Tuesday
Wednesday
Thursday
Missing assignments

Figure 17.1   Assignment Sheet for Elementary Students

the student's responsibility to write down his or her assignments on a daily assignment sheet and present the sheet to the teacher. The teacher checks it for accuracy, initials it, and notes any outstanding assignments or incomplete work at the bottom of the form (see figure 17.2). It's the student's job to bring the sheet home.

Date _____

Class: _____ Assignment due: _____
Assignment:

Teacher's
initials: _____

Class: _____ Assignment due: _____
Assignment:

Teacher's
initials: _____

Class: _____ Assignment due: _____
Assignment:

Teacher's
initials: _____

Class: _____ Assignment due: _____
Assignment:

Teacher's
initials: _____

Class: _____ Assignment due: _____
Assignment:

Teacher's
initials: _____

Figure 17.2   Assignment Sheet for Secondary Students

If the student fails to bring his or her initialed assignment sheet home, then consequences should go into effect that afternoon. If the student does bring the initialed sheet home and does the work during the time required, then parents simply compare work assigned to work completed and allocate privileges.

Does monitoring take away some of the child's responsibility? Yes, it does, but very little in comparison to the amount of responsibility it keeps on the child for doing the rest of his or her jobs. Monitoring simply removes the gray area about what jobs need to be done and provides parents with a basis for evaluating if assigned work has been completed.

Now, let's look at the second part of the accountability system—consequences. When applied consistently, logical consequences help children learn responsibility and lesson 2 by holding them accountable for their choices. All parents need to do is follow through and enforce the consequence without dancing. No lectures. No threats. No reminders or angry displays. When children hold the hot potato, they learn from their own mistakes.

What is a logical consequence for not doing homework? If homework is the child's job and after-school privileges are the paycheck for a job completed, then temporary loss of after-school privileges is an effective logical consequence.

The system is really very simple. Privileges are based on performance. If the child brings home all of his or her assignments and completes all assigned work during the designated time, then he or she receives full after-school privileges for that day. If the child completes all of his or her homework assignments for the entire week, then he or she earns full weekend privileges.

If, on the other hand, the child fails to bring home his or her assignments or fails to complete his or her work within the agreed-on time, then parents should follow through and withhold some or all of that child's after-school privileges. Call it "a quiet time in the house" and take it one day at a time. Incomplete work should be completed during a designated time on Saturday or Sunday, but not both. In short, each school day, the child earns privileges not only for that day but for the weekend as well.

Consequences for Elementary School Students

No after-school play privileges

No visiting with friends

No TV or video games

Spend time in the house doing quiet activities

Consequences for Secondary Students

No after-school free-time privileges

No visiting with friends

No telephone privileges

No TV or video game privileges

Spend quiet time in the house doing quiet activities

Revised limits on curfew, dating, car use, or telephone privileges based on level of compliance

Step 3: Stay Off the Dance Floor

After parents clarify the jobs to be done and put their accountability measures in place, they are ready to back off and let their homework system teach its lessons. The hot potato is now in the child's lap, and parents should see that it stays there. How do they do that? By limiting their involvement to their own jobs and by enforcing their accountability system.

What You Should Expect

"HOW LONG WILL it take to get things back in balance once we put this new system into effect?" asked Darren's father.

Every parent wants to hear the good news that things will get better quickly. But some problems, such as homework dances, don't lend themselves to a quick fix. Changing old habits takes time. I had confidence Darren's parents would be successful, because they were motivated to do what was needed. But, I wanted to be sure that they left my office with a realistic set of expectations. I tried to put things in perspective.

"Your homework dances have been going on for quite a while," I observed. "Things will probably get worse before they get better. That is, Darren will need to experience repeatedly the consequences associated with his poor choices before he is likely to change his behavior. This takes time, perhaps three to six weeks or more. When it does happen, and it should, you will also begin to see a lot more of lesson 1."

During the transition period, parents should expect testing. Their children will probably continue to make excuses about lost or forgotten assignments, dawdle, procrastinate, or put on displays of confusion or helplessness. They may even intensify their routines in a desperate attempt to get Mom and Dad to rescue, lecture, punish, or do more than just their rightful part.

> During the transition period, parents should expect testing.

As tempting as the bait may be, encourage parents to keep their limits firm and follow through with the three-step plan. The testing won't last forever. It's just a normal, but stressful, part of the change process.

As suggested, Darren's parents reviewed their new homework system with Darren and put it into effect the next day. They established a four o'clock start time with an upper limit of five o'clock. Neither parent would be available to help after five o'clock unless arrangements were made in advance. The schedule allowed Darren plenty of time to have a snack after school and time to play with friends or watch TV if he finished his work promptly.

Darren's father set up a desk in Darren's room upstairs and provisioned it with all the necessary supplies. If Darren needed help, it was his job to go downstairs and ask for it, and then return to his room to do the work.

For accountability, Darren's parents and teacher decided to use the weekly assignment sheet and the monitoring system I recommended. They informed Darren that it was his responsibility to bring the sheet home on Monday. If that didn't happen, his after-school play privileges were suspended each day until it did. No excuses were accepted.

If Darren completed all his jobs each day and did his own work within the allotted time, he received full privileges for that day. He could visit with friends, go outside and play, watch TV, and enjoy his evening without restrictions.

If Darren chose not to do his jobs, he lost his privileges for that day and spent the hour before dinner from five until six in his room. After dinner, he spent a quiet time in the house without TV or video games. On Saturdays, between nine o'clock and one o'clock, he was expected to finish all of his incomplete work for the week before he could play with his friends.

Two weeks after our first session, Darren's parents returned for a follow-up visit. "How did it go?" I asked.

"Well, we didn't see much homework completed until very recently," said Darren's father, "but we didn't hear much fighting, either."

"He's right," agreed Darren's mother. "For the first time in months, my stomach hasn't been in knots after dinner. Our home has been a much more peaceful place to live."

"Did Darren do much testing?" I inquired.

"As predicted," said his mother. "He didn't bring his assignment sheet home until Wednesday of the first week, but we followed through with consequences—no play privileges. When he finally did bring it home, he informed us that he wasn't going to do it. 'That's up to you,' I said. When four o'clock rolled around each day, I made sure he was in his room. Then I announced that I would be available until five to help but not afterward. He never asked. In fact, he didn't do any homework that first week," she continued. "He just sat there. So, we followed through—no play privileges. He spent the hour before dinner in his room, and after dinner, it was quiet time. On Saturday, he made no efforts to do the work, so he was restricted to the house. When his friends came by, we informed them that he couldn't play."

"How did he handle all that?" I inquired.

"At first, he said he didn't care," said Darren's father, "but later, he cried and told us we were mean and unfair. This past week, he's been scowling and glaring at us a lot in the evenings."

"You mentioned that he did complete some work toward the end of the two-week period?" I inquired.

"Yes, on Thursday, he just went up to his room and did it!" said his mother. "I thought he was pouting, so you can imagine my surprise at five o'clock when he handed over his completed work and headed out to play. The strange thing was, it was no big deal to him. That evening, we all watched a program together, and he acted like nothing happened.

"On Saturday, he surprised us again. He had accumulated a fair amount of leftover homework during the week. We anticipated another day of moping and scowling and turning friends away at the door. But after breakfast, Darren headed up to his room and finished all of his work by ten-thirty. Three days' worth! Then, off he went. No big deal."

Their homework system was working. For two weeks, Darren held the hot potato by himself with no one to pass it to. He tried avoidance, then defiance, and then waited for the rescue that never came. Lesson 2 was beginning to sink in, and lesson 1 wasn't far behind.

Darren and his parents were well on their way to a successful outcome. They just needed more time for their system to teach its lessons. I agreed to meet with them every two weeks and follow their progress.

The improvement continued. By the end of week 4, Darren completed more homework than he left unfinished and did the mop-up work quickly on Saturdays. The pattern continued into week 6. His grades were improving. In week 8, all homework assignments were completed on time. A milestone! Saturday wasn't needed.

By week 10, Darren was showing initiative and independence by heading off to his room before the usual prompt of "Time for homework." His parents decided to reduce their monitoring to random spot checks of completed work. Darren was so eager to get out to play each day that he didn't even notice. By week 12, Darren showed full compliance. Their system was in balance.

When they came in for their final follow-up session, Darren's parents were pleased, and with good reason. The homework battles that dominated their house had been gone for many weeks. Darren was doing his part independently, and his grades showed it. Things seemed to be fixed. But were they really?

Change can be fragile, particularly during the early stages of implementing a homework system. Lapses sometimes occur, and they can happen to parents just as easily as to children. It begins with a missed assignment here and a reminder there, more missed assignments, more reminders, maybe a lecture or two, and before they know it, parents are dancing again!

Keeping a system in balance requires vigilance on the parents' part. I encouraged Darren's parents to be on guard for lapses and relapses and to be prepared to increase their monitoring procedures if Darren slipped back into old patterns. They had worked hard to put things back in balance. I wanted them to leave with the tools to see that things stayed that way.

When Professional Help Is Needed

IN DARREN'S CASE, the three-step system was an effective remedy because homework really was the primary problem and not just a symptom of something larger going on. But this is not always easy to determine. If parents do not see significant improvement during the first six weeks, then they may need assistance from a qualified professional.

If you recall, I began my work with Darren and his parents by conducting an evaluation. A number of factors were considered: possible learning problems; behavioral problems; emotional issues; family, communication, and relationship problems. With teens, I routinely investigate possible problems with depression, drugs, or alcohol. After reviewing Darren's background information, I felt comfortable that homework was the primary concern.

You may need to recommend the same type of evaluation when parents do not encounter anticipated progress during the first six weeks. Encourage them to make an appointment with a licensed psychologist, educational psychologist, or other qualified helping professional.

Questions and Answers About Homework

Q : How do parents get children started with good homework habits?

A : The best way is to begin with a homework system in
balance. That is, parents and children should do their
own jobs, and only their jobs, at regular times and in
regular places.

Q : When should parents implement the three-step homework system?

A : If a child avoids his or her homework responsibilities
on a regular basis, then it's time to implement the
three-step system.

Q : When parents inform me that their children do homework late in the evening at the dining room table,
should I encourage them to change this practice?

A : As you know, I don't recommend late homework
schedules or allowing children to do homework in busy
family areas, but these habits do not always lead to
problems. If lessons 1 and 2 are taking place, then I don't recommend tampering with their system.

Q : Do younger children need more help getting started
with their homework?

A : Yes, and this is a major reason why many parents get
overinvolved early on. Younger children usually do require more prompts to get started and more assistance

with directions. If parents keep their prompts and assistance to a minimum, then they will be sending the right messages.

Q What can teachers do in the classroom to hold students accountable for completing their homework?

A At the elementary school level, classroom teachers can encourage good homework habits with a clever accountability procedure called Fun Friday. Fun Friday is a preferred activity period, held on Friday afternoons. Students become eligible for Fun Friday when they have completed all of their homework assignments for the week. Those who are not eligible use the time to catch up on their unfinished homework. In effect, Fun Friday becomes an incentive for compliance and an instructive logical consequence for noncompliance. Although the procedure supports parents' efforts, it is not a suitable substitute for an effective accountability system in the home.

Q Should I ask the parents of all of my students to initial completed homework assignments to help them become more aware of their child's compliance with homework?

A The gesture is well intentioned, but probably not very helpful. The practice may even send the wrong message to your compliant students by encouraging parent overinvolvement.

Q If parents implement the three-step system with good results, how long should they wait before they discontinue monitoring?

A I recommend that parents taper off gradually rather than drop their monitoring all at once. After four to six weeks of full compliance, parents should conduct random spot checks for another eight to twelve weeks. If full compliance continues, then they are probably ready to discontinue monitoring altogether. They should be ready to reinstate the procedure if needed.

Q : **Do lapses on the child's part indicate that the system doesn't work?**

A : No. Lapses indicate that the child still has more learning to do. Lesson 2 is not complete. It's time to resume the three-step system.

Q : **What should parents do when they check their child's work for compliance and discover that most of it was done hurriedly and carelessly?**

A : This is probably limit testing or the child's attempt to determine the parent's minimum standards for acceptable work. If the child's work doesn't satisfy the parent's definition of a good effort, then the parent should be clear about what is expected and ask the child to go back and finish up.

Q : **Do you recommend that parents give prizes or special rewards when children complete their homework on time?**

A : No. This sends the wrong message. Usually, special rewards are reserved for special accomplishments. The parent is not asking that they do anything special. Positive acknowledgment and the usual privileges should be enough.

Chapter Summary

HOMEWORK TAKES PLACE in a system involving three participants: the parents, the teacher, and the child. Each has his or her own set of jobs to carry out if the system is to operate smoothly and remain in balance. The system can break down, and often does, when its members do less than or more than their own part. Teachers are in an ideal position to help parents put their system back in balance.

The key to a balanced homework system is helping parents do their part, and only their part, without taking responsibility away from the child or the teacher. Parents should establish a regular time for homework, a regular place for homework, and logical consequences for noncompliance. Once the system is set up, all parents need to do is follow through and let the system teach the lessons it was intended to teach. Homework can, and should, be a lesson in responsibility, independence, perseverance, and time management.

18

Developing a
Schoolwide
Guidance Plan

Throughout this book, the focus has been on helping teachers develop effective guidance practices in the
classroom. Now, it's time to expand our focus and address
guidance and discipline from a schoolwide perspective. We
know the tools that work. Our next challenge is to incorporate
these tools into a schoolwide guidance plan.

We'll begin by asking some important questions about
your school's guidance program. Is it effective with all students
or just the compliant ones? Is it effective at all levels: the administrative level, the classroom level, and the school site level?
Does it need a tune-up or a major overhaul?

This chapter will help you answer these questions.
Whether your guidance system needs a tune-up or a major
overhaul, this chapter will show you how to put the parts back
together so your program operates in a cohesive, integrated,
and highly effective manner.

Guidance Services from an Organizational Perspective

MOST SCHOOLS ORGANIZE and deliver their guidance services based on a three-tier organizational model. Let's look at an organizational diagram of a typical school guidance program (see figure 18.1). Notice that the organizational pyramid is divided into three levels, reflecting the ways guidance services are organized and delivered in most schools.

At the administrative level, the school principal, vice principal, and guidance counselors are responsible for providing guidance services—that is, if your school is fortunate enough to have a vice principal or guidance counselors. In many schools, the principal handles all guidance services at this level. Teachers are primarily responsible for providing guidance services at the classroom level. The lower level of the pyramid represents guidance services outside the classroom such as on the playground and in hallways, bathrooms, cafeteria, library, and bus pickup

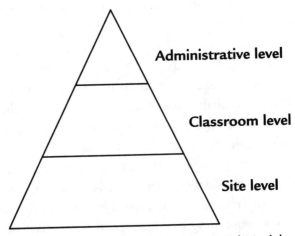

Figure 18.1   Three-Tiered Organizational Model

areas. Once again, site administrators are responsible for managing and coordinating guidance services in these areas.

How Effective Is Your School's Guidance Program?

WITH AN UNDERSTANDING of how most schools organize their guidance services, let's conduct an informal assessment of your school's guidance and discipline practices. We'll look at each level of your school's guidance system and answer a series of questions that should help you rate your program's effectiveness in each area. The more questions you can answer "yes" to, the more effective your school's guidance system is likely to be. We'll begin with the administrative level.

Guidance Practices at the Administrative Level

1. Does your school discipline policy specify the steps teachers are expected to take to resolve discipline problems in the classroom before sending students to the office?

2. Does your school discipline policy specify the steps your site administrator or office support staff is expected to take to resolve discipline problems in the office?

3. Do guidance practices in the office support guidance practices in the classroom? Are guidance practices in the office effective with the 10 to 15 percent of students who cause most of the school discipline problems?

4. Does your site administrator provide an adequate level of back-up support for classroom teachers?

5. Does your site administrator discourage staff from sending students to the office for disciplinary reasons?

6. Does your site administrator discourage the use of lectures, writing sentences, picking up trash, detentions, or off-campus suspensions as regular disciplinary interventions?

7. Does your site administrator encourage classroom teachers to invest time at the beginning of the year in developing effective structure for their classrooms?

8. Does your site administrator discourage using the school's office as a revolving door for the 10 to 15 percent of students who cause most of the school's discipline problems?

9. Does your school have procedures for handling crises in the classroom such as extreme disruption, extreme defiance, and violent or destructive behavior?

10. Does your site administrator provide in-service training for staff in effective guidance and discipline?

Based on your answers to the above questions, rate the effectiveness of guidance practices at the administrative level:

Highly effective	Moderately effective	Ineffective	Very ineffective

Guidance Practices at the Classroom Level

1. Are you adequately trained to handle the full range of discipline problems you encounter in your classroom? Are your guidance methods effective with the 10 to 15 percent who cause most of your classroom discipline problems? Do you believe most of your colleagues are adequately trained in classroom management?

2. Does your school offer in-service training in effective limit setting, responsibility training, team building, teaching social skills, or using incentive systems?

3. Is in-service training required rather than optional for staff? Are salary or job advancement incentives available to staff who upgrade their guidance skills?

4. Do you set aside time at the beginning of each year or semester to create effective structure for your classroom? Do you send a copy of your classroom rules and expectations for student conduct home to parents? Do most of your colleagues follow these practices?

5. Do you notify parents within the first four weeks when their child shows extreme or persistent behavioral problems, rather than waiting until the next regularly scheduled teacher-parent conference to share the news?

6. Are the guidance and discipline practices at your school consistent from one classroom to another, rather than everyone doing their own thing with their own students?

7. Is there a prescribed series of steps you're expected to take before sending students to the office? If so, are most of your colleagues aware of these steps?

8. When you send students to the office for disciplinary reasons, do you know what steps your site administrator or office support staff will take to resolve the problem?

9. Do you send students to the office only as a last resort or final step in your guidance and discipline process?

10. Do you believe guidance and discipline should be part of your job description? Do your colleagues share this belief?

Based on your answers to the above questions, rate the effectiveness of your school's guidance practices at the classroom level:

| Highly effective | Moderately effective | Ineffective | Very ineffective |

Guidance Practices Outside the Classroom (Site Level)

1. Are the playground and hallway supervisors at your school trained in effective guidance and discipline?

2. Are staff members in the library and cafeteria trained in effective guidance and discipline? Are they adequately trained to handle the types of problems they encounter?

3. Do the yard duty supervisors at your school avoid sending misbehaving students to the office or issuing citations for misbehavior?

4. Does your school discipline policy specify the guidance roles teachers are expected to play in settings outside the classroom?

5. Does your school discipline policy specify the guidance and discipline methods staff are expected to use in settings outside the classroom?

6. Does your school have a discipline committee?

7. If so, does your school discipline committee support classroom teachers with challenging discipline problems?

8. Does your school discipline committee regularly communicate with your site administrator regarding schoolwide discipline concerns?

9. Does your school site discipline committee assist with in-service training for staff?

10. Are there members of your staff who are qualified to provide in-house training in effective guidance and discipline to new staff?

Based on your answers to the above questions, rate the effectiveness of your school's guidance practices outside the classroom:

Highly effective	Moderately effective	Ineffective	Very ineffective

Assessment Summary

Enter your ratings here for each of the three levels:

Administrative level: _____

Classroom level: _____

Site level: _____

How Are These Ratings Useful?

The ratings help you identify the effectiveness of your school's guidance program at each level of the guidance process and target your repair work. For example, if you rated your school's guidance program as ineffective at either the administrative or classroom levels, then your program likely requires a major overhaul. Fundamental changes are required in the way your school organizes and delivers guidance services. Refer back to the questions that indicate the breakdowns to target your repair work.

If you rated your program as moderately effective at the administrative and classroom levels but ineffective at the site level, then your program can probably get by with a tune-up and some bodywork. Refer back to the questions that indicate the breakdowns to target your repair efforts. If you rated your program as moderately effective at all three levels, a simple tune-up should put your program back on the road to recovery. You've identified the breakdowns in your guidance program; now let's look at the replacement parts.

Components of an Effective Guidance Program

IN AN EFFECTIVE program, the parts work together in a cohesive and integrated manner. Each level supports the others, and everyone works from the same guidance plan. All members of the system receive the same effective training, speak the same guidance language, and share a common set of effective guidance methods. Roles and responsibilities are clear and evenly distributed. Everyone understands the steps they're expected to take before passing the problem on to others. Now, let's look at the specific program components at each level of the process.

Components at the Administrative Level

- A clear, well-thought-out, and well-developed school discipline policy that specifies roles, responsibilities, and procedures at each level of the guidance process for all staff and parents

- A school discipline policy based on effective methods that work with the full range of students, not just the compliant ones

- A discipline policy that defines "an appropriate referral" and specifies the steps staff are expected to take to resolve discipline problems before sending students to the office or requesting administrative involvement

- A discipline policy that requires staff to complete an incident report documenting steps taken to resolve problems before sending students to the office

- In-service training for site administrators in effective limit setting, crisis intervention, relationship building, responsibility training, social skill training, problem solving, positive motivation, and the use of incentive systems

- Crisis intervention back-up support for classroom teachers and site-level staff

- Back-up support for classroom teachers in cases of extreme disruption, extreme defiance, and destructive or violent behavior

- Assistance with the planning and coordination of in-service training for staff

- Assistance with the coordination of supervision of areas outside the classroom

- Ongoing consultation with the school discipline committee

- Salary incentives for site administrators for upgrading their guidance and discipline skills

Components at the Classroom Level

- A discipline policy that clearly specifies guidance and discipline as part of each classroom teacher's job description

- In-service training on developing effective structure for the classroom

- In-service training in effective limit setting, problem solving, and the use of natural and logical consequences

- In-service training on positive motivation, incentive systems, relationship building, and skill training

- In-service training on crisis intervention procedures

- Salary or job advancement incentives for staff who upgrade their guidance skills

- Incidents reports for teachers to complete before sending students to the office or requesting administrative involvement

- Access to the school site discipline committee for advisory input or training on challenging discipline problems

- Access to back-up support from administrative staff or other designated persons in cases of emergencies or extreme behavior problems

Components at the Site Level

- A school discipline policy that specifies roles, responsibilities, and procedures for staff outside the classroom

- In-service training in effective guidance and discipline for playground and hallway supervisors, office clerical staff, library staff, and cafeteria staff

- Salary or job advancement incentives for staff who upgrade their guidance skills

- Incident reports for staff to complete documenting steps taken to resolve problems before sending students to the office

- A site-level discipline committee composed of staff from each level of the guidance system

- A site-level discipline committee that provides advisory support for classroom teachers or other staff regarding difficult discipline problems

- A site-level discipline committee that acts as liaison to teacher and parent groups and provides advisory input to site administrator regarding school discipline concerns

- A site-level discipline committee that assists site administrator with planning and coordinating in-service training for all staff

- A site-level discipline committee that assists site administrator with planning and coordinating crisis intervention procedures

Principles to Guide Your Repair Work

YOU'VE IDENTIFIED THE breakdowns, and you've examined the replacement parts. The next step is to put the parts back together so your program can operate as a cohesive and integrated unit. As you begin this task, there are some principles you should keep in mind to guide your repair work:

1. Make it efficient.
2. Make it effective.
3. Make it simple.
4. Make it affordable.

Let's begin with efficiency.

Make It Efficient

You may have already discovered that some of the replacement parts don't fit within the conventional three-tier organizational model. Why? Because the three-tier model has design flaws that all but guarantee inefficiency and expense. Let's revisit the typical organizational model (see figure 18.2).

In the three-tier model, discipline problems are passed up the system but seldom passed down. The higher they go, the more expensive they are to resolve. When you consider the numbers of people at each level of the system, another problem emerges. There are fewer people at the top of the pyramid to deal with the problems. What does this diagram tell you about the way guidance services are distributed throughout the school? Who handles most of the problems and the most difficult problems? It's the administrator. The diagram reveals a fundamental flaw in the way most guidance systems are set up. Too much of the load is concentrated at the highest and most expensive level.

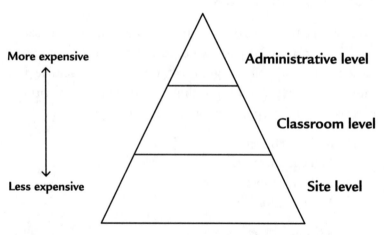

Figure 18.2   Three-Tiered Organizational Model

The three-tier model might be efficient in small schools with a low incidence of discipline problems, but the model is not efficient in larger schools with a high incidence of discipline problems. Too much of the load ends up in the laps of too few people.

What's the solution? The solution is to better distribute the load so more discipline problems can be handled at the lowest and least expensive levels. We should abandon the old three-tier model in favor of a four-tier model (see figure 18.3).

Adding a school site discipline committee to the organizational model improves guidance services at every level. It takes pressure off the administrator, distributes workload, increases support for staff both inside and outside the classroom, and provides an open channel for communication between all levels of the system. Now, the levels of the system can support each other at less cost and with more efficiency.

Who should be part of the school site discipline committee? The committee should be composed of staff from each level of the system and preferably staff with the most expertise

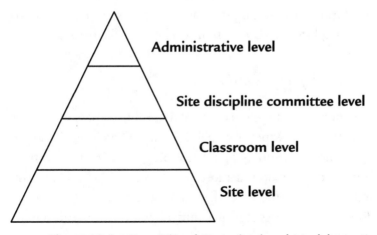

Figure 18.3   Four-Tiered Organizational Model

in guidance and discipline, because they'll likely be called on to provide back-up support for their colleagues.

Make It Effective

An effective guidance program works with all students, not just the compliant ones, and achieves all our guidance goals. It stops misbehavior. It resolves discipline problems at the lowest levels, and it teaches students the skills they need to improve their behavior. Most important, the guidance program supports the instructional program by minimizing costly disruption and making more time available for teaching and learning.

Make It Simple

In most organizations, the simple, straightforward plan is the plan people are most likely to use. Your site administrator and school discipline committee should take this into consideration when revising your school's discipline policy and guidance procedures. If your policy and guidance procedures resemble an IRS form, you're setting the stage for confusion. Keep it simple and straightforward. Your staff will be more likely to use it.

Make It Affordable

We know that the higher discipline problems pass up the system, the more expensive they become. Therefore, the key to operating an affordable guidance program is to resolve problems at the lowest and most cost-effective levels. To do this, staff must have the necessary training and skills to get the job done. This requires a greater initial investment in staff training to bring everyone in the system up to an acceptable skills level, but the investment will yield big returns and cost savings to the whole system later on. Pay up front or pay as you go, but paying up front is always the cheapest option.

Enjoying the Rewards

IF THIS BOOK has fulfilled its mission, you and your school should have the tools and information you need to correct your old mistakes and begin setting limits more effectively. You've discovered many of the obstacles to effective teaching and learning: punitive and permissive guidance styles, soft limits, negative motivational approaches, and the classroom dances that wear us out and make our jobs so difficult.

You've learned a variety of effective methods to help you achieve your guidance goals. You know how to prevent power struggles by giving clear messages, how to inspire cooperation with encouraging messages, how to increase on-task time with PAT, how to teach responsibility and good work habits, and how to support your rules with effective consequences that don't injure feelings or damage relationships. You've also learned how to solve problems with homework.

Your preparation is complete. The next step is to put your skills into practice and begin enjoying the rewards of your efforts.

The immediate rewards will be stopping misbehavior quickly and effectively, getting better cooperation from your students, and eliminating all those stressful dances that wear you down and leave you feeling so frustrated and discouraged. Soon, you'll be hassling less and enjoying your students more. You'll also have the satisfaction of knowing that you're teaching your guidance lessons in the clearest and most understandable way.

The long-term rewards of your efforts should be the most satisfying of all, because your methods will be laying a foundation for cooperative and satisfying relationships with students for years to come. By your example, you will be teaching a cooperative process of communication and problem solving your students will need to be successful, not only at school but out in the world. The skills you teach in the classroom are the skills your students will carry forward. Enjoy setting limits.

SUGGESTIONS FOR GETTING STARTED

● ●

I RECOMMEND STARTING OFF with the skills listed in the following tables for students of different ages. I've also included a suggested schedule for adding new skills. These suggestions are based on my experiences with teachers in my staff development workshops, but you may prefer to add new skills to your repertoire at a faster or slower rate.

I encourage you to go at a pace that is comfortable for you. For some, this may mean adding one or two new skills each week, but for others it may mean adding one new skill every two or three weeks. There is no one correct way, but I caution you against trying to learn too much too quickly.

You should expect to make mistakes as you begin practicing the methods. That's okay. The more you practice, the more proficient you will become. If you are having particular difficulty with any one method, refer back to the pertinent chapter for assistance. Note the specific language used to set up and carry out each technique in the examples.

Getting Started with Preschool Students

Week 1	
Clear verbal messages	Chapter 6
Check-in, cut-off, cooldown	Chapter 7
Encouraging messages	Chapter 14
Logical consequences	Chapter 10
Two-stage time-out procedure	Chapter 11
Week 2	
Add "try it again"	Chapter 16
Add role modeling	Chapter 16
Week 3	
Add limited choices	Chapter 7
Week 4	
Add natural consequences	Chapter 9

Getting Started with Elementary School Students

Week 1

Clear verbal messages	Chapter 6
Check-in, cut-off, cooldown	Chapter 7
Encouraging messages	Chapter 14
Logical consequences	Chapter 10
Two-stage time-out procedure	Chapter 11

Week 2

Add "try it again"	Chapter 16
Add role-modeling	Chapter 16

Week 3

Add limited choices	Chapter 7

Week 4

Add exploring choices	Chapter 16

Getting Started with Secondary Students

Week 1

Clear verbal messages	Chapter 6
Check-in, cut-off, cooldown	Chapter 7
Encouraging messages	Chapter 14
Logical consequences	Chapter 10

Week 2

Exploring choices	Chapter 16
Two-stage time-out procedure	Chapter 11

Week 3

Add limited choices	Chapter 7

Week 4

Add natural consequences	Chapter 9

TEACHER STUDY-GROUP GUIDE

....

T HIS BOOK IS designed to be used as a skills-training manual for teacher study groups. Study groups provide a supportive format for practicing and improving your guidance and discipline skills during the critical first eight weeks of your skills-training experience. The following suggestions will help you get started.

> **Suggested Length:** The recommended length for the group is eight weeks. Group sessions are usually sixty to ninety minutes long.

> **Preparation for Study Groups:** I recommend that all participants read the entire book prior to becoming involved in a group. This preparation will lead to a much richer experience.

> **Study Group Leaders:** Ideally, a teacher study-group leader will have a solid working command of the material in the book as well as formal training in child development, education, or child guidance. Teachers, guidance counselors, school psychologists, school administrators, and special education support staff are all good candidates for study-group leaders.

Overview of Study Sessions

Week 1

> **Objective:** Participants will develop an understanding of importance of structure and learn specific strategies for improving structure in their classrooms.

> **Preparation:** Review chapter 1.

Week 2

> **Objective:** Participants will discover their guidance approach, how students learn classroom rules, the importance of effective teaching in the guidance process, and the classroom dance they may use to get cooperation.

> **Preparation:** Review chapters 2, 3, and 4.

Week 3

Objective: Participants will learn to identify the type of limits they use in the classroom, how to give clear messages, and how to stop power struggles and classroom dances.

Preparation: Review chapters 5, 6, and 7.

Week 4

Objective: Participants will learn how to use natural and logical consequences.

Preparation: Review chapters 8, 9, and 10

Week 5

Objective: Participants will learn how to use the two-stage time-out procedure, strategies for managing extreme behavior, and the appropriate use of the office for back-up support.

Preparation: Review chapters 11, 12, and 13.

Week 6

Objective: Participants will learn how to inspire cooperation with positive motivational strategies and how to teach responsibility and increase time on task with PAT.

Preparation: Review chapters 14 and 15.

Week 7

Objective: Participants will learn simple and effective approaches for teaching social skills to students who lack the skills to behave acceptably.

Preparation: Review chapter 16.

Week 8

Objective: Participants will learn how to solve problems with homework and help students develop good work habits.

Preparation: Review chapter 17.

Study-Group Discussion Questions

STUDY QUESTIONS THAT cover themes and methods are provided for each chapter. The questions are intended to get participants involved with the skill-training material and to give them opportunities to discuss their experiences in a supportive setting. All study-group participants are encouraged to practice the methods with their students in their classrooms and share their experiences with the group.

Don't feel limited by the questions I've provided. These are only suggestions for discussion. Feel free to add additional questions that might help participants become better acquainted with the material. I also recommend setting aside the last fifteen to twenty minutes of each session for a question-and-answer period.

Chapter 1

1. Discuss the ten mistaken beliefs many teachers hold about structure. Have you neglected structure for any of these reasons? What changes will you make in the way you approach structure in the future?

2. Discuss rules in theory versus rules in practice. What type of rules do you teach your students? Which of the three teachers in the examples do you most closely resemble? Mrs. Atkins? Miss Stallings? Or Mr. Larson?

3. How much time do you set aside at the beginning of each new year for teaching your rules, expectations, and classroom procedures? What changes do you intend to make?

4. What are your expectations regarding your students' work habits and organizational skills? How do you teach these skills? How do you communicate your expectations to parents?

5. What accountability procedures do you use to teach your students to be responsible for arriving to class promptly and prepared? What steps can you take when students fail to complete assigned class work or homework? What steps can you take when your students repeatedly fail to follow classroom procedures such as lining up, entering, or exiting the classroom properly?

6. What steps can you take to enlist parent support and cooperation? Do you clearly articulate to parents your classroom rules, guidance procedures,

homework and grading policy, and expectations for work habits at the beginning of the year? Do you make early contact to discuss behavioral concerns or wait until the first teacher-parent conference or end of a report period? What changes will you make? What factors do you take into consideration when developing a seating plan?

Chapter 2

1. Can you identify your guidance approach? Are you permissive? Punitive or autocratic? Mixed? Or do you tend to be more democratic? Describe the specific things you say and what you do when your students misbehave. Then, diagram the steps. Ask for feedback from others. Does the feedback validate your suspicions?

2. Why are the punitive, permissive, and mixed training models poorly matched to those students who cause most of the classroom discipline problems and need guidance the most—strong-willed students? How do they respond? What lessons do they learn?

3. Is your guidance approach a good match for all of your students, or does it predispose you to certain types of conflicts with certain types of students?

4. How do students respond to permissive guidance practices? What lessons does this approach teach children about rules, authority, power, and control? What type of learning environment do permissive guidance practices promote? What kind of relationships usually develop?

5. How do students respond to punitive guidance practices? Is shaming, blaming, and humiliation appropriate in the classroom? What type of learning environment do these practices promote? What type of relationships usually develop?

6. Discuss the advantages of democratic guidance practices. Why is the democratic approach best matched to the full range of students? What type of learning environment do these practices promote? What type of relationships do these practices foster?

7. What lessons do children learn about cooperation, respect, power, and authority in democratic learning environments?

8. Describe the range of guidance practices among your staff. How would you rate the level of consistency among staff members at your school? Low?

Moderate? High? What effect does the consistency or inconsistency have on students at your school?

Chapter 3

1. Mr. Harris is a substitute teacher in a fifth-grade classroom. After recess, several students enter the classroom in a loud and disruptive manner. Mr. Harris approaches them and announces that he expects students to enter the classroom quietly and ready to learn. Is he teaching his rules concretely? Is his message complete?

2. Is limit-testing normal behavior? Why do students do it? What questions are they trying to answer?

3. How does temperament influence limit-testing and learning styles? Discuss the different ways that compliant and strong-willed students test limits. Why are strong-willed students referred to as aggressive researchers?

4. How do you respond to the aggressive researchers in your class? Do you react with annoyance and irritation? Do you sometimes personalize their aggressive research? How do you react to their disrespectful attitude?

5. Based on what you know about your guidance approach, are you teaching your rules in the clearest and most understandable way for the strong-willed students in your class?

Chapter 4

1. Have you been stuck in a classroom dance? If so, let's diagram the steps you usually take to handle classroom misbehavior. Write down how you begin your dance. Do you begin with a clear message? Is the focus of your message on the behavior you want to stop or increase, or is the focus on attitude, feelings, or something else? How do you usually feel when you start your dance? Calm and controlled? Irritated and annoyed? Angry or upset? Write this down at the beginning of your diagram.

2. Write down all of the steps in your dance that rely primarily on words. If you can, write them in the order they typically occur. Next, write down the steps in your dance that involve action or consequences. If you become irritated, annoyed, or angry during your dance, indicate that on your diagram.

3. Draw a circle around all the steps in your dance that rely primarily on words. Then, draw a box around all the steps in your dance that involve action.

4. Count the total number of steps you take in a typical dance. How many involve words? How many involve action? Let's see what steps are working for you. Are your verbal steps effective in stopping the misbehavior of your strong-willed or difficult-to-manage students? Are your action steps effective in stopping their misbehavior?

5. Let's analyze your dance. Based on what you've read in this chapter, how would you describe your dance? Permissive? Punitive? Mixed? Estimate how many times you perform this dance each day and each week and each month. Multiply the monthly estimate by nine to get an annual figure. Now, rate how much stress you feel during your dances. Low? Moderate? High? Are you beginning to get a better picture of the wear and tear you're experiencing? Are you at risk for burnout?

6. Do you think your dance might be entertaining for some of your students? Discuss the concept of "reinforcement error." Does it apply in your case?

7. What changes do you need to make to help your verbal steps become clearer?

8. How do students usually respond to your action steps? With cooperation? With anger and resentment? Do they sometimes retaliate? What changes do you need to make to help your action steps become more effective?

9. Draw a new diagram reflecting the changes you need to make.

10. Is your new message clear, firm, and respectful? Do you communicate it succinctly without anger, drama, or strong emotion? Congratulations! You're beginning to chart a new course toward effectiveness.

Chapter 5

1. Have you been using soft limits in the classroom? If so, what messages are these ineffective signals giving your students about your rules, your authority, and cooperation?

2. What are teachers really saying when they repeat and remind students to cooperate?

3. Why are speeches and lectures not meaningful consequences for many students? What's missing from these messages?

4. What message do we send students when we ignore misbehavior in the classroom? Is the absence of a red light equivalent to a green light?

5. When we argue, bargain, or negotiate with students about our rules, what are we really saying about our rules and our authority?

6. What are the disadvantages of using bribes and special rewards to gain cooperation in the classroom?

7. Miss Roberts, a tenth-grade geometry teacher, teaches her lesson while several of her students carry on conversations and distract others. She intervenes. "I need a little less talking and a little more listening," she says, with an annoyed look on her face. What does "a little less talking" mean? What kind of message is she giving? What kind of response can she anticipate from her disruptive students?

Chapter 6

Directions: In each of the following situations, an unacceptable student behavior is followed by an ineffective message from the teacher. Analyze each message. Is it clear and specific? Is the focus on behavior? Is the message communicated in matter-of-fact terms? Does the student have all the information he or she needs to correct the behavior? Replace the ineffective message with a clear message.

1. Mr. Carol's third-grade class lines up for recess, when he notices that one of his students, Jeff, has left books and papers lying all over his desk. Mr. Carol asks Jeff to return to his desk to put the items away. Jeff complies, but when he returns to the line, several students refuse to let him have his old place back. Jeff becomes angry and gives one of them a push. Mr. Carol intervenes: "I'll bet Tim didn't like that, Jeff. I really wish you'd try to be more considerate."

2. Steve, a fourth grader, leans back in his chair to the point of falling over. His concerned teacher intervenes: "I'll bet your parents wouldn't let you sit like that at home," says the teacher. "I'm afraid you might get hurt."

3. James, a seventh grader, is annoyed with the student who sits behind him. James turns around and calls the student a shithead. The teacher intervenes:

"James, I wonder what the principal would think if he heard that kind of language. Do you think we can allow students to talk that way in class? Come on. Think for a change."

4. Sharon, a second grader, interrupts her teacher during instruction by blurting out comments without raising her hand. Her teacher responds: "When you interrupt, it makes it difficult for me to teach, and it's not fair to others who raise their hands and wait to be called on."

5. Late reading group is finishing up when several students enter the classroom laughing, talking loudly, and disrupting. The teacher intervenes: "Hey, guys, can't you see there is learning going on in here? I'd appreciate it if you would try to come in a little more quietly."

Chapter 7

1. Shawna, a sixth grader, reads a teen magazine during instruction. When her teacher asks Shawna to put it away, Shawna attempts to engage her teacher in an argument about whether reading magazines in class should be allowed. How should Shawna's teacher handle this?

2. When his teacher asks him to turn around and stop talking, Miles, a fourth grader, responds angrily. "Why are you always picking on me?" he shouts. How should his teacher handle this?

3. When the teacher asks the class to clear off their desks and get ready for recess, he notices one student doesn't respond. "Did he hear my instructions?" the teacher wonders. What should the teacher say next?

4. Jake, a third grader, cheats in a game of four square. Several students complain. Jake insists he's innocent. What should the teacher say to Jake?

5. There are ten minutes until recess, and Jana, a second grader, hasn't even started copying her spelling words from the board. Her teacher suspects Jana is trying to avoid the task altogether. How should the teacher handle it?

6. Cheryl, a tenth grader, talks to a classmate during the first fifteen minutes of instruction. The teacher asks Cheryl to take a seat at the back table. Reluctantly, Cheryl complies but gives the teacher a look of disgust. How should the teacher handle this?

7. Keenan, a ninth grader, gets caught playing with his pocket-size video game during instruction. When the teacher asks Keenan to hand it over,

he apologizes and pleads for a second chance. How should the teacher handle this?

8. Mr. Brunson, a middle school PE teacher, is frustrated with one of his overweight students, who is consistently late to suit up and get out on the blacktop for roll call. "Come on, Harold," Mr. Brunson shouts as Harold takes his usual spot at the back of the line. "I could train a monkey to get suited up for PE faster than you," adds Mr. Brunson. Everyone laughs. Mr. Brunson can see from the look on Harold's face that the comment went too far. How should Mr. Brunson handle this?

9. Discuss the difference between attitude and misbehavior. How do you respond to displays of poor attitude? Do you get hooked? Where do you draw the line between poor attitude and misbehavior? Do you agree that role-modeling firmness and respect is more effective than reacting to provocative attitude?

10. Do you tend to personalize your students' misbehavior? Do you sometimes lose your composure and say or do more than is needed? Is it liberating for you to step back and view misbehavior as the student's problem, not yours?

Chapter 8

1. Why are consequences a necessary element in the teaching and learning process?

2. What are the advantages and disadvantages of using punitive consequences in the classroom?

3. How is punitive thinking different from logical thinking? Discuss your observations about how students respond to punitive consequences in the classroom based on their temperaments. How do compliant students usually respond? How do strong-willed students respond? How do you respond to punitive consequences?

4. What sets apart logical consequences from punitive consequences? Where's the focus? How do students perceive logical consequences? What are the advantages of using logical consequences in the classroom?

5. Clarey, a second grader, disrupts repeatedly during the day. Each time she does, her teacher writes her name on the blackboard under the frown face.

Discuss the effectiveness of this guidance procedure. How could you handle this more effectively?

6. Mrs. Huntington uses a color card guidance system in her classroom. The first time students misbehave, she asks them to pull a yellow card and place it under their name on a board. The second time, she asks them to pull a green card. The third time, she asks them to pull a red card, and they lose their next recess. Then, they start over again. Discuss the advantages and disadvantages of this guidance approach.

7. Grant, a ninth grader, receives his third tardy slip of the quarter in Mr. Garren's English class. Grant knows he'll have to spend an hour in detention after school that day. The next day after class, Mr. Garren pulls Grant aside and gives him a lecture on the importance of promptness. Was this effective? If not, why?

8. Manny, a fourth grader, is informed by his teacher that he won't be allowed to participate in the class field trip to Marine World in May because he has been so disruptive in class. It's February. Discuss the disadvantages of this guidance approach. What can Manny's teacher expect?

9. What are the disadvantages of simplistic classroom guidance systems that use the same consequence such as loss of recess for all minor misbehaviors?

10. What problems can you anticipate when the classroom teacher and office administrator operate from very different guidance models? What problems can you anticipate when staff operate from very different guidance models?

Chapter 9

1. Denny, a first grader, tends to be bossy and controlling with his playmates during recess. He insists on being the leader or having the first turn in whatever game he plays. Denny's playmates have had enough. Nobody wants to play with him. What is Denny experiencing? If you were Denny's teacher, what would you say if he approached you and complained that his classmates didn't want to play with him?

2. Selena, a tenth grader, has two weeks to write a research paper but waits until two days before the paper is due to get started. As she begins the project, she realizes how much work is actually involved and pleads with her

teacher for a deadline extension. If you were Selena's teacher, how would you handle this? What would you say? What would you do?

3. Drew, a fifth grader, knows it's against school rules to bring Gameboys or other electronic video games to school but decides to do it anyway. "Nobody will catch me," he thinks. "I'll play with it on the playground." The plan goes well until Drew has to use the bathroom during recess. He puts the game in his backpack and sets it on the bench, but when he returns from the bathroom, his Gameboy is gone. If you were Drew's teacher and he brought the problem to you, how would you handle it? What would you say? What would you do?

4. Gordon, a ninth grader, thinks he has mastered the art of forging his parents' signatures, but after the tenth excuse note in a four-week period, the attendance clerk becomes suspicious. She calls his parents. Gordon is caught, and the matter is turned over to the vice principal, who makes Gordon serve one hour of after-school detention for each forged note. In addition, Gordon's parents are asked to verify all future absences with a phone call. Gordon complains that the phone call is unfair. "Other students don't have to go through this procedure," he argues. If you were the vice principal, how would you respond to Gordon?

5. What are the natural consequences associated with cheating? Stealing? Name-calling? Breaking a promise? Betraying trust? Shaming or humiliating others?

Chapter 10

1. What types of consequences do you use to handle problems such as disruption, attention seeking, unacceptable language, tardies, truancies, or hurtful behavior? Are your consequences logically related to the unacceptable behavior? How do your compliant students respond? How do your strong-willed students respond?

2. Do you have difficulty thinking of an appropriate logical consequence in guidance and discipline situations? If so, you're probably thinking too hard or reacting without thinking. How can you help yourself come up with an appropriate logical consequence?

3. Sean, a seventh grader, knows it's not okay to bring comic books to class, but he decides to do it anyway and gets caught. If you were Sean's teacher,

how would you handle the situation? What would you say? What would you do?

4. Carla, a kindergartner, can't seem to keep her hands and feet off her classmates during morning circle time. If you were Carla's teacher, how would you handle this? What would you say? What would you do?

5. Randall, a third grader, pretends to pick his nose and then wipe it on the child who sits next to him in his table group. If you were Randall's teacher, how would you handle this? What would you say? What would you do?

6. Maria, a sixth grader, collects homework assignments from her classmates as part of her weekly classroom job. When she comes to students she doesn't like, she snatches their assignments from their hands. If you were Maria's teacher, how would you handle this? What would you say? What would you do?

7. Sam, a fourth grader, arrives to class five minutes late after recess without an excuse. If you were Sam's teacher, how would you handle this? What would you say? What would you do?

8. There are ten minutes left until recess, and Sherry, a first grader, hasn't started copying the spelling words from the blackboard. If you were Sherry's teacher, how would you handle this? What would you say? What would you do?

9. Taylor, a third grader, is supposed to be working quietly at his desk but decides to clown around and disturb others in his desk group. His teacher sends Taylor to the back table to work by himself. As he heads to the back table, his teacher adds, "If you continue to behave like a brat, you're going to find yourself at the back table a lot." Is this an example of a logical consequence? What would make this consequence more effective?

10. The students in Mrs. Wallace's fifth-grade class know they're not supposed to bring Pokémon cards to class, but Jeremy decides to do it anyway and gets caught. "What did I say I would do if I catch you with Pokémon cards?" asks his teacher. "You said you would take them away," replies Jeremy. "That's right, and I will too," she insists. "Now put them away. That's your last warning." Is this an example of a logical consequence? How could you improve the lesson?

Chapter 11

1. What are the goals of time-out? Is the procedure appropriate for students who quietly refuse to do their work?

2. What target behaviors are appropriate and inappropriate for time-out?

3. What are the disadvantages of using time-out in a punitive manner?

4. What are the disadvantages of using time-out in a permissive manner?

5. What considerations should you keep in mind when selecting a buddy teacher for stage 2 time-outs?

6. When should you use stage 2 in the time-out process? What additional steps should you take to involve parents after a stage 2 time-out?

7. Are the office and hallway appropriate areas for time-out? If not, why?

8. What should you say or do when students refuse to go to the time-out area?

9. If you ask a student to go to the time-out area, and he complies but rolls his eyes and gives you a look of disgust as he heads there, should you add more time to the time-out?

10. What should you say and do when the time-out is over?

Chapter 12

1. Mrs. DeLong, a tenth-grade English teacher, sees two of her students fighting in the classroom and runs to the class next door to summon help. What is the problem with this step? What steps should she take instead?

2. Mr. Barrows, a fourth-grade teacher, stands more than six feet tall and weighs over two hundred pounds. When one of his students refuses to go to the time-out area, Mr. Barrows's first thought is to physically force the student to go the time-out area. What is the problem with this approach? What are the legal and safety implications?

3. From a safety and risk management point of view, why is it better to separate an entire classroom of students from one defiant or assaultive student than to attempt to move the student in crisis?

4. Why are cooldowns such an important step in crisis management? What purpose do they serve? What happens if we neglect this step and move on too quickly to problem solving?

5. What back-up support systems are available at your school site? Are they trained to use restraint procedures? Are they available during school hours? If not, are there other persons who can serve this role? Are they trained to use restraint procedures?

6. Does your classroom have an intercom? If not, how would you notify the office in the event of an emergency?

7. Steve and Thomas, two sixth graders, are caught fighting on the playground. The yard duty supervisor stops the fight and promptly sends both of them to the office. The boys are still hot and start fighting again on their way to the office. One child gets injured. What important step or steps were omitted from this intervention? How could this situation be handled more effectively?

8. Julia, a tenth grader, arrives at third-period class looking very depressed. She has two cuts on her right wrist. Her teacher asks Julia to have a seat in the hallway and calls the office for help. No one is available, but the school secretary promises to find the vice principal as quickly as possible. Julia sits in the hallway while the teacher begins her lesson. Is there a potential problem here? What other steps could the teacher take to ensure Julia's safety?

Chapter 13

1. Is the office in your school used as a place for handling disciplinary problems? If so, how is it used? Discuss the problem of reinforcement errors. Do you think this might be occurring in your school?

2. Does your school have a clear discipline policy, one that spells out the guidance procedures all staff members are expected to follow? Are roles and responsibilities clear? At what point in the guidance process is the office or site administrator involved? Is the policy based on effective or ineffective practices?

3. What steps are teachers in your school expected to take to resolve disciplinary problems in the classroom before passing them on to the office or to the administrator?

4. When you send a student to the office for disciplinary reasons, does your administrator know what steps you've taken to resolve the problem at the classroom level? When the student returns from the office, do you know what steps your administrator has taken to resolve the problem? Are your disciplinary approaches compatible, or do they send mixed messages to your students?

5. How consistent is your staff with regards to their guidance and discipline practices? If they're not consistent, what problems does this create for your site administrator and other staff members?

6. Does your school require staff to complete an incident form prior to sending students to the office for disciplinary reasons? Discuss this practice. What are the advantages and disadvantages of requiring staff to complete an incident report prior to passing discipline referrals on to the office?

7. Discuss the training you received during your teacher preparation program in the area of guidance and discipline. Was it adequate? Did it prepare you for the range of discipline problems you encounter in the classroom?

8. What provisions does your site administrator make for in-service training in the area of guidance and discipline? Does the in-service training promote uniform or consistent practices among staff? Are these practices effective?

9. Does the game of hot potato take place at your school? If so, what are the causes of this destructive practice? What is the remedy?

10. Do you believe guidance and discipline should be part of your job description? Before you became a teacher, did you have any idea guidance and discipline would require so much of your time and energy? How do you feel about that now? What advice would you give someone considering a career as a teacher?

Chapter 14

1. Can you identify your motivational style? What type of motivational messages do you use in the classroom? Positive messages? Negative messages? Do you spend as much time catching your students being good as you do catching them being bad? Is your motivational approach effective with compliant students, strong-willed students, and those in between?

2. Why do negative, discouraging messages often backfire as motivational tools? Discuss the limitations of negative motivational messages? Share your observations based on your experiences with children.

3. Imagine you're at a staff meeting, and the agenda topic is ineffective guidance practices. Without warning, your supervisor shares an ineffective practice he observed you use in your classroom. How would you respond? Would you feel embarrassed? Ashamed? Singled out? Humiliated? Would this motivate you to try harder to improve? Would you approach your supervisor after the meeting and tell him that you really appreciated his comments and that you'll be a much better teacher because of it? Put yourself in the position of a student, and imagine what it feels like to be singled out and humiliated in front of your peers.

4. Why are positive, encouraging messages more likely to achieve their intended motivational effect? What basic needs do these messages address?

5. Discuss guidelines for using positive, encouraging messages. Where should the focus of our encouraging messages be?

6. How can teachers increase the motivational power of their efforts to encourage? Discuss strategies for involving parents in the encouragement process.

Chapter 15

1. Discuss the benefits of the PAT group incentive system. What lessons is it designed to teach? What are some of the built-in components that contribute to its effectiveness?

2. Why are time bonuses plus time penalties more effective than bonuses alone?

3. Is PAT intended to replace your limit-setting practices? Describe typical off-task behaviors in your classroom that might warrant time penalties? How should attention-seeking and disruptive behavior be handled?

4. What are automatic time bonuses? When are they used? Make a list of possible situations for awarding automatic time bonuses in your classroom and assign a time amount to each one.

5. What is an unexpected time bonus? Discuss possible situations for awarding time bonuses in your classroom. How much time should be awarded?

6. What is a "hurry-up" time bonus? Discuss possible situations for awarding hurry-up time bonuses in your classroom.

7. Why is the teacher's role as timekeeper such a critically important aspect of the PAT system? What's the best way to record time and prevent arguments or protests of unfairness?

8. What are some of the considerations to keep in mind when using time penalties? What tone of voice should you take? How much time should you deduct? Are critical or shaming comments by the teacher ever appropriate?

9. Generate a list of possible PAT activities your students might enjoy. How should you approach this topic? What types of learning activities are fun for you?

10. Discuss some of the mistakes teachers make that sabotage the effectiveness of the PAT group-incentive system.

Chapter 16

1. Do you sometimes become stuck on the discipline treadmill with your students? Make a list of the situations in which you use consequences to manage recurring misbehavior. Can you improve these situations by teaching your students the skills they need to behave acceptably? What steps should you take?

2. Recess ends, and a group of students enters your classroom yelling and fooling around. How should you handle this? What should you say and do?

3. Karen, a seventh grader, is annoyed with the boy sitting behind her because he keeps tapping her chair with his foot. Finally, she turns around and shouts, "Would you cut it out?" Then, she gives his chair a kick and says, "How do you like it?" What could you say and do to help Karen learn the skills she needs to handle this situation more appropriately?

4. Raymond, a fourth grader, waits in line to go to lunch, when he realizes he forgot his lunch money in his desk. He leaves the line to get it. When he returns, someone else has taken his spot. "Get out of my spot," says Raymond as he gives the other student a shove. If you were Raymond's teacher, what could you say and do to help him learn the skills he needs to handle this situation more effectively?

5. Susan, a third grader, approaches her teacher after class and complains that several students in her desk group tease and bother her while she tries to work. "Just ignore them," says the teacher. Susan walks away in frustration. Is the teacher's suggestion helpful? Does it go far enough? What more could Susan's teacher say or do to help Susan learn some skills to handle this problem?

Chapter 17

1. What steps can you take in the classroom to help your students develop good homework study habits?

2. What steps can you take to help parents establish a good homework routine?

3. What is an effective monitoring system to ensure that students write down their homework assignments and bring them home?

4. What consequences should you encourage parents to use when students fail to complete their homework at home?

5. Is an F grade for incomplete homework an effective natural consequence for all students? If not, why?

6. What is the best place for students to do their homework? Why?

7. What are the best times for students to do their homework? Why?

8. What should you advise parents when their child gets in the habit of doing a hurried, sloppy, or less than adequate job with homework?

9. When good homework habits and good grades deteriorate with secondary level students, what contributing factors should you suspect?

10. When is professional help recommended?

INDEX

Robert J. MacKenzie, Ed.D., is an educational psychologist and family therapist with more than twenty years of experience helping teachers and parents solve children's learning and behavioral adjustment problems. He is the author of two other books, *Setting Limits* and *Setting Limits with Your Strong-Willed Child,* as well as numerous magazine and newspaper  articles. Dr. MacKenzie provides teacher training, parent education, and family counseling. He consults privately with school districts, teacher-parent organizations, hospitals, and a wide variety of community service agencies. He leads more than fifty workshops each year nationwide on his Setting Limits program. Dr. MacKenzie lives in Davis, California, with his wife and sons.

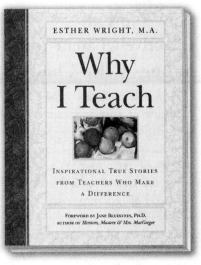